NOTES ON LITERARY STRUCTURE

Daniel Burke, F.S.C.
La Salle College

UNIVERSITY
PRESS OF
AMERICA

Library of Congress Catalog Card Number: 81-40645

DEDICATION

To the many students who, over some thirty
years of my college teaching, have helped
me to clarify and organize ideas presented
here; to name a few--Vincent Anderson,
Anthony Battaglia, Joseph Beatty, Paul Betz,
James Butler, Paul Deasy, Michael Ditchkofsky,
John Egan, Per-Otto Ericksen, Patrick
Gleason, Hanspeter Hodel, Paul Howe, Matthew
Janczewski, Lester Keyser, Lori Kradzinski,
Bernard Krimm, John Langan, Mary Anne
Lutz, Joseph McAuliffe, Michael McGinniss, FSC,
Philip McGuire, William O'Toole, William
Misticelli, Gabriel Moran, FSC, Robert Pushaw,
John Rodden, John Seydow, Donna Skalicky,
Peter Speaker, Michael Tanney, Leonard Terr,
Richard Tiedeken, Joseph Wisenfarth, Thomas
Wickens, Robert Wilsbach, FSC, and Shawn
Witmer.

ACKNOWLEDGEMENTS

I am grateful to the following publishers for permission to quote from or reprint the materials listed here:

The Athlone Press for quotations from Winifred Nowottny, The Language Poets Use (1962);

Ardis for a quotation from Yury Lotman, Analysis of the Poetic Text (1976);

The Catholic University of America Press for quotations from Robert M. Browne, Theories of Convention in Contemporary American Criticism (1956) and William J. Rooney, The Problem of Poetry and Belief in Contemporary Criticism (1949);

Faber and Faber for Ted Hughes, "The Thought Fox" from The Hawk in the Rain (1959);

Fédération Internationale des Langues et Litteratures Moderne for excerpts from Craig La Drière, "Literary Form and Form in the Other Arts" in Stil- und Formprobleme in der Literatur (1959);

Georgetown University Press for excerpts from Jan Mukařovský, "Standard Language and Poetic Language" in A Prague School Reader in Esthetics, Literary Structure, and Style edited by Paul Garvin (1964);

Grolier, Inc. for a reprint of Daniel Burke, FSC, "Versification" in Encyclopedia Americana (1981);

Harcourt Brace Jovanovich, Inc. for Ned O'Gorman, "The Rose and the Body of the Rose" in The Night of the Hammer (1959) and a quotation from Katherine Anne Porter, Pale Horse, Pale Rider (1939);

Alfred A. Knopf, Inc. for Wallace Stevens, "The Disillusionment of Ten O'Clock" in The Collected Poems of Wallace Stevens (1955);

Macmillan Publishing Co. for John Masefield, "Cargoes" in Poems (1953);

MIT Press and John Wiley for quotations from Roman Jakobson, "Linguistics and Poetics" in _Style in Language_, edited by Thomas A. Sebeok (1960);

Modern Fiction Studies for material from Daniel Burke, FSC, "Salinger's Esmé: Some Matters of Balance" (1966);

National Art Education Association for a reprint of Monroe C. Beardsley, "The Classification of Critical Reasons" in _Art Education_ (1967);

New Literary History for a reprint of Seymour Chatman, "On Defining 'Form'" (1971);

Oxford University Press for a quotation from M.H. Abrams, _The Mirror and the Lamp_ (1953);

Quarterly Journal of Speech for a reprint of Robert M. Browne, "The Shropshire Lad as Funeral Orator" (1971);

Spirit for a reprint of Craig La Drière, "The Role of the Critic" (1947);

The Writer, Inc. for reprints of Craig La Drière, "Fitness," "Form," "Scientific Method in Criticism," and "Voice and Address" in _Dictionary of World Literary Terms_, (c) 1943, 1953, 1970 by Joseph T. Shipley.

CONTENTS

PREFACE

These notes have been the basis of an "introduction to literary theory and criticism" for advanced undergraduates and beginning graduate students. As the first chapter indicates, they are not
intended as a survey of various theories, modern or
ancient. Rather they concentrate on one structuralist
approach which has roots in Aristotle and other
classical writers, in the twentieth century schools
of Russian and Czech theorists, and most particularly
in the work of the late J. Craig La Drière of Harvard's
Comparative Literature Department.

The notes, of course, are frequently sketchy,
since further development in the lectures and discussions of the course is envisioned. The suggested
readings and the selections in the appendices indicate a basic aim of the course: to introduce students to a variety of materials that support, but
occasionally contradict, the positions developed here.
In the first instance, the selections include several
of La Drière's seminal articles, which first appeared
in 1943 and which anticipated many of the concerns
of theorists since that time.

As the footnotes at least begin to make clear,
I am indebted to many writers in the field as well
as to my earlier teachers at the Catholic University,
particularly Craig La Drière and Rev. William Rooney,
to present and past colleagues, especially Charles
Scheve, and, as the Dedication should make clear,
to many of my own students.

I APPROACHES TO LITERATURE

It is the evident characteristic of modern genius to study and enjoy expression--the suggestion of the not-given--rather than form, the harmony of the given.

George Santayana
The Sense of Beauty (1896)

After many years of reading literature and a few years, more recently, of studying it, the college student can still find himself with a nagging "why bother?" at the back of his mind as he begins another course. Perhaps literature itself seems worth bothering about: one remembers an increasing number of novels, plays, short-stories, even poems perhaps, that he has enjoyed, that he has seen widen and deepen his experience. To some extent, learning about the works, their authors and backgrounds, has had an obvious rationale: more understanding has meant more enjoyment. But as for close analysis of the work itself or the attempt to judge whether it is good or bad? At this point especially the worry begins that our feeling for the work is in danger, that more is being pressed from the work than is really there, that any judgment about it is after all purely subjective.

Such attitudes are widespread and entrenched even among people who devote much time to literature. The present notes and readings will question these attitudes and assumptions and, if not displace them, will at least suggest some viable alternatives to them. In particular, the major effort will be to examine the nature of the literary value, whatever it is that makes literature different from ordinary writing, and to suggest that this value isn't entirely subjective, but is open to some degree of public inspection and weighing.

Experience and Analysis

People use literature for many different purposes. Psychiatrists sometimes use novels in therapy; teachers of moral theology may use them to point up vividly a moral situation. By far the most common use of literature, however, is simply to read and enjoy it. Perhaps "simply" is not the right word here. For both reading and enjoyment are very complex operations involving the human intellect and sensibility. Normally, though, once a person has learned how to read and continues to read only within a certain range of difficulty, the process itself seems relatively simple.

The enjoyment which accompanies and follows the understanding of literature, while it is automatic enough, too, is an especially complex mixture of intellectual and emotional elements. It is plain enough, however, that we know what we enjoy and when we enjoy something. When we put down a good story, a pleasant resonance remains from our whole reading. In a crowd emerging from a theatre after a good show or movie, you can hear expressions of general satisfaction as well as exclamations about particular scenes, or characters, or lines that have been especially appreciated. And in the normal run of enjoyment, there are those more exalted moments of reacting to literature we speak of as "aesthetic experiences."

The reading and enjoyment of literature, what we call its "appreciation," is, together with the rarer moments of aesthetic experience, its most typical use. Literature is intended primarily for this.

The other approach to literature with which we are concerned here is admittedly more eccentirc, less typical: not too many people pursue it or pursue it very frequently or very far. This is the approach of the student and the scholar. The approach is, of course, essentially intellectual. It may seek simply to understand a work better. At times the work may present only minimal obstacles to this end in, say, for instance, the discontinuity between parts or the lack of explicit commentary on the three ships in Masefield's poem called "Cargoes":

Quinquireme of Nineveh from distant Ophir,
Rowing home to haven in sunny Palestine,
With a cargo of ivory,
And apes and peacocks,
Sandalwood, cedarwood, and sweet white wine.

Stately Spanish galleon coming from the Isthmus,
Dipping through the Tropics by the palm-green
    shores,
With a cargo of diamonds,
Emeralds, amethysts,
Topazes, and cinnamon, and gold moidores.

Dirty British coaster with a salt-caked smoke
    stack,
Butting through the Channel in the mad March
    days,

```
     With a cargo of Tyne coal,
     Road-rails, pig-lead,
     Firewood, iron-ware, and cheap tin trays.1
```

Not much reflection is needed to see that the contrast between the last cargo and the first two implies the speaker's strong dislike of modern indus-
trialization and the sense of values in industrialized
society. Unfortunately--or fortunately--the difficulties of poems are usually more formidable and concentrated (and that fact might be sufficient to account
for the relatively smaller following lyric poetry has
usually had compared to novels, say, or plays). Take
Wallace Stevens' "Disillusionment of Ten O'Clock":

```
     The houses are haunted
     By white night-gowns.
     None are green,
     Or purple with green rings,
     Or green with yellow rings,
     Or yellow with blue rings.
     None of them are strange,
     With socks of lace
     And beaded ceintures.
     People are not going
     To dream of baboons and periwinkles.
     Only, here and there, an old sailor,
     Drunk and asleep in his boots,
     Catches tigers
     In red weather.2
```

     More than superficial reflection is obviously
required here; attention must be given to hints supplied by the title and, again, to the contrast of
major parts in the poem. From these elements it
emerges that the poem is not too different in its
general direction from Masefield's: it is a comment
on the drabness of modern society represented now by
the way people go to bed--early, in plain night-
clothes, to dream very ordinary dreams, all that is,
except the old sailor. Such points, of course, are
simply the beginning of analysis that can illuminate
the details of meaning, of pattern and relationship,
that can search ultimately for reasons that can help
explain the poem's charm or oddity, its success or
failure.

     And study may go beyond the work itself in search

of knowledge about it: to determine whether the text
itself is correct; to study its author, his background,
and the influences upon him; to analyze what kind of
literature it is and how the kind developed--or what
literature itself is. In dealing with the literary
work itself, scholars know that some assertions can
be proved simply by pointing to, by describing the
text ("there are four stanzas in the poem"), whereas
the evidence for other assertions of fact or judgment,
of interpreting or evaluating the text ("the peacocks
are symbols of death," "the ending of the poem is
weak") is much more difficult to marshall. But, in
general, literary students and scholars behave like
students and scholars in other disciplines, proceeding
to establish facts wherever possible, and generalizing
about them with as much logic and objectivity as possible.

   We have, therefore, appreciation and study or,
from another viewpoint, experience and the analysis
of experience. These are distinct things. One cannot be chosen to the exclusion of the other, at least
by students of English; for these people, both are
indispensable. Nor is there any conflict between the
two approaches--except that we cannot ordinarily do
both at the same time. For the study of a literary
work should lead to a deeper and richer experience of
it. What we have studied in the flat can be appreciated again and better in the round:

          Analysis is never in any sense
       a substitution for the poem. The
       best any analysis can do is to pre-
       pare the reader to enter the poem
       more perceptively. By isolating
       for special consideration some of
       the many simultaneous elements of
       the poem, analysis makes them more
       visible in one sense, and less in-
       teresting in another. It is up to
       the reader, once the analysis is
       completed, to reread the poem in
       a way that will restore the simul-
       taneity and therefore the liveli-
       ness and interest of the poetic
       structure. The only reason for
       taking a poem apart is that it may
       then be put back together again

more richly.[3]

Perhaps the last sentence here goes too far in saying "the only reason." Just as important is the fact that literary study and the knowledge we derive from it are their own justification. The physicist explores inanimate nature, its microscopic structure, its mystery--and he rejoices in whatever knowledge he achieves. So, too, the literary student studying one of man's most important arts, one which has its own unique value and at the same time embodies other precious human values, can be satisfied in what he learns about this object of his study. The study of atoms and the study of poems are alike part of man's intellectual enterprise and his intellectual history.

Literary Study: Theory, History, and Criticism

A paragraph above suggests some of the questions which students of literature pursue. Despite their variety, they fall within the scope of a limited number of disciplines. Some of these disciplines are preliminary (textual criticism, bibliography, library science) or ancillary (psychology, aesthetics, political history) to literary study properly so called. In the first instance, these studies insure that the literary student has a text which is as close as possible to what the author intended; that he knows the development of the text and its history in successive editions; that he has it and works related to it conveniently catalogued and at hand. Ancillary disciplines, on the other hand, provide relevant insights, facts, principles for illuminating particular meanings in texts, or some of the processes involved in creating literature or appreciating it, or even about its very nature.

The basic disciplines of literary study, however, are literary history and literary theory. Here the standard procedures of all science and systematic study are employed: literary objects are observed as part of reality; they are described, interpreted, analyzed with as much accuracy as possible (though the exact measurements of physical science are not usually necessary or possible); they are related to similar phenomena and so are classified; finally, they yield conclusions about their historical character or generalizations about their more universal nature.

From these intellectual labors, we derive knowledge
of literature--of historical particulars and of theoretical principles, of what the sources of <u>Hamlet</u>
were and of what tragedy is.

Radically different from, though not independent
of, literary history and literary theory is literary
criticism. It is indeed somewhat akin to literary
history in that it is concerned with particular literary works. However, it is not concerned with gaining
knowledge about the work or its bakcground, but rather
with coming to terms with its value. While the work
of criticism is essentially cognitive and while, as
we shall see, it involves as much knowledge as it
needs, it is also concerned with preference and with
judgment, with choice between alternative ways of es-
teeming and evaluating the work it confronts. However, whether criticism performs operations which are
actually distinct from literary history and theory
has been a matter of some dispute.

The Possibility of Criticism

From the time of Plato's <u>Ion</u>, it has been questioned whether a literary critic has any work which
is properly his own.[4] On the one hand, it is suggested that he is only a literary theorist dealing with
general questions or a literary historian who explains individual works or distinguishes their classes
and types. On the other hand, it is asserted that
since taste varies from epoch to epoch, since there
are no universal standards of judgment, and since
the critic is limited by his own likes and dislikes
--there is no possibility of an objective judgment
of literary works. What gives further proof of the
fact, is that those who have put forward supposedly
absolute and definitive judgments have, even when
these agreed, arrived at them by quite different and
opposed methods and by assuming quite different concepts of what the essential value of literature is.
On the latter point, some have suggested that this
value is literature's faithfulness to life; its insight into the complexity of reality; its ability to
create a wholly new, imaginative world or an inten-
sified, endlessly organized simulacrum of its own;
its function as an escape from reality, and so on
and so on.

Clearly there has been much diversity in what men have considered to be the value of literature; indeed the line to be taken in the present notes present still another possibility. However, to assume that literature has some value peculiarly and distinctly its own and to attempt to probe this value in particular works seems a sufficiently distinct task for the critic. These requirements are enough, at least, to distinguish the work of the critic from that of the literary historian and the literary theorist.

The Nature of Criticism

What then is literary criticism? What is the real nature of the work which the critic does? One of the most illuminating answers to these questions is the rather simple one that "Criticism is evaluation of evaluations." This definition implies that, while everyone makes judgments and evaluations of novels, movies, plays (and of any number of non-literary situations and events), it is the critic who returns to his initial evaluation and explores, tests, analyzes that judgment:

> Criticism, then, is not just evaluation. It is a reflex operation by which we examine a spontaneous evaluation and evaluate this evaluation. How is this operation performed? By bringing to bear upon the first evaluation all the relevant knowledge possible. Knowledge of the processes involved in evaluating itself; knowledge of the thing evaluated--of things of that kind in general and of this specimen in particular; knowledge of the evaluator and his capacities and limitations; knowledge of the situation in which the evaluation occured and the pressures it exerted upon the evaluator; knowledge of everything that might possibly affect the evaluation or enter into its composition.[5]

Of all these various types of knowledge which the critic may bring into play in providing reasons for his evaluation, in making assertions to support it, none is more important than knowledge of the object itself. For ultimately the literary object itself will contain within itself the reasons for its goodness--and it will continue to exhibit these reasons not only to the critic but also to those he may be attempting to persuade about its goodness. Thus, the literary object is necessarily the focus of concern for the critic. Whatever method he develops must take the object as its point of departure, must indeed be elaborated as a technique for enlarging, as systematically and relevantly as possible, the knowledge he can have of the object. To criticize, said Henry James, "is to appreciate, to appropriate, to take intellectual possession, to establish in fine a relation with the criticized thing and to make it one's own."

The Present Approach

The general approach to theory here, and its application in criticism, is structuralist; it deals with the elements of the literary work and how they are put together. The notion of the literary work as a structure is at least as old as Aristotle's _Poetics_, and it has had a recurrent popularity in the tradition. In our century, structuralism has been a major, at times a dominating, interest of theorists and critics. But this interest has shifted in recent decades from the individual work (as with New Criticism) to the whole body of literature and its codes (as with French structuralism and deconstructionism) and, most recently, to the patterned responses of individuals (as in theories of reading).

These changes in emphasis and fashion do not necessarily mean that definitive conclusions have been reached in any particular area or that we are now progressing to a more valuable field of investigation. The position taken here, in fact, is that analysis of individual literary structures requires continuing attention, and is likely to remain the most fruitful line of inquiry for theory and for critical method.

Even within this single focus, however, theorists take different approaches. If only one approach is stressed here--it is a line which extends from Aristotle to modern Russian and Czech struc-

9

turalists and, more specifically, to the late Craig
La Drière--the purpose is to show the development of
a theory from its premises. The basic premise here
differs from that of other structuralist theories,
which are typically concerned with the number or complexity of relationships in a work, particularly in
its structures of meaning. Here, however, the quality of these relationships is stressed, specifically
their fitness, and this quality is traced through
small and intermediate elements, and finally in the
total structure of meaning and sound. By concentrating on one theory, students may also have more opportunity to integrate the sometimes fragmented and
miscellaneous details of their previous literary
study in its larger principles and frameworks.

Notes

[1] John Masefield, _Poems_ (New York: Macmillan, 1960), pp. 43-44.

[2] Wallace Stevens, "Disillusionment of Ten O'Clock," _The Collected Poems of Wallace Stevens_ (New York: Alfred Knopf, 1955), p. 66.

[3] John Ciardi, _How Does a Poem Mean?_   (Boston: Houghton Mifflin, 1959), pp. 663-664.

[4] Craig La Drière, "The Problem of Plato's _Ion_," _Journal of Aesthetics and Art Criticism_, 10 (1951), 26-34.

[5] Craig La Drière, "The Role of the Critic," _Spirit_, 3 (1946), 180.

Suggested Readings

Beardsley, Monroe C.   _The Possibility of Criticism_. Detroit: Wayne State University Press, 1970, pp. 9-15, 62-88.

Culler, Jonathan.   _Structuralist Poetics: Structuralism, Linguistics, and the Study of Language_.   London: Routledge and Kegan Paul, 1975.

Ruthven, K.K.   _Critical Assumptions_.   Cambridge: Cambridge University Press, 1979, pp. 195-197.

Sutter, Ronald.   _Six Answers to the Problem of Taste_.   Washington: University Press of America, 1979, pp. 1-36.

Tompkins, Jane T., ed.   _Reader-Response Criticism_. Baltimore: The Johns Hopkins University Press, 1980.

Wellek, René, and Austin Warren.   _Theory of Literature_.   New York: Harcourt Brace, 1949, pp. 3-8.

II LANGUAGE AND THE STRUCTURE OF SPEECHES

The matter out of which a poet makes his poem is a
language as it exists in his time and place. But
this language is by no means a wholly formless matter when the poet begins to work with it; it is itself the product of more or less art, of ages of
human imposition of forms upon matter. In language
the basic matter, a matter so solidly material as to
fall within the province of the physicist, is sound.
This is given form by selection, differentiation
(e.g., of consonant from vowel), and construction
(syllable, phrase), by having significations, natural
or conventional, attached to it (the word), and by
conventional systematization of all these things
(grammatical and syntactic "constructions"). When
the writer begins to work, therefore, his material
is already full of formal elements. But these, though
they remain always formal elements and as such appear
still in his finished work, are for him part of the
matter which he is to inform; the form of his work
is a form he imposes upon this mass of forms and
purer matters by shaping it as a whole to a structure
and a meaning determined by himself. The form he
imposes is the peculiar total character of the speech
he makes.

Craig La Drière
"Form," Dictionary of
World Literature (1953)

13

Language, the Material of Speeches

   To develop a method for analyzing and evaluating
literary works, it is first necessary to understand
their matter, language, and their natural parts simply as speeches.[1]

   Language is the vocal and audible medium of human communication. Language has several possible
mediums or states of existence, but its primary, if
not essential, state is simply in sound. Thus, writing, printing, phonograph records, and so forth, are
not varieties of language; they are ways of recording
language. Again, language is supported by and in-
teracts with gesture. But the major weight and the
complexity of communication is carried by language.

   From the viewpoint of its speakers, a language
is a set of competencies and of habits which they
have learned by imitation and by being trained. Children are born with an instinct for language in general. They develop a competence for a particular
language by learning several sets of habits: of producing certain sounds, of associating concrete realities or ideas and other subjective experiences with
these sounds, and, finally, of combining meaningful
sounds in acceptable ways in the syntax of sentences.
In the second instance, as John Dewey suggested, a
baby may at first cry simply from pain and his parents
interpret and understand his cry. But once the baby
understands the connection between its cry and the
results it gets, once it intends to evoke a response
from the parents, it is on the threshold of language.

   Thus, the association of particular sounds with
particular things (subjective ideas, emotions, desires or objective realities) is the essence of
meaning in language. This association, moreover, is
not natural as it would be between the sound of rain
we could not see and the rain itself or between smoke
and fire. Rather, the connection is man-made or conventional. Man makes of the sounds he produces signs,
which manifest and make known other things for which
they stand. In conventional sign, the relation between the sign and the thing it signifies is a product of mind, not of nature--and not of one mind but
of a group. Hence, while these relations are mental,
they are not private; they are social. They are not

something entirely objective, the way physical objects
are objective. Nor are they completely subjective,
like our private moods and emotions. Rather they are
objective-subjective, a mixture of both, something
which has become objective because many persons (sub-
jects) share in it. Thus, we say that language has
an intersubjective existence. In a true sense, then,
words have or possess meaning, words interacting in
the contexts of sentences, that is. It is because
verbal meaning has this objective social reality that
speeches can communicate ideas from one person's head
to another's. And it is with verbal meaning and its
development in texts that the literary student has
first and primarily to deal.

Needless to say, there is a subjective side to
meaning as well. When an individual perceives that
a sound involves a connection with a thing, his perception itself constitutes a mental sign or idea.
The birth of ideas in an individual, in fact, seems
bound up with the signifying value of words. Helen
Keller describes a famous scene that marked for her
a new beginning:

> We walked down the path to the well-
> house, attracted by the fragrance
> of the honeysuckle with which it was
> covered. Some one was drawing water
> and my teacher placed my hand under
> the spout. As the cool stream gushed
> over one hand she spelled into the
> other the word water, first slowly,
> then rapidly. I stood still, my
> whole attention fixed upon the mo-
> tions of her fingers. Suddenly I
> felt a misty consciousness as of
> something forgotten--a thrill of re-
> turning thought; and somehow the my-
> stery of language was revealed to me.
> I knew then that "w-a-t-e-r" meant
> the wonderful cool something that
> was flowing over my hand. That living
> word awakened my soul, gave it light,
> hope, joy, set it free!...I left the
> well-house eager to learn. Everything
> had a name, and each name gave birth
> to a new thought. As we returned to
> the house every object which I touched

seemed to quiver with life.[2]

Miss Keller had experienced two of these realities many times previously: the tracing of the letters in one hand, the water in the other. But a third reality, the perceived relationship between the two, the idea that the letters referred to the water, was a new mental experience. The perception of such relationships we call psychological meaning.

From another point of view, language must be considered as a system of specific but rather flexible procedures and norms:

> Language as a historical object
> is the well-ordered changing set
> of norms ruling the association
> between signs and thought. When-
> ever we want to express what is
> in our minds or to make it known
> to others, we have to translate
> our thoughts into physical signs
> perceptible to others, in com-
> pliance with certain norms which
> are, at least implicitly, known
> to the emitter and to the addres-
> sees; that is, we must cipher them
> into sounds...And whenever we
> want to understand such ciphers,
> we have to decode and re-translate
> them into meanings according to the
> same norms. In consequence of this
> relation, whenever we want to under-
> stand speech expressed in a language
> we do not know we have to acquire
> knowledge of the norms according
> to which that language associates
> signs with signified ideas.[3]

The norms which are systematized in a language are actually rather wide-scoped rules and conventions. Within their range of tolerance for how sounds may be pronounced, combined in larger groups, associated with meaning in words and larger constructions, a variety of dialects and the peculiarities of individual speakers and their particular speeches can exist and be understood. This complex set of norms is something no one completely masters; in its totality, it

16

is the possession only of the whole linguistic community.

To insist, in this fashion, that language is independent of speakers, and speeches from the situations that produce them, is not to detract from the realities of speaker or situation or from the human values which may be involved in either. It is to insist, however, that speeches have certain values, perhaps at times very minimal values, independent of the values to which they refer. Thus, an educated speaker may refer to commonplaces in the most grammatically correct language; on the other hand, a foreigner may speak of vast and sublime realities in ungrammatical English. An elegant and rhetorically effective advertisement may be persuading to some triviality; a poor sermon may deal with redemption and beatitude. A speech, simply as a construction of language, that is, can have grammatical correctness and rhetorical effectiveness, and thus, grammatical and rhetorical values--and, what we will be more concerned with here, may also have literary values.

Speeches

While we have made significant advances in this century in understanding language and its own structure, there is still much unexplained about it. There is even more mystery, perhaps, about the process of speaking, the most common experience we have with other persons in human society, an important path, in fact, to our becoming human. We use the term speech for this process.

We use the term speech also to refer to the product of the process, any one of the great variety of utterances a person produces and interprets during the course of a day. A speech is "any stretch of talk by one person," as Zellig Harris says, "before and after which there is silence on the part of that person."[4] Hence, for the present purpose, conversations, reports, advertisements, sermons, editorials, lectures, stories, announcements will all be considered "speeches." What characterizes all speeches aside from the fact that they are constructions in language, is that even the most complex have a certain unity and even the briefest have an independent character. The range is from simple exclamations (John!)

17

to lengthy works with many parts (<u>War and Peace</u>).

While this much is true about speeches, it is
also clear that we do not ordinarily think of most
speeches we utter and hear as "constructions." This
term suggests more stability and permanence than our
daily speech has. For we naturally forget most of
what we say and hear; very few speeches apparently
are worth recording and preserving. What this fact
points up is that our speeches are part of processes
we are more concerned about; they have been directed
to other practical goals than their simple production; they have been temporary instruments to those
goals. Our speeches, that is, have been addressed
to other persons whom, frequently at least, we have
attempted to influence by what we say and how we say
it. Once our speech has been noted and understood,
then the way lies open to informing, interesting,
persuading, or affecting in some fashion or other the
person we are addressing. The ordinary speech situation, therefore, is fluid and dynamic; it <u>is</u> a process. A speaker is using constructions of language
to address another.

The notion of address is most obvious in questions ("Are you coming?") and commands ("Close the
windows first."). But in statements and even exclamations, the speaker is drawing someone's attention to what he is saying. Thus, the <u>purpose</u> to
address someone (though that someone may be a very
general anyone who will listen or read) is basic to
any speech, is reflected in its meanings to a greater
or less extent, and is a basic factor modifying and
qualifying it.

Besides a speaker, therefore, a speech always
implies an addressee and it always and most obviously includes reference to other realities. As a result, speaking cannot be reduced to a single kind
of activity. Rather, it involves several activities
for which the speech is purely an instrument: expression of the speaker, appeal to an addressee, reference to some reality. Depending on the thing he
wants to express or the kind of appeal he is making,
the speaker will give his speech a particular slant
or shape. The crucial thing is that the resulting
speech has <u>within itself</u> reflections of its speaker,
its addressee, the part of the world it concerns.

These, in fact, are its major kinds of meaning, and
they are the kinds of meanings grammarians long ago
labelled first, second, and third person meanings. But
there is more involved in the structure of speeches.

The Natural Structure of Speeches

To describe any structure it is necessary to isolate the parts or elements of the structure, to describe the relations between these parts, and thus, to
suggest the principles by which the whole is organized.

In a speech, the most basic elements are the
sounds and meanings which operate in a particular language. These elements, especially meaning, are not
always easy to analyze. Meanings do not always come
one to a word; they are not neat and definable units;
they do not combine into larger constructions of
meaning the way bricks combine in a wall.

However elusive they may be, meanings are given
their first shape in a speech by the grammatical
rules operating in the language. Such rules (and un-
formulated conventions) assure that the speech will
achieve the basic function of all language, to achieve
meaning. The relating of words in phrases, of modifiers to modified, of subject to predicate, of smaller
to larger constructions, of deep to surface structure
--all this gives a speech a grammatical structure.
This structure may incorporate the stylistic peculiarities of the speaker at the grammatical level, but
it nevertheless assumes that the speech is correct
according to the norms of the language, that it has
achieved a meaning which can be shared by those who
know the language.

Speeches, we have seen, however, are not produced simply as constructions of meaning, but rather
as purposeful instruments in practical life situations. Speeches are directed to goals, they are used
to influence others. The pressures of such directions
and purposes do not destroy the grammatical structure
of a speech, but indeed pattern its elements to create
an additional rhetorical shape or structure. Thus,
the order of ideas, the relation of sentence to paragraph, the deductive and inductive sequence of particular and general statements, the marshalling of
evidence and proof, the distribution of emphasis, the

appeals to emotion, the manipulation of occasional figures of speech--all this creates a new series of relationships that assure not only communication but <u>effective</u> communication.

(A speech may, more infrequently, be specialized by a tightening of the relationships between ideas so that it achieves a high degree of logic; this is typical of scientific and philosophic discourse. On the other hand, figures of meaning and sound found in rhetorical structures may be increased or developed so systematically that the speech is moved toward the poetic. But this will be our major concern hereafter.)

A speech is naturally structured, too, as basic kinds of meaning accumulate in it and are interrelated. We have noted already the most general kinds of these meanings: every speech, we said, involves meaning about a speaker, an addressee, and the realities they are concerned with.

Voice and address in a speech involves all direct references to and implications of an "I" and a "you" --and the relation between them.[5] In formal and objective writing and speaking (e.g., textbooks, editorials), these persons and their relationship may be quite indefinite and general; anyone is speaking to anyone. At other times the persons may be presented quite extensively and vividly, the play of attitudes and purposes between them may be quite specific and detailed.

Within the framework provided by this relation of speaker to addressee, other references are presented and developed--references which may be to objective or subjective realities, to mountains or murders, to anger or hope. At a minimum, these meanings, and the concurrent implications of voice and address, may be presented in a sentence:

> All men are created equal.
> The woods are lovely, dark, and deep.
> The king wrote the letter feverishly.
> O to be in England now!

Such sentences (expository, descriptive, narrative, exclamatory) may combine with sentences of other types but may eventually be accumulated in such a way as to

give the dominant character to longer speeches. We
may have, for example, a whole speech which is domi-
nantly exposition (that is, most of the things talked
about are ideas and their logical relations), or description (about physical things and their perceptual
qualities, presented according to temporal or spatial
patterns), or narration (about a series of actions,
presented in a temporal and causal pattern).

Furthermore, as any such speech is constructed,
it develops its own stages of presentation, its major parts, as, for example, the introduction, body,
and conclusion of an expository speech. Similarly,
it may develop structures which cross and accumulate
over its major sequential parts, as, for example, the
setting, characters, series of actions, and "themes"
of a narrative speech.

It is by describing such parts, the accumulation
of meanings that constitute them, and their interrelations, that we indicate the natural structure of a
speech. For the rhetorician, interested as he is in
the effectiveness of speeches and the way their structures contribute to that effectiveness, such analysis
is basic. But the student who is interested in the
literary value of a text must, as we shall see, go
beyond. A firm sense of the natural structure of a
text, however, can help to highlight by contrast the
poetic or literary structure; it can, at the same
time, give a sense of what natural elements are being
used to create the poetic structure. For indeed the
grammatical and rhetorical patterning of any speech
constitute its essential or natural structure. The
following outline summarizes some of the ways that
meanings are given a grammatical and rhetorical structure.

21

NATURAL STRUCTURE OF SPEECHES

Every speech has meanings which (I) reflect the essentials of a speech situation and which (II) are formed into larger, more complex meanings as they are structured according to grammatical and rhetorical norms.

I The Meanings Structured

    A. First Person Meanings (Speaker)

       Who speaks; evidencing what kind of personality, character, attitudes (tone), purpose for the speech, management of the speech in this situation?

    B. Second Person Meanings (Addressee)

       Who is spoken to (singular, plural, real, fictional); what kind of audience is the speaker trying to reach; what reactions of the addressee are suggested, what relationship to the speaker?

    C. Third Person Meanings (Other persons, things)

       What general-specific; concrete-abstract; objective (other persons, things)-subjective (ideas, volitions, emotions); static-dynamic realities are referred to?

II The Structure of Meanings

    A. Grammatical Structure

       Patterning of the speech according to the rules and conventions of the language to insure that meaning is achieved. Meaning is achieved in structures of varying size and complexity, notably at the level of phrase and sentence and of the whole discourse. But as specific types of meaning accumulate, they also form intermediate structures which are cumulative, continuous, and discrete, at least by abstracting the related meanings scattered through the discourse.

1. Sentence

| All men are created equal. | The woods are dark and grim. | The king wrote feverishly. |

2. Intermediate Parts

Speaker	Speaker	Speaker
Addressee	Addressee	Addressee
Ideas developed in lines of thought, assertions established by arguments	Persons, Places, and/or Things	Actions (involving persons, places, things, ideas)

3. Total Discourse

| Exposition | Description | Narration |

B. Rhetorical Structure

Patterning of a speech to a particular addressee, to achieve a specific purpose effectively.

1. By emphasis on or special use of parts of speech, modifiers, sentence patterns, or deviations from them; by developing varieties or levels of diction; by use of imagery, figures, and tropes.

2. By special emphasis on or use of the intermediate parts of the discourse.

3. By the management of rhetorical patterns of presentation or the sequential parts of the discourse.

a.
| Extended definition, classification, and so forth in Exposition | Fixed point of view, moving point of view, and so forth in Description | Natural order, Artificial order and so forth in Narration |

b.
Beginning	Beginning	Beginning
Middle	Middle	Middle
End	End	End

Notes

[1] The present discussion touches only a few points in the vastly expanding modern field of language study. Among introductory texts one can recommend to the literary student are Dwight Bolinger, Aspects of Language (New York: Harcourt Brace Jovanovich, 1975) and John Lyons, Language and Linguistics: An Introduction (New York: Cambridge University Press, 1981). In the last twenty years especially there have been numerous applications of linguistic analysis to literary works. Such applications have often given greater precision to traditional literary analysis, though at other times have simply provided abundant but largely irrelevant detail. See useful collections of such studies by Seymour Chatman, Literary Style: A Symposium (New York: Oxford University Press, 1971); Roger Fowler, Style and Structure in Literature (Oxford: Blackwell, 1975); Marvin Ching, Linguistic Perspectives on Literature (London: Routledge and Kegan Paul, 1980); and Geoffrey Leech and Michael Short, Style in Fiction (London: Longman, 1981).

[2] Helen Keller, The Story of My Life (Boston: Houghton Mifflin, 1928), pp. 23-24.

[3] Paul Schrecker, Work and History (Princeton: Princeton University Press, 1948), p. 89.

[4] Zellig Harris, Methods in Structural Linguistics (Chicago: University of Chicago Press, 1951), p. 14. Harris was an early investigator of what is now called discourse or text analysis, that is, the grammatical analysis of the development of meaning in whole speeches. See, for example, Margaret Coulthard, An Introduction to Discourse Analysis (London: Longman, 1977) and Teun A. van Dijk, Text and Context (London: Longman, 1980).

[5] See Craig La Drière, "Voice and Address" (Appendix II here); Walker Gibson, Persona: A Style Study for Readers and Writers (New York: Random House, 1969); D. Crystal and D. Davy, Investigating English Style (Bloomington: Indiana University Press, 1969), pp. 64-83; and Raymond Queneau, Exercises in Style, tr. Barbara Wright (New York: New Directions, 1981).

24

Suggested Readings

Hall, Robert A., Jr. <u>Introductory Linguistics</u>.
    Philadelphia: Chilton, 1964, pp. 14-17.

Aristotle. <u>The Rhetoric</u>. Book I, Chapter 2.

Brockreide, Wayne. "Dimensions of the Concept of
    Rhetoric." <u>Quarterly Journal of Speech</u>, 54
    (1968), 1-12.

Black, Edwin. <u>Rhetorical Criticism</u>. New York:
    Macmillan, 1965, pp. 132-147.

Corbett, Edward P.J. <u>Rhetorical Analysis of Literary
    Works</u>. New York: Oxford University Press,
    1969.

III   THE SMALL POETIC STRUCTURE

Every work of art is "a Form (<u>Gestalt</u>), but one which, besides having those characteristics that mark the Form as such, has others, which assimilate it to those peculiar Forms called living organisms; and presents these characteristics...not only when it is taken in its entirety, nor even in those parts of it which one might call its limbs or organs and which are themselves Forms, but even its microstructure, in its flesh of living cells which are as many units of tension (such as the alternation of long and short, of strong and weak tenses or the balanced coexistence of mutually opposed elements in a spatial work)."

Wladimir Weidlé
"Art and Language" (1969)

The Small Poetic Structure

The following paragraph opens J.D. Salinger's story "For Esme--with Love and Squalor":

> Just recently, by air mail, I received an invitation to a wedding that will take place in England on April 18th. It happens to be a wedding I'd give a lot to be able to get to, and when the invitation first arrived, I thought it might just be possible for me to make the trip abroad, by plane, expenses be hanged. However, I've since discussed the matter rather extensively with my wife, a breathtakingly levelheaded girl, and we've decided against it--for one thing, I'd completely forgotten that my mother-in-law is looking forward to spending the last two weeks in April with us. I really don't get to see Mother Grencher terribly often, and she's not getting any younger. She's fifty-eight. (As she'd be the first to admit.)[1]

Perhaps the most striking phrase in the paragraph is the reference to the speaker's wife as "a breathtakingly levelheaded girl." The description is clever and humorous. We could pin down its specific varieties of hyperbole and irony with the tools of classical rhetoric. But the attractiveness of the phrase and its success over other bits of wry humor and keen observation that surround it need more explanation.

Something further might be said for the improbability of the phrase. Normally, we would expect "beautiful" or a very close synonym to follow "breathtakingly." But "breathtakingly levelheaded" is different, fresh, original. And such qualities have always been considered hallmarks of literature, of poetry in particular. Aristotle stressed the "unusual" nature of literary language; the Romantics searched for "novelty and freshness"; the modern critic asks the writer to "make it new."

Among the more interesting modern discussions
of this quality have been those of the Russian and
Czech formalists. Victor Shklovsky, a member of the
Leningrad "Society for the Study of Poetic Language"
(founded in 1916), spoke of literature as "defamiliar-
izing" our ordinary experience. Most often, he said,
our experience of language and other realities is
dulled and narrowed by habit, but the novelty, odd-
ness, and even difficulty, of literary language shar-
pens and expands our awareness.[2] Czech formalists
like Mukořovský adapted the notion of "defamiliariza-
tion" and stressed the contrast between "foregrounded"
elements in the text and the more ordinary "automatized" language which acted as their background.[3]

The notion of "foregrounding" is a good one because it stresses what seems to be so obviously true
about literature: that something unusual is being
done with meanings and sounds to create a literary
structure. The concept gives some insight, too, into
the fact that poems or short stories are not a continuous tissue of dazzling phrases, but rather an interplay of the extraordinary moment and more commonplace passages. In this view, moreover, both "foreground" and "background" play essential roles in the
literary effect; analogously, a painting could not
do without its background. Hence it is that some rather commonplace and prosaic passages become essential
to the literary effect.

The concept is helpful, too, because it can be
applied to such different aspects of the literary
work. Barbara Smith, for example, observes that
Shakespeare's Sonnet 73

> contains two subtle surprises, one
> thematic and one formal.
>
> That time of year thou mayst in
> me behold
> When yellow leaves, <u>or</u> <u>none</u>, <u>or</u>
> <u>few</u>, do hang
> Upon those boughs which shake
> against the cold,
> <u>Bare</u> <u>ruined</u> <u>choirs</u>, where late
> the sweet birds sang.

Our experience with the logical con-

ventions of discourse makes the
series "yellow leaves, or few, or
none" much more probable than the
present series; and I think that
the affective quality of the line
which results from this nonlogical
sequence is still available at the
hundredth reading of the sonnet.
Similarly, even though one has the
quatrain absolutely fixed in one's
memory, the deviation from the iambic norm at the beginning of the
fourth line will continue to be experienced as an expressive deviation
during any particular reading of
the poem--a reading, that is, in
which one allows oneself to respond
to the poem as a total structure.[4]

There is a serious problem, however, with the
concept that simply saying something in a new or different way can assure the writer that he has achieved
a literary quality--though some of the wilder experiments of our century seem to assume this. In our
present example from Salinger, for example, "breathtakingly left-handed" would be different, but also
nonsensical; "breathtakingly conservative" might be
mildly interesting.

Other Russian and Czech formalists have hints to
answer this problem. Mukařovský, for example, in
talking about "foregrounding" and the way it involves
the smallest aspects of the linguistic material in a
network of interrelations says that

there is thus always present, in
communicative speech as well, the
potential relationship of the word
as a meaningful unit to the phonetic
structure of the text, to other
words as units of meaning in the context of the same sentence. It can
be said that each linguistic component is by means of these multiple
interrelationships in some way, directly or indirectly, linked to
every other component. In communicative speech, relationships are

30

for the most part merely potential,
because attention is not called to
their presence and to their mutual
relationship. It is, however, enough
to disturb the equilibrium of this
system at some point and the entire
network of relationships is slanted
in a certain direction and follows
it in its internal organization:
tension arises in one portion of
this network (by consistent unidirectional foregrounding), while
the remaining portions of the net-
work are relaxed (by automatization
perceived as an intentionally arranged background).[5]

The key words here for our present purposes are
relationships and consistent. When the novel phrase
is indeed literary, one becomes unusually aware of the
many smaller relationships it has in itself and with
its context. Perhaps "aware" is too much; "one seems
to respond to these heightened relationships" would
be a better way of putting it.

For Roman Jakobson, this awareness is created by
a system of repetitions or balances in a text. The
"organized violence committed on ordinary speech" involves a shift in the usual principles by which words
are selected and arranged in speech. The principle
governing the selection of a word for use in a particular point in a sentence--the principle, that is,
of the identity or rough equivalence of synonyms or
related terms in a semantic group--is now used in
the successive arrangement of phrases and sentences.
Repetitions or identities of sounds and meanings now
become more important than their contiguity or the
grammatical cohesiveness of their successive arrangement. "The poetic function," says Jakobson, "projects the principle of equivalence from the axis of
selection into the axis of combination."[6]

Other theorists, however, object that many repetitions of sound and meaning in a literary text are
below the threshold of artistic control and seem un-
related to its aesthetic effects.[7] Still others feel
that contrast rather than balance lies at the heart
of the literary structure.[8]

A more promising approach to such problems requires us to return to the second key term suggested
in Mukařovský's text above, the term <u>consistent</u>.
While elements of sound and meaning are indeed patterned by both balance and contrast in a literary
structure and are foregrounded in the process (though,
perhaps, not in the "unidirectional" way suggested),
what is more crucial to their artistic effect is that
they be adjusted consistently, adjusted, that is, so
appropriately in their context, that they have a new
and special sense of belonging together, of forming
a new unity.

In Salinger's phrase, what is particularly appropriate is the <u>extreme</u> contrast between the exaggerated qualities of the sequence normally expected
with <u>breathtakingly</u> and the pedestrian and undigni-
fied qualities of the irony that actually occurs.
Synonyms for <u>levelheaded</u> might get the essential idea
across--"wise," "commonsense," "rational," "reasonable." But nothing has quite the force in this contrast that <u>levelheaded</u> has. And there is, further,
the string of heavy stresses in the phrase as it is
that ever-so-slightly suggests more of the ironic
flatness of <u>levelheaded</u>--a good relation, that is,
between meaning and sound. There are relations between sounds themselves to consider, the short <u>e's</u>
and <u>l's</u> asserting their pattern in the present phrase.
And there are, of course, other relations of meaning
as we get into the larger context--the thrust of irony here highlighted by the stereotyped milque-toast
remarks to either side, the contrast of <u>wife</u> with
<u>girl</u>, and so forth.

If we were to list the bits of meanings and
their relations in the phrase, therefore, we could
say that <u>breathtakingly</u> <u>levelheaded</u> is:

1. a set of semantic markers, distinguishers,
   and other bits of meanings that give the
   major grammatical relations, denotations,
   and connotations of the phrase

2. a set of meanings, traditionally called irony, contrasting what sounds like a compliment
   to the wife with the implication that the
   "girl" is actually very unimaginative.

3. a set of (slighter) meanings in <u>levelheaded</u>, suggesting a metaphorical equivalence between good <u>mental</u> balance and some type of <u>physical</u> stability or, at the level of implication, with some type of flatness.

4. with the additional contrast of hyperbole, between the stated exaggeration of <u>breathtaking-ly</u> and the implication simply of "very"

5. with humor deriving from the irony and hyperbole

6. with deviations from ordinary norms of usage

   a) a frustration of a probability of sequence ("breathtakingly beautiful"), that is, of a bit of meaning attached to <u>breathtakingly</u>

   b) and perhaps, a more extreme improbability than other possible combinations (e.g., "terribly rational," "thrillingly commonsense")

   c) hence, a foregrounding against a more ordinary background in the context.

7. with an interesting interplay of meanings and patterns, e.g.,

   a) the balance of the physical connotations of <u>breath</u>takingly and levelheaded (as opposed to e.g., "breathtak<u>ing</u>ly wise")

   b) the balance of size between the two polysyllabic words and the contrast with the monosyllabic <u>wife...girl</u>

   c) with perhaps the best sound pattern in itself (as opposed, say, to "breathtakingly wise" or "thrillingly commonsense")

   d) with perhaps the best fit of sound pattern to meaning, especially the series of level stresses

It is important to emphasize again that only with the

last four items of (7) do we have relations which are
of interest for their own sake, rather than for any
semantic complexity they give to the phrase. Perhaps,
it would be more accurate to say that, while the alternative phrasings suggested here would preserve much
of the hyperbole, irony, humor, and even foregrounding,
the actual phrase heightens these elements in a set
of especially appropriate relations and unifies them
in a way which even "breathtakingly commonsense,"
close though it is, fails to achieve.

(After such a lengthy analysis, one also hastens
to add two cautions. The first is that no assumption
is being made about how conscious or unconscious the
choices involved in such patterning are.[9] The assumption is simply that, in one way or another, a good
result has been achieved--and it is worth analyzing.
The second caution is that a phrase-by-phrase analysis
of larger literary works in this fashion would be neither possible nor desirable. Hopefully, what will
emerge in this discussion, however, is the concept of
a larger-scale analysis that will include the same
principles operating here.)

It is clear, nevertheless, that sensitive critical analysis, whether in dealing with some local effect in a work or in an important aspect of a larger
structure, has often been concerned with the smallest
bits of meaning and sound and the ways they interre-
late. Winifred Nowottny, for example, comments on the
narrator's conclusion to a hymn in the third canto of
Byron's Don Juan, particularly the first line:

> Thus sung, or would, or could,
>   or should have sung,
> The modern Greek, in tolerable
>   verse;
> If not like Orpheus quite, when
>   Greece was young,
> Yet in these times he might have
>   done much worse.

"Thus sung" is the epic "dixit" which
marks the termination of a heroic speech
and prepares for the move from oratio
recta to narrative or descriptive verse.
To "thus sung" Byron adds "or would,
or could, or should have sung" and the

purpose of this addition is to de-
flate, but not too suddenly, the
dignity of what has gone before;
this sequence, putting ludicrous
stress on the auxiliaries of the
verb, draws attention to the fact
that the sardonic Byron is coming
back into the poem, the Byron who
casts a cold eye on the Muse and
who represents himself as finding
it so difficult to write poetry in
a modern setting that he is always
having involved debates with himself about the propriety or impro-
priety of what he has just written
or what he might write or what
other people think he ought to write.
This aspect of the Byronic personality
re-enters the poem not with a bang,
but a stutter, a deliberate grinding
of the gears of language as the poem
changes over again from romantic
to satiric writing. The stutter,
of course, is not just a metrical
filler in a desperate situation;
it is only supposed to be that; it
is ironically offered as a helpless
bit of writing. Its real purpose
is to modulate to the satirical tone
again and to the already established
Byronic manner in which the deliberate
exposure of poetic machinery is part
of the satiric technique.[10]

Of course, the small poetic structure occurs
as frequently and with as telling effect in "serious"
texts. In his perceptive analysis of Blake's famous
poem, E.D. Hirsch, Jr., remarks, for instance, that
the most daring phrase of "The Tyger" is "forests of
the night." To some extent, the phrase balances connotations of fear and mystery carried by both forests
and night. But to some extent, too, "forests" like
"bright" transfigures all that dread. Blake's usual
and more threatening word for a tiger's habitat was
"desart" and it

was the word normally used by Blake's
contemporaries, if we may judge from

Charles Lamb's misquotation of the
line: "In the desarts of the night."
"Forests," on the other hand, suggests
tall straight forms, a world that
for all its terror has the orderliness
of the tiger's stripes or Blake's
perfectly balanced verses. The phrase
for such an animal in such a world
is "fearful symmetry," and it would
be a critical error to give prepon-
derance either to that terror or that
beauty.[11]

   The range from <u>breathtakingly</u> <u>levelheaded</u> to
<u>forests</u> <u>of</u> <u>the</u> <u>night</u> may confirm again the experience
of many people, that the literary quality has great
variety. It can be as plain as Williams' "This is
Just to Say"

        I have eaten
        the plums
        that were in
        the icebox[12]

or as pyrotechnic as Ted Hughes' description of small
but savage fish:

        Pike, three inches long, perfect
        Pike in all parts, green tigering
            the gold.
        Killers from the egg: the male-
            volent aged grin.
        They dance on the surface among
            the flies.

        Or move, stunned by their own gran-
            deur,
        Over a bed of emerald, silhouette
        Of submarine delicacy and horror.
        A hundred feet long in their world.[13]

It can be as elegant as Henry James:

        The casements between the arches
        were open, the ledge of the bal-
        cony broad, the sweep of the ca-
        nal, so overhung, admirable, and
        the flutter toward them of the

loose white curtain an invitation
to she scarce could have said what.
But there was no mystery, after a
moment; she had never felt so invited
to anything as to make that, and
that only, just where she was, her
adventure.[14]

or as folksy and boisterous as Mark Twain:

You don't know about me without you
have read a book by the name of
The Adventures of Tom Sawyer; but
that ain't no matter. That book
was made by Mr. Mark Twain, and
he told the truth, mainly. There
was things which he stretched, but
mainly he told the truth.[15]

While a heightened sense of relationship is only
minimally present in the phrases and short passages
being examined here (as opposed to the tremendously
complex structure of a character or a whole novel),
it does have radical effects. For it tends to make
the language opaque, as it were, and to dominate the
normal communicative purposes of speech. It tends to
detach speech from the utility of a communication
which does go on, of course, but seems less important
than the extraordinary interest of the speech itself.
And it doesn't take much to slant speech in this direction. As Valéry explains it:

For poetry to be a certainty (or at
least for us to feel ourselves in
imminent danger of poetry), it is
necessary, and indeed sufficient, for
the simple arrangement of words
which we have been reading as spoken,
to compel our voice, even the inner
voice, to leave the tone and rhythm
of ordinary speech and to enter a
quite different key and, as it were,
a quite different time. This inner
coercion to a pulse and a rhythmical
action profoundly transforms all the
values of the text that imposes it.
All at once this text is no longer
one of those intended to teach us

37

something and to vanish as soon
as that something is understood;
its effect is to make us live a
different life.[16]

"Detachment," "divergence," "extraordinariness,"
"foregrounding," are indeed rather clinically pale
terms for explaining the excitement and pleasure we
find in literature. But such terms have their more
positive counterparts--concepts like "originality,"
"craftsmanship," "beauty." And all such terms are
proposed here simply as pointers to the basic literary
value itself that necessarily retains much of its mystery, its own "life." What is argued here is that
the most promising avenue of investigation into that
mystery is simply our sense that meanings and sounds
have been put together exceptionally well.

Poetic Devices

The literary quality is, of course, a property
of whole works. It characterizes a small part of a
work only in ultimate relation to the whole. In the
final stages of his tribulation, for instance, Lear
reflects bitterly on the double standard of justice
for rich and poor:

> Through tatter'd clothes small
> vices do appear
> Robes and furr'd gowns hide all.
> (IV, iv, 168-169).

While there are communicative, not to say persuasive,
values in this statement (the kind of insight, in
fact, that a modern humanist prizes for its educational
value), the primary literary value of the sentence as
a small poetic structure is its success as a set of
harmonizing and contrasting patterns of sound and
meaning. Ultimately, however, this value depends on
the function the sentence has as a fitting part of
Lear's characterization and of other larger patterns
of meaning (the clothes motif, motifs of injustice
and of sin) which were developed from the beginning
of the play.

What our examination of a small poetic structure
suggests, again, is not that a whole work achieves
literary quality by simply multiplying small poetic

structures but rather by systematically creating the same sense of structure and fit relation in the whole speech that we have seen in phrases and sentences.

On the other hand, it is clear that some small structures may be successful primarily in themselves, or that they may emerge forcefully from less successful contexts. Such small structures, the poetic and stylistic "devices" of the tradition, have, in any event, received major attention in rhetorical and poetic theory. From the time of the Greeks, the poetic devices have been catalogued, classified into several broad types, analyzed in their nature and function.[17] Unfortunately, such study has always been plagued by a lack of agreement about the basic terms used--the term "image" in our time, for instance, being used very generally for any small poetic structure; or more specifically for a limited number including metaphor and symbol; or most specifically perhaps for a reference to a concrete specific thing or its qualities--<u>moon</u> or <u>gnarled oak</u>. Only recently, too, have linguistic discriminations become fine enough, particularly in semantics, to give much clarity to such analysis.[18]

Nevertheless, the traditional definitions and classifications remain serviceable for some of the major jobs that engage critics--tracing recurrences of specific devices in analyziang individual works and abstracting sets of such recurrences from many works to characterize the syles of authors, genres, or periods.[19]

The traditional classifications are also helpful in coping with the enormous variety and complex combinations of the devices: <u>unusual words</u>--rare, slang, imagistic in the restricted sense (where one of the sememes carried by the word may be heightened in context); <u>figures</u>--anaphora, polysyndeton or whatever (where recurrence and arrangement of word, phrase, or clause is essential); <u>tropes</u>--metaphor, synecdoche, symbol (where substitution of one term for another, the unusual combining of semantic features, is crucial).

While the lists of devices are quite long, there are numerous other ways, unnamed and unclassified, by which a small part of speech and a whole utterance can shift emphasis from its communicative to its aesthetic function. Such deviations can involve the speaker or other specific kinds of meaning, elements of syntax, devices for increasing the intensity of meaning, the full range of rhythmic and melodic sound patterns. In some sense, one regrets the amount of work that has been done on the smaller, and perhaps more easily analyzed, structures; attention to the larger structures has suffered by comparison.

What can be said about the smaller structures, finally, is that they are simply ways in which meaning and sound can be patterned to present the literary quality in speech. This structuring, to repeat, can occur in the meaning of the smallest phrase ("the white radiance of eternity") or the sounds of the shortest line ("Lully, lulley"). In a very real sense, a metaphor is a small poem. Perhaps we should say, however, that it is potentially a poem. For while all but the most frozen of metaphors or the "deadest" poetic devices will present some divergence from general linguistic and contextual norms and some sense of pattern, only the truly artful will go beyond the convention of the "device" to achieve the special sense of relation which is the attraction of literature. Of themselves, simile, metaphor, hyperbole, irony and all the rest are conventions, general and empty formulas that need the touch of the poet's originality to become interesting structures.

Modes of Language

We have said that a poem or a short story is not developed as a piece of literature simply by multiplying and accumulating small poetic structures. There is some point, nevertheless, to considering poetry or literary language (and those are rather generalized abstractions) in terms of how frequently and consistently the poetic devices appear. At least, the problem of different kinds or modes of language has frequently been approached this way.[20] The "language of prose is distinct from that of poetry," says Aristotle, and no one uses the devices of style "in teaching mathematics."

There are, of course, many modes of language for there are many specializations in its use: scientific, legal, technological, political, and so forth.

But there is some value to proposals that have been made (as wide stylistic generalizations) for a very limited number of basic modes. Each of these basic modes would then embrace a variety of more specialized uses of language.

At the beginning of such theorizing on modes of language, we find Aristotle writing a _rhetoric_ and a _poetics_, though not a complete _grammar_ of ordinary language. There are sufficient indications in his work, however, that he considered these three as the basic modes. In any event, this triad dominates most of the later tradition, with rhetoric, more often than not, preoccuping writers on the subject and absorbing any separate poetics. In modern times, there has been a return to something like the three-fold division of grammatical, rhetorical, and poetic language.[21]

For the present purpose, the question is simply how the small poetic structure is used in each mode. In the grammatical mode (which ranges from everyday conversation to scientific discourse), the plainest kind of speech, such structures are avoided: "the shortest distance between two points is a straight line." In the rhetorical mode, a middle-ground mixing plainess with unusualness, they are used to some degree: "The world will little note, nor long remember, what we say here, but it can never forget what they did here." In the poetical mode, the most unusual kind of speech, the small poetic structure is used most frequently and most consistently: "Life, like a dome of many-colored glass, stains the white radiance of Eternity, Until death tramples it to fragments." The following passages suggest the differences of the modes at greater length:

Grammatical:

The motor correlate of the phonemic syllable has been most adequately described by Stetson as "a puff of air forced upward through the vocal channel by a compression of the inter-costal muscles." According to this description, every syllable invariably consists of three successive factors: release,

culmination, and arrest of the pulse.
The middle one of these three phases
is the nuclear factor of the syllable
while the other two are marginal.
Both marginal factors--inititation and
termination--are effected either by
the mere action of the chest muscles
or by speech sounds, usually consonants. If both marginal factors are
effected by the action of the chest
muscles alone, the nuclear phase of
the syllable is the only audible one;
if, however, the release and/or the
arrest is effected by speech sounds,
the nuclear phase of the syllable
is the most audible. In other words,
the nuclear part of the syllable is
in contrast to its marginal part as
the crest to the slopes.[22]

Rhetorical:

    Dickens entered the theatre of this
world by the stage door; the shabby
little adventures of the actors in
their private capacity replace for him
the mock tragedies which they enact
before a dreaming public. Mediocrity
of circumstances and mediocrity of
soul for ever return to the centre of
his stage; a more wretched or a grander existence is sometimes broached,
but the pendulum soon swings back, and
we return, with the relief with which
we put on our slippers after the most
romantic excursion, to a golden me-
diocrity--to mutton and beer, and
to love and babies in a suburban villa
with one frowsy maid. Dickens is the
poet of those acres of yellow brick
streets which the traveller sees from
the railway viaducts as he approaches
London; they need a poet, and they de-
serve one, since a complete human life
may very well be lived there.[23]

Poetic:

Miranda, enchanted, altogether
believing, looked upon a deep clear
landscape of sea and sand, of soft
meadow and sky, freshly washed and
glistening with transparencies of
blue. Why, of course, of course,
said Miranda, without surprise but
with serene rapture as if some promise made to her had been kept long
after she had ceased to hope for it.
She rose from her narrow ledge and
ran lightly through the tall portals
of the great bow that arched in its
splendor over the burning blue of
the sea and the cool green of the
meadow on either hand.

The small waves rolled in and over
unhurriedly, lapped upon the sand in
silence and retreated; the grasses
flurried before a breeze that made no
sound. Moving towards her leisurely
as clouds through the shimmering air
came a great company of human beings,
and Miranda saw in an amazement of
joy that they were all the living she
had known. Their faces were trans-
figured, each in its own beauty, beyond
what she remembered of them, their
eyes were clear and untroubled as
good weather, and they cast no shadows.
They were pure identities and she knew
them every one without calling their
names or remembering what relation she
bore to them. They surrounded her smooth-
ly on silent feet, then turned their
entranced faces again towards the sea,
and she moved among them easily as a
wave among waves. The drifting circle
widened, separated, and each figure
was alone but not solitary; Miranda,
alone too, questioning nothing, desiring
nothing, in the quietude of her ecstasy,
stayed where she was, eyes fixed on
the overwhelming deep sky where it was
always morning.[24]

43

It can be noticed that as a speech moves from
the grammatical mode toward the poetic mode, it moves
from common usage, from ordinariness to extraordinariness, from using words to playing with them and on
them. It can be said, therefore, that grammar uses
words as much as it has to; rhetoric plays with words
as much as it uses them; poetry plays with words as
much as it can. We should note, too, that there are
obvious differences of purpose among these three
modes. It is the purpose of the grammatical mode simply to present ideas and, at the scientific extreme,
to demonstrate these. Hence, the virtue of the grammatical mode is <u>clarity</u>. As Charles Wheeler puts it:
"we read <u>through</u> prose; we want it to be transparent
and not to get in the way of the message it is communicating, the subject matter it conveys."25

In the rhetorical mode, the purposes are obviously more concerned with the listener or the reader--to
interest him, to move him emotionally, to convince
or persuade him, and so forth; the virtue language
has in this mode is <u>efficiency</u> toward these practical
ends. In poetic speech, words are no longer primarily instruments but are objects, especially as they
function as parts of a whole object which is aesthetic; thus their virtue is <u>beauty</u>, if we may use the
traditional term.

To clarify further the notion of three basic
modes in language, let us consider the following
analogies:

I. Gestures:

    A. Gestures may be given meaning by a group
      and may have a communicative function,
      e.g., pointing. They may even be syste-
      matized into an alphabet such as that used
      by deaf mutes.

    B. Gestures may be given meaning by a group
      and may have a persuasive function, e.g.,
      the gestures of a policeman directing
      traffic or a conductor directing an orches-
      tra.

    C. Gestures, more or less meaningful, may be
      ordered in aesthetically pleasing combi-

nations, e.g., a dance, or a mime.

II. Sounds:

    A. Mechanically produced sounds may be given meaning by a group and may have a communicative value, e.g., a bell indicating the time. Such sound may even be systematized into an alphabet as in the Morse code.

    B. Mechanically produced sounds may be given meaning by a group and may have a "persuasive" function, e.g., horns and sirens.

    C. Mechanically produced sounds, more or less meaningful, may be ordered in aesthetically pleasing combinations, e.g., a symphony.

III. Colors and Shapes

    A. Colors and shapes, more or less meaningful by the fact that they reproduce some reality more or less accurately may have a communicative function, e.g., a news photograph. Crude pictures have also been systematized in a method of writing, the pictographic.

    B. Colors and shapes, more or less meaningful in their organization into pictures, may have a persuasive function, e.g., advertisements.

    C. Colors and shapes, more or less meaningful in their organization into pictures, may be so well ordered as to become aesthetically pleasing objects, e.g., paintings.

Our excursions here into the variety of small poetic structures and their role in different modes of language have been somewhat digressive. Our major concern has been to see what is happening in the small poetic structure--and to suggest that the same principles operate at other levels of the whole literary work. A metaphor, a couplet, a brief alliteration--they have their own order and unity, but they do, of course, figure as part of much larger constructions--plots, characters, stanzas, acts, settings. And these larger structures we shall look at next.

Notes

[1] J.D. Salinger, Nine Stories (Boston: Little, Brown and Company, 1953), p. 91.

[2] Victor Shklovsky, "Art as Technique," in Russian Formalist Criticism, trans. Lee T. Lemon and Marion J. Reis (Lincoln: University of Nebraska Press, 1968), pp. 12, 22-23.

[3] Jan Mukařovský, "Standard Language and Poetic Language," in A Prague School Reader on Esthetics, Literary Structure, and Style, trans. Paul L. Garvin (Washington: Georgetown University Press, 1964), p. 19.

[4] Barbara Herrnstein Smith, Poetic Closure (Chicago: University of Chicago Press, 1968), p.55.

[5] Mukařovský, pp. 20-21.

[6] Roman Jakobson, "Linguistics and Poetics," in Style in Language, ed. Thomas A. Sebeok (New York: MIT Press and John Wiley, 1960), p. 358: "If 'child' is the topic of the message, the speaker selects one among the extant, more or less similar, nouns like child, kid, youngster, tot, all of them equivalent in a certain respect, and then, to comment on this topic, he may select one of the semantically cognate verbs--sleeps, dozes, nods, naps. Both chosen words combine in the speech chain. The selection is produced on the base of equivalence, similarity and dissimilarity, synonymity and antonymity, while the combination, the build up of the sequence, is based on contiguity. The poetic function projects the principle of equivalence from the axis of selection into the axis of combination. Equivalence is promoted to the constitutive device of the sequence. In poetry one syllable is equalized with any other syllable of the same sequence; word stress is assumed to equal word stress, as unstress equals unstress; prosodic long is matched with long, and short with short; word boundary equals word boundary, no boundary equals no boundary; syntactic pause equals syntactic pause, no pause equals no pause. Syllables are converted into units of measure, and so are morae or stresses." Jakobson's theory is, of course, more com-

46

plicated than this single principle; see, for example,
"Poetry of Grammar and Grammar of Poetry," Lingua,
21 (1968), 597-609; "On the Verbal Art of William
Blake and Other Poet-Painters," Linguistic Inquiry,
1 (1970), 3-23; and, with Lawrence Jones, Shakespeare's
Verbal Art in Th' expence of spirit (The Hague: Mouton, 1970). An interesting combination of Jakobson's
theory with communication theory has been made by
Yuri Lotman, who argues that the shift of principles
discussed by Jakobson creates a new code in any literary work and that the resulting intersection of
several codes increases the quantity and density of
information. See his Analysis of the Poetic Text,
trans. D. Barton Johnson (Ann Arbor: Ardis, 1976)
and The Structure of the Artistic Text, trans. Ronald
Vroon (Ann Arbor: Michigan Slavic Publications, 1977).

7 Michael Riffaterre, "Describing Poetic Structures," Yale French Studies, 36-7 (1966), 200-242;
but cf. Jonathan Culler, Structuralist Poetics
(Ithaca: Cornell University Press, 1975), p. 67.
Riffaterre has been helpful in analyzing the way a
small poetic structure deviates from norms established
in the text; see especially his "Stylistic Context,"
Word, 16 (1960), 270 ff. and, more recently, Semiotics
of Poetry (Bloomington: Indiana University Press,
1978).

8 See Michael Shapiro, Asymmetry: An Inquiry
into the Linguistic Structure of Poetry (New York:
North Holland, 1976).

9 See Louis T. Milic, "Rhetorical Choice and
Stylistic Option: the Conscious and Unconscious
Poles," in Literary Style: A Symposium (New York:
Oxford University Press, 1971), pp. 77-78, and the
interesting discussion of the paper, pp. 88-94.

10 Winifred Nowottny, The Language Poets Use
(London: Athlone Press, 1962), p. 47.

11 E.D. Hirsch, Innocence and Experience: An
Introduction to Blake (New Haven: Yale University
Press, 1964), p. 247.

12 William Carlos Williams, The Collected Earlier Poems (New York: New Directions, 1951), p. 354.

47

[13] Ted Hughes, Lupercal (London: Faber and Faber, 1960), p. 56.

[14] Henry James, The Wings of the Dove (New York: Modern Library, 1946), p. 163.

[15] Mark Twain, Huckleberry Finn, ed. Henry N. Smith (Boston: Houghton Mifflin, 1958), p. 3.

[16] Paul Valéry, The Art of Poetry, trans. D. Folliot (New York: Pantheon Books, 1961), p. 285.

[17] See the examples drawn from the Ad Herrenium in Appendix III.

[18] While there have been some suggestive beginnings--see, for example, G.W. Leech, "Linguistics and the Figures of Rhetoric," in Essays on Style and Language, ed. Roger Fowler (London: Routledge and Kegan Paul, 1966) and J. Dubois et al., A General Rhetoric, trans. Paul B. Burnell and Edgar M. Slotkin (Baltimore: Johns Hopkins University Press, 1981)-- we do not yet have a comprehensive analysis of the whole range of rhetorical devices. Among the devices, metaphor has had the lion's share of attention in recent years, not only from literary theorists but also from linguists and logicians; see, for example, Sheldon Sacks, ed., On Metaphor (Chicago: University of Chicago Press, 1979) and David W. Hirsch, "Dwelling in Metaphor," Sewanee Review 89 (1981), 93-110.

[19] Two classical efforts are Caroline Spurgeon, Shakespeare's Imagery and What It Tells Us (Cambridge: Cambridge University Press, 1935) and W.H. Clemen, The Development of Shakespeare's Imagery (Cambridge, Mass.: Harvard University Press, 1951).

[20] See James Kinneavy, A Theory of Discourse (Englewood Cliffs, NJ: Prentice-Hall, Inc., 1971).

[21] See, for example, Charles Morris, "Science, Art, and Technology," Kenyon Review 1 (1939).

[22] Roman Jakobson and Morris Halle, Fundamentals of Language (The Hague: Mouton, 1956), p. 21.

[23] George Santayana, "Dickens," in Irving

Singer, Essays in Literary Criticism of George Santayana (New York: Scribner, 1956), p. 216.

24 Katherine Anne Porter, Pale Horse, Pale Rider
(New York: Harcourt Brace, 1939), pp. 253-254.

25 Charles B. Wheeler, The Design of Poetry (New
York: Norton, 1966), p. 45.

Suggested Readings

Brower, Reuben.   The Fields of Light.   New York:
    Oxford University Press, 1962, pp. 31-57.

Ciardi, John.   How Does a Poem Mean?   Boston: Hough-
    ton Mifflin, 1959, pp. 709-721, 864-875.

Culler, Jonathan.   Structuralist Poetics.   Ithaca:
    Cornell University Press, 1975, pp. 3-35,
    55-74.

Hawkes, Terence.   Structuralism and Semiotics.
    Berkeley: University of California Press, 1977,
    pp. 57-76.

Jakobson, Roman.   "Linguistics and Poetics," in
    Style in Language, ed. Thomas A. Sebeok.   New
    York: MIT Press and John Wiley, 1960, pp. 350-
    377.

IV THE INTERMEDIATE POETIC
STRUCTURE

I cannot imagine composition existing in a
series of blocks, nor conceive, in any
novel worth discussing at all, of a passage
of description that is not in its intention
narrative, a passage of dialogue that is
not in its intention descriptive, a touch
of truth of any sort that does not partake
of the nature of incident, or an incident
that derives its interest from any other
source than the general and only source
of the success of a work of art--that of
being illustrative. A novel is a living
thing, all one and continuous, like any
other organism, and in proportion as it
lives will it be found, I think, that in
each of the parts there is something of
each of the other parts. The critic who
over the close texture of a finished
work shall pretend to trace a geography
of items will mark some frontiers as
artificial, I fear, as any that have been
known to history.

> Henry James
> "The Art of Fiction" (1884)

The Intermediate Poetic Structure

From a strictly theoretical viewpoint, we might imagine that the phrase we examined in the last section resulted, in condensed fashion, from the following steps:

1. basic meaning (grammatical structure): "my wife--a rather unimaginative person"

2. convention of hyperbole (rhetorical structure) "my wife--a terribly unimaginative person"

3. convention of irony (rhetorical structure): "my wife--a terribly commonsense person"

4. originality (poetic structure): "my wife-- a breathtakingly levelheaded girl"

Of course, this probably wasn't how it happened; the intuition of a good writer is much quicker and to the point--as often as not. What spinning things out in this way does suggest, again, is that the poetic structure builds with the natural structure of the speech, with essential structures that will remain and perform their communicating function while a dominating literary structure is developed in, around, and through them. What it also suggests is that there are "intervening" stages of pattern or structure. These patterns reflect very frequently the general, the accepted ways of doing something, the conventions.

Consider an example from another area. Between the raw wood cut from trees and the good Chippendale chair, there intervene a certain number of natural structures and conventions in the process of creation. Besides the shaping into planks and working pieces of material, there is, for instance, simply the convention of "dining room chair" itself--as opposed to that of "desk," say--that dictate that the material be worked up in a particular fashion for the legs of this piece of furniture. And the legs, of course, are an intermediate structure in the whole chair.

From an abstract point of view, again, something similar happens in the development of a plot or a character--or a stanza in a lyric. There is an interplay, that is, between certain basic materials (meanings and sounds of language), certain conventions, and a measure of the artist's own originality. Murray Krieger describes the interaction in these terms:

> The poet begins with a vague impulse, a vague something-he-wants-to-say; but this something need have little relation to what his work finally will say. It seems to be something new to him, something unique and important. He cannot say precisely what it is, or else his poem would already be written...
>
> The poet then submits this vague idea to his ability to work in language. He is controlled here by certain fixities, and yet he has certain freedoms within these fixities. First, he must be limited to some extent by the everyday uses of language, by the elementary laws which cannot be ignored if his work is to have any meaning at all for other users of his language; he must to some extent respect the meanings of words and the conventions of syntax. Secondly, he must be limited to some extent by the artistic traditions which have grown about the art form he has chosen, by the conventions with which he cannot break too sharply if his work is to have any aesthetic meaning for the members of his culture...
>
> But merely to submit the initial impulse to the demands of everyday semantics and syntax and to the demands of artistic traditions would ensure the poet's coming up with an utter stereotype; he could hardly create, could hardly bring something uniquely new into the world if he merely glided down these parallel sets of grooves...

Here the poet's freedom must enter the picture as a counterbalance
to these tendencies toward the stereo-
type. His unique, felt purpose,
though still vague, yet in some mysterious manner also controls the poet
to the extent that he is a creative
artist...He must often bend dangerous-
ly, indeed at times to the breaking
point, the rigidities of everyday
language and poetic tradition.[1]

Thus, there are several types of structure simultaneously involved in what we think of as the literary
structure:

	Literary Structure
Artistic Structure:	Original Patterns
Material:	Patterns from Literary Conventions
Natural Structure:	Patterns from Grammatical and Rhetorical Conventions.
Material:	Sound and Meanings

Ordinarily, of course, we don't advert to the most
basic materials or even the intervening conventional
patterns, any more than we advert to raw or milled
wood in a Chippendale chair or simply to the fact
that it has the general shape of a chair. What is of
prime importance for us is its Chippendale-ness--and
beyond that, the fact that it is a good, not a run-
of-the-mill Chippendale, one that reflects some degree of original achievement by its creator.

Even at that, it must be said that the expert in
antiques and the furniture craftsman might at times
be interested in one or another part of the chair.
And so, too, an informed reader or a critic might be
interested in one or another intermediate part of a
novel or a lyric, as the author very probably was in
the act of composition. For a writer may create a
plot or a character that is intrinsically interesting
or indeed superior to other parts of the story as an
interesting development of standard convention and

54

his own originality. In another sense however, as Henry James suggests, the plot, character, or any other intermediate part will succeed completely only if it contributes to the other parts and is appropriately adapted and adjusted to the context, to the multiple relationships of the whole work. But to get some sense of the development of such intermediate parts, it may be worthwhile to examine a few here, specifically one of the meaning structures of a narrative, a characterization, and the two basic sound structures of a lyric.

Character in the Narrative

We have seen already that the rhetorical structure of a narrative necessarily involves certain parts, each of them resulting from the accumulation of certain kinds of meaning in the speech, most particularly, first, second, and third person meanings.

In a literary narrative, these parts are developed further by convention and artistic originality so that they are indeed different in a short-story from what they would be in a news story. For example, in a brief account of an attempted theft which appeared in the New York Times a few years ago, one can see how the essential "grammatical" meanings have been given a rhetorical structure, particularly by highlighting some of the lighter aspects of urban crime:

> An alleged attempt to steal a piano from a Harlem school ended in a brief block party on a street nearby. The incident started in the post-midnight hours when three patrolmen saw several youths wheeling an upright piano across the intersection of Lenox Avenue and West 117th Street. The youths, spotting the patrolmen's unmarked car, fled in several directions. The patrolmen chased them into several buildings but left the piano in the middle of Lennox Avenue.
>
> One 15-year old was arrested. When the patrolmen returned to the piano, they found a block party had sprung

up around it. Neighbors were singing
and dancing, the police said, as
a man played "I Left My Heart in
San Francisco" on the keyboard.

More police were summoned, and
the piano was wheeled away. It had
apparently been stolen, the police
said, from Public School 149, which
is at the intersection. The 15-
year-old was charged with juvenile
delinquency and the police said they
were searching for his alleged ac-
complices.

If the account were to be used, however, as the kernel of a short story, most of the parts would have
to be expanded according to the general and current
conventions of that narrative genre--and, hopefully,
developed with some originality:

Natural Narrative Structure	Literary Narrative Structure
1. Speaker	1. Narrator
2. Addressee	2. Addressee
3. Persons	3. Characters
Series of Actions	Plot
Time, Place	Setting
Ideas	Themes

Just what the conventions are that influence
the creation of one or another of these parts of a
story is of increasing interest to literary historians
and critics. The reader who is aware of them is also
in a better position to appreciate what a writer has
done with them and just where the writer's originality is at work.

Sometimes the convention affects only one element
of a literary work, for instance, the fashion of having
a narrator present a novel through a series of letters.
At other times, the convention might affect characterization in the novel, short story, verse narrative,
or even lyric. Thus Wellek and Warren comment on bru-
nettes and blonds in various forms of nineteenth century literature:

> The blond is the home-maker,
> unexciting but sweet. The bru-
> nette—passionate, violent, mys-
> terious, alluring, and untrust-
> worthy—gathers up the charac-
> teristics of the Oriental, the
> Jewish, the Spanish, and the
> Italian as seen from the point
> of view of the "Anglo-Saxon."[2]

A nineteenth century short story wasn't automatically
a success when it had a heroine, and it was also a
matter of some indifference whether she was brunette
or blond. The critical decisions came after such
initial choices of conventions by the writer, decisions
about how he was to develop the character and, especially, how he was to fit her into the rest of the story.

But what is a character in a story? Objectively
speaking, "he" or "she" is a set of meanings we usually call "traits," that is, qualities presented as
differentiating, persistent elements in the fictional
personality, whether they be mental, emotional, or
even physical. Such traits are typically scattered
through a story, some presented directly by the narrator in description, others left to be inferred from
what a character says or does or how others react.
Consider, for example, the introduction of Esmé in
Salinger's short story.[3]

> She was about thirteen, with straight
> ash-blond hair of ear-lobe length,
> an exquisite forehead, and blasé
> eyes that, I thought, might very
> possibly have counted the house.
> Her voice was distinctly separate
> from the other children's voices,
> and not just because she was seated
> nearest me. It had the best upper
> register, the sweetest-sounding,
> the surest, and it automatically led
> the way. The young lady, however,
> seemed slightly bored with her own
> singing ability, or perhaps just
> with the time and place; twice, be-
> tween verses, I saw her yawn. It
> was a lady-like yawn, a closed-
> mouth yawn, but you couldn't miss it;

her nostril wings gave her away.[4]

We have here a mix of somewhat exaggerated positive qualities and some slightly negative features.
As the story proceeds, other weaknesses are attributed to Esme—some vanity about her appearance, the
self-consciousness and nervousness expressed by her
nail-biting, the snobbishness challenged by X. But
what dominates the negative side of her characterization is the fact that Esme is also lonely—or at least
isolated. At first, this is simply a matter of her
end position in the first row of the choir and the
separateness of her voice in the singing. But in her
tea-room conversation, it emerges that she is isolated
in various ways from Charles, her parents, aunt, and
governess. In her own analysis of her situation,
her relationship with her father, who had been slain
in the war, seems especially important; what becomes
unconsciously operative, the story suggests, is her
identification of X with her father. There is, in
particular, her father's observation that she hadn't
the sense of humor necessary to face life, a remark
similar to her aunt's about her coldness, and to her
own that she wasn't "terribly gregarious." If Esme
finds solace in her brief meeting with a reassuring
father-figure, therefore, it is against the background
of how she is isolated and insecure, how she wants to
be accepted, how she is experiencing, and accomodating
herself to, a certain amount of life's squalor. These
are some of the "extenuating circumstances" in which
she meets X.

What is emphasized in this mix of positive and
negative features, however, is that Esme is exceptional
—a bright, perceptive,and pleasantly candid young
person. For the controlling conventions in the characterization are those of the attractive, precocious,
lively, but proper, English girl, the figure that appears in such diverse roles as Alice in Wonderland or
Laura in "The Garden Party." Simply to establish such
a convention, therefore, requires that positive and
negative features be selected within a certain range.
If there is to be some pathos in Esme's characterization, it may do to make her a war-time orphan, but,
given the contrasting comic element, it might not do
to have her blind or crippled. She may have the little
habit of counting things, but, for the same reason,
it would be too much to have science be her consuming

58

interest.

Again, such a character might be developed with even more romantic exaggeration or her failings made funnier in a caricature or even, perhaps, left to the flatness of soap-opera melodrama. What also operates in the Salinger story, however, are the conventions of modern realism: Esmé may be memorable, but she must also be believable as an upper class child of mid-twentieth century England.

A mix of positive and negative traits patterned according to recognizable conventions, thus, gets us well on the way to an acceptable characterization. But beyond this stage, we have still to consider literary structures as such, the result of originality in adapting these conventions. One could point here to the freshly observed detail (the lady-like yawn, for example), the flamboyance of Esmé's fantasies about Ohio, or her comic fracturing of adult vocabulary, her amateur psychologizing of her own character traits, the mixture of sympathy, admiration, and amused tolerance in X's reactions to her.

What is also important is that, as Esmé's traits have been repeated, varied, and contrasted, there has been neither too little nor too much (too many repetitions, for example, of her favorite adverb, "extremely"); that the development has internal consistency, that it "hangs together"; that expectations about her have been raised and fulfilled--though not without occasional surprises; that the various elements of the portrait are unified, that they belong together.

Finally, it must be said that Esmé is a successful literary character and that she is not, as some critics suggest, snobbish or tiresomely cute, but rather courageous and generous. Despite her weaknesses and her comic attempts to be grown-up, she is presented as one who adjusts to the difficulties of her situation in a way that X does not. It is she who takes the initiative in kindness by approaching X and who makes perhaps the most subtle of several generous moves by asking for a short story after X has intimated that editors have not been enthusiastic about his work. And it is her letter which reintroduces her so vividly that it provides climax and salvation.

Analysis of a character has finally led us to some of the intersections with other characters, with other meanings in the plot, setting, thematic structure--and these will be discussed in the following chapter. While the character may be interesting and successful in itself, one senses that its final success lies in the way it contrasts with and complements other elements in the story that have to do with love and squalor, compassion and loneliness.

As we will see, the web of convincingly adjusted relations between such parts can be as extensive and as complex as those of Hamlet in his enormous variety and in his commerce with practically every other character in the tragedy, or they can be as relatively simple as that between the dog and the mother seeking revenge (the dog mirroring her fanatical devotion and determination) in Maupassant's little story, "Vendetta." Or it may be relations are concurrently established with settings--as in the extended classical example of Hardy's Return of the Native or, more briefly, with summer and winter settings that echo the love and hate of Maupassant's "Mère Sauvage."

Again, one intermediate structure of a narrative can be more important or successful than another. But the ultimate dependencies which are being emphasized in this discussion imply that any discriminating and open-ended analysis of such a part will lead eventually to important intersections and interactions with other parts in the total structure. And such relations are tremendously more important for the literary value of the work than are questions of whether the character is realistic or fantastic, a psychological or social type, with or without symbolic significance. Again, it may be important to recognize such conventions as they affect the intermediate parts, but it is more important to see what has been done with them.[5]

Sound Structure in the Lyric

In most of our discussions to this point, we have been preoccupied with meanings in the literary work and with the ways these are arranged in smaller and larger designs. However, for the short story writer, the playwright (in verse especially), even the novelist in occasional passages, but most frequent-

ly for the lyric poet, the sounds of the work and
their design become a major challenge and opportunity.

The lyric poet, above all, is always confronted
with the necessity of providing a melodic structure
(in which traditional figures of rime, alliteration,
consonance, assonance will perhaps be conspicuous)
and a rhythmic structure (involving stress verse, metrical verse, or at least free verse) for his poem.
These structures are continuous in the work; they
extend from the first to the last syllable. In terms
of the whole structure, they are, like a character,
the narrative voice, or the plot, "intermediate" parts,
and they have their own stages, parts, and interrelations.

The structures of sound in a poem occur simultaneously with and are variously related to the structures of meaning. In most cases, they are not as conspicuous or as important as the meaning structures.
But they are there and they do influence the total
system of relationships in the poem--for good or ill.
Readings in Appendix IV afford more detailed information about the theory and history of sound structures
in English poetry and about procedures for analyzing
their design and function.

For the present purpose, it may be more important
to look at the sound structure of a particular lyric,
to see how it is put together, and how it is related
to other elements in the poem. Let us consider the
example of Blake's "Tyger":

THE TYGER

Tiger! Tiger! burning bright
In the forests of the night,
What immortal hand or eye
Could frame thy fearful symmetry?

In what distant deeps or skies
Burnt the fire of thine eyes?
On what wings dare he aspire?
What the hand dare seize the fire?

And what shoulder, and what art,
Could twist the sinews of thy heart?
And when thy heart began to beat,

What dread hand? and what dread feet?

What the hammer? what the chain?
In what furnace was thy brain?
What the anvil? what dread grasp
Dare its deadly terrors grasp?

When the stars threw down their spears,
And water'd heaven with their tears,
Did he smile his work to see?
Did he who made the Lamb make thee?

Tiger! Tiger! burning bright
In the forests of the night,
What immortal hand or eye,
Dare frame thy fearful symmetry?

To begin with rather general qualities, it would
be agreed that this poem has mysterious depths and
yet has much simplicity about it. On the one hand its
wonder and awe are rather child-like, on the other
its vision is dramatic, intense, over-powering. Our
goal here and in the following chapter is to see how
such contraries have been coherently structured in a
work that has about it the authentic ring of greatness.

As far as the sound structure is concerned, it
seems to be rather simple but it is effective. Consider the meter. It is basically a conventional
trochaic meter that Blake adapted, perhaps, from the
simple hymn tunes of Issac Watts. (It is also, incidentally, the meter of "Twinkle, Twinkle Little Star,"
and that fact suggests how impossible it is to make
any generalization about meters in themselves.) The
meter is, moreover, developed in a highly repetitive
fashion, though not to the extent of becoming sing-
song. The basic lineal form is that of the opening
line, three trochees and an additional stressed syllable: <u>Tiger! Tiger! burning</u> bright (oo oo oo o).
That line is repeated eighteen times in the twenty-
four line poem; there are only slight variations
"below" the level of the meter itself in the size of
stress, additional secondary stresses, and the size
and cadence of groups which form the base of the metrical pattern. The rather high degree of regularity
which results seems very much a part of the impression of simplicity which the poem develops as a
whole.

Considering other relations of sound pattern to meaning in the poem, we might note first that the allusion which the meter itself makes to the 18th century religious song (usually more pietistic—and orthodox) is deliberate. For "The Tyger" is a theological speculation, from one point of view, one that finally throws innocence and experience, the Lamb and the Tiger into such violent opposition that the speaker wonders whether even God can reconcile them—or be responsible for both. In strictly poetic terms, however, to throw such profound meaning against such simplistic sound structure is to play a dangerous game. For any hint of a childish jingle, of triviality instead of innocence and true simplicity will destroy the serious mood attempted; and that is just what happens in some of Blake's poems. That it doesn't happen here may be credited, perhaps, to the daring extremity in the contrasting elements and to the careful control exercised to make sure the repetition does not become a simple-minded monotony.

There are three factors operating in that control. First, six lines of iambic meter are placed strategically throughout the poem (last line of the first stanza; lines 2 and 3 of the third stanza); lines 2 and 4 of the fifth stanza; last line of the last stanza). The meter is thus varied as well as the way it regularly combines into trochaic couplets and quatrains. Second, there is a major metrical variation, a spondaic foot, with the climactic phrase of the whole poem—dare frame—which is, moreover, the only change in the otherwise complete repetition of the first stanza. Third, since the poem is set against "The Lamb" in the whole collection, there is some point perhaps in noting that the masculine ending of the metrical line in "The Tyger" is particularly appropriate. Given the intense meanings of the poem, a falling cadence at line end, say "Tiger! Tiger! burning brightly" (which would correspond to "Little Lamb, who made thee, oo oo oo) would not do as well.[6]

The melodic structure is, perhaps, more rich and complex than the metrical structure in "Tyger." It does not, however, become obtrusive nor does it much disturb the basic impression of simplicity. Frequent and regular rhyme in verse, in fact, often reinforces this very connotation—and it would seem to do so here.

As with most poems, end-rime is the most prominent figure in Blake's "Tyger." It is couplet-rime
and what is first apparent is that its range of vowel
sounds is quite narrow. Ten of twenty-four rimed
words involve a long i sound; eight a long e sound;
and six a variety of a. There is also a large amount
of internal rime, because words are repeated so frequently in the poem in the same or adjacent lines:
Tiger, tiger; what the; what dread; and so forth.
And there is rich alliteration especially in the fifth
stanza. I count sixteen cases in the whole twenty-
four lines: burning-bright; frame-fearful; distant-
deeps; what-wings; began-beat; what-was; done-deadly;
the-their; water'd-with; he-his; he-who; made-make;
the-thee--and again, burning-bright and frame-fearful.
What deserves special note, too, is the frequent use
of ramdom consonatal patterns involving sibilants,
dentals, and especially r and n. The fourth stanza
is a good example of an elaborate figuration of r
and n particularly:

What the hammer? what the chain?
In what furnace was thy brain?
What the anvil? what dread grasp?
Dare its deadly terrors clasp.

These same consonants, incidentally, provide additional
links to the rime scheme of "Tyger" which escapes the
casualness, as also the inconsequence and jiggling,
of other riming patterns in Blake's poems, which I
do not think would do here. The r and n also provide
an appropriate clipped quality to the masculine rimes.

What generalizations can be made about such details? It should first be said again that the melodic
structure is rather highly figured, but that the impression it carries is not of baroque elaboration,
rather of a compelling repetition. While Blake repeats only a few sounds in the major figures, he does
achieve a degree of variation within the range he com-
mits himself to; he does avoid monotony, that is,
while achieving a controlled simplicity. And again,
the sound pattern is structured appropriately in relation to his meanings.

Sounds and meanings are two quite different materials in a literary work--though the principles of
their structuring, as we shall see further, are in-

64

deed similar. But as with the development of Esmé,
we see in the structuring of sound here, metrically
and melodically, the establishment of striking relations within the structures themselves and the
successful adjustment of those structures to others
in the whole work.

Notes

[1] Murray Krieger, The New Apologists for Poetry (Minneapolis: University of Minnesota Press, 1956), pp. 69-71.

[2] René Wellek and Austin Warren, Theory of Literature (New York: Harcourt Brace, 1949), p. 228.

[3] Analysis for the short story here and in the next chapter is drawn from Daniel Burke, FSC, "Salinger's Esme: Some Matters of Balance," Modern Fiction Studies, 12 (1966), 341-347.

[4] Salinger, p. 94.

[5] Modern structuralists have done extensive work in analysis of narrative; see the bibliographical references at the conclusion of Daniel Burke, FSC, "Some Questions for Narrative Analysis" (Appendix IV).

[6] See Note A following here for metrical analysis of the poem. The first column of the transcription gives the natural grouping of syllables; the second column indicates the meter in the first stanza and, thereafter, only in the variant liens.

Suggested Readings

Chatman, Seymour. Story and Discourse. Ithaca: Cornell University Press, 1978, pp. 15-42.

La Drière, Craig. "Prosody," in Dictionary of World Literature, ed. Joseph T. Shipley, 2nd edition. New York: Philosophical Library, 1953.

Wellek, René and Austin Warren. Theory of Literature. New York: Harcourt, Brace, 1949, pp. 219-234.

Welty, Eudora. "Place in Fiction," in The Eye of the Story. New York: Random House, 1978, pp. 116-133.

NOTE A   Metrical Structure

"The Tyger"

Tiger! Tiger! burning bright

In the forests of the night,

What immortal hand or eye

Could frame thy fearful symmetry?

In what distant deeps or skies

Burnt the fire of thine eyes?

On what wings dare he aspire?

What the hand dare seize the fire?

And what shoulder, and what art,

Could twist the sinews of thy heart?

And when thy heart began to beat?

What dread hand? and what dread feet?

67

NOTE A (continued):

What the hammer what the chain?

In what furnace was thy brain?

What the anvil? what dread grasp?

Dare its deadly terrors clasp?

When the stars threw down their spears,

And water'd heaven with their tears,

Did he smile his work to see?

Did he who made the Lamb make thee?

Tiger! Tiger! burning bright

In the forests of the night,

What immortal hand or eye,

Dare frame thy fearful symmetry?

68

V   THE TOTAL POETIC STRUCTURE

The plot, being an imitation of an action, must imitate one action, and that a whole, the structural union of the parts being such that, if any one of them is displaced or removed, the whole will be disjointed and disturbed. For a thing whose presence or absence makes no visible difference, is not an organic part of the whole.

Aristotle,
The Poetics

Our approaches in the last two chapters to the
small and intermediate poetic structures have, in a
certain sense, been rather beside the point. At least
they have yielded only partial answers to what constitutes a poetic structure. In a very radical way,
the whole work of art has to be our concern. For the
whole work determines the function and value of each
of its parts, and it is the ultimate basis for whatever is achieved of artistic value. It is often said,
in fact, that the total work transcends the parts, is
more than the sum of the parts:

> The function of a poem, i.e., what
> makes it a work of art, is to create,
> in the mind of the hearer or reader,
> a gestalt, comparable to a melody
> in music. The gestalt of a poem is
> an organized whole or configuration
> of aesthetic experiences. Just as
> a melody is distinct from the sepa-
> rate tones, the gestalt of a poem
> is different from the sum total of
> its linguistic features.[1]

Only by experiencing the whole work, therefore, and
its unique qualities can we be in a position to judge
it or to justify our judgment of it. What our attention to smaller parts thus far has done, however, is
to introduce us to the principles which operate in
the whole structure. For actually the same principles
are involved at any level of that structure and in
any of its parts.

The Conventions of Total Structure

We have seen that a small or intermediate poetic
structure evolves from the interplay, so to speak,
of natural structure (with its grammatical and rhetorical conventions) and artistic structure (with a
further interplay of literary convention and the writer's originality). With a total structure, a set
of literary conventions now comes into play, a set
that corresponds in its effects, however, to the conventions affecting smaller structures. For example,
there are analogies among conventions of metaphor,
conventions of plot, and conventions of tragedy.

The conventions which most frequently influence

the larger structures of a work are precisely those of the forms and genres to which, sitting before a blank piece of paper, the writer decides to address himself. What are forms and genres? From the viewpoint of the writer--and the reader as well--they are traditions, sets of conventions, abstract and general patterns or models for writing (or appreciating) a story, a novel, a domestic tragedy--or any other distinguishable "kind" of literature.

Most of us, if we were set the task, could write a list of things that usually happen, settings or types of characters than can be expected, plot endings that are inevitable in television westerns, courtroom dramas, or spy melodramas. These are the fashions now in these particular genres; there may be even more ephemeral fashions that vary from year to year but which, for a while at least, exert their influence on television writers--and viewers.

There are, however, more basic conventions of writing particular types of literature that have arisen at some point in history, have been imitated by others, and thus have eventually become traditions. Hence, a character or plot will have to be developed in certain ways in a short story simply because it is that and not a novel. Every type of literature, therefore, has its own possibilities and limitations and with these sets of characteristics the creative writer, as we have observed, must come to terms. As he develops a character in a short story, for instance, he is elaborating, first, what is an inevitable and natural part of any narrative speech. But in doing it sketchily he is, in the second place, limited by the conventions of the short story; or in making the character a slow-witted foil for a brilliant detective, he is following the conventions of a specific genre.[2]

Analyzing Total Structure

It is clear that everything in a work contributes to or detracts from what it is attempting to be. It is not just the melodies of a symphony that make it successful, but everything in it, every note. So, too, every inch of painted canvas contributes to the art masterpiece; nothing can be ignored when we discuss its success. Thus, the effect of any work depends upon its total structure, its total design. It in-

cludes all of the parts in the work and all the relations between those parts. It is not simply the general or the so-called "external" formal elements, for
example, the rime scheme of a sonnet, but everything
--meaning, sound, their patterning, their inter-rela-
tions--that gives specific character or uniqueness
to a piece.

What is needed for literary criticism, therefore,
is a method of analysis which is comprehensive but
which also helps to suggest the uniqueness of a piece,
as ineffable as that may ultimately be. On the one
hand, every possible use of sound and meaning has to
be potentially provided for by the method; on the
other, the character of the specific work and its design have to remain the focus.

What satisfies these two opposed demands is a
structural analysis. Such an analysis assumes that,
in Aristotelian terms, matter (sound and meaning) and
form (the relationships sound and meaning enter) are
found throughout the piece and that they can be separated, for purposes of analysis, only by mental abstraction. This analysis assumes, secondly, that any
structure is an organization of smaller structures:
a syllable is a structure of individual sounds; a verse
line, a structure of feet; a phrase, a structure of
words--and so on through the most elaborate structures
(e.g., the plot of a novel) of literary pieces. Thirdly, this analysis assumes that in every structure some
element is initially presented, then, typically, is
repeated or varied and that, appropriately related,
these patterned elements become a special unity.

The most basic principle of such poetic structure
is, unfortunately, not easily stated or readily open
to analysis. It is simply that the work gives a
special sense of structure, a special sense that parts
have been well related. The difficulty with the principle is that it does not appear in any ready-made
formulas--the fit relation of one character to another,
for example, of setting to plot, of one event to another in a plot and so forth. These relations are indeed central to the poetic structure, but there are
many possibilities of where and how relations may be
established and may dominate the grammatical and rhetorical structures of the speech--and these possibilities, in fact, are infinite and unpredictable. For

these possibilities are created differently in each work of art, and their very uniqueness and complexity, especially in larger works, insures them against any absolutely complete or definitive analysis. When we do examine a work, therefore, whose value impresses us, what we do is probe the structure in this or that aspect to test its coherence, in some sense to retrace the paths a good artist has taken and the choices he has made.

John Dewey has said that the artist must have "a grasp of the connection between what he has done and what he is to do next."[3] What this implies is that the most important criteria for what is right or wrong in a work of art are those which are uniquely developed within the work itself. A move in a chess game or a shot in billiards is not right or wrong in itself, but only in relation to the situation which has developed to that point. In the same way, the structuring of a poem is a progressive feat of art in which certain possibilities arise once the poet begins and, then, are capitalized upon or not. When what ought to be done is done, the relationships established radiate that fitness which is the essential achievement of art. Poetic structure, therefore, is a net-work of uniquely realized potentialities, of possibilities that have been generated within this work and then fitly realized in terms of the developing context. Our aesthetic satisfaction and pleasure in the work is a response to this system of relation, to the sense of structure simply as itself, of a happy fitness which has dominated any particular convention or meaning which it involves.

The idea of a "net-work" of fit relations should not be interpreted to mean that the total poetic structure is simply a loose accumulation of such relations among the smaller parts of the literary work. The unity of any piece of art suggests rather that a design has been worked out among its largest parts--the sequence of beginning, middle, and end; the coordination of narration, characterization, and plot; the individualized divisions and shapings of the unique form--or among the smallest elements of meaning and sound.

Consider, for example, Shakespeare's Sonnet 73:

That time of year thou mayst in me behold
When yellow leaves, or none, or few, do hang
Upon those boughs which shake against the cold,
Bare ruin'd choirs, where late the sweet birds
        sang.
In me thou see'st the twilight of such day
As after sunset fadeth in the west,
Which by and by black night doth take away,
Death's second self, that seals up all in rest.
In me thou see'st the glowing of such fire
That on the ashes of his youth doth lie,
As the death-bed whereon it must expire
Consum'd with that which it was nourish'd by,
    This thou perceiv'st, which makes thy love
        more strong,
    To love that well which thou must leave ere
        long.

The four-part division of the English sonnet-form is
quite obvious here: three quatrains repeating different images of "decline" with many parallels in
the way each question is set up and then, a couplet
making an application. These clear divisions serve
the rhetoric of a speaker who is very emotionally
and dramatically involved but who pursues his purpose
with deceptively simple means and patterns. But practically anyone who has read the sonnet with care has
noted many relationships beyond those among the major parts, and so, perhaps, has sensed the basic contrast between "surface" plainness and the deeper complexity of the individual images. Nowottny, for
example, notes several relations involved in the repeated ideogram of "decline" and shows how the second
quatrain mediates many of the more specific relations:

                But that common ideogram, however
                compulsively given by the poem,
                leaves out other movements going
                on within the particulars of the
                metaphors, moving as they do from
                a cold, bare, ruined season to a
                glowing fire, from a time of year
                to a crucial moment, from what has
                gone to what is imminent, from the
                separate perceptions and simple
                reference in the first quatrain
                ("yellow leaves"..."boughs which
                shake against the cold") to the one

complex image, highly figurative
in expression and irradiated with
intellection, in the last quatrain.
These movements are no less controlled than is the emergence of a
"common" abstraction under the im-
petus of the "in me..." formula.
For if we inspect the second quatrain
closely we shall see that in the
case of each of the movements (from
cold to fire, past to future, diffuse to concentrated, etc.) the second quatrain occupies a stage in-
termediary between the first quatrain
and the third. The glide from "cold"
through "fadeth in the west" to
"glowing of...fire," easiest to point
to, is not more important than the
other glides the quatrain executes,
though these take longer to translate
into critical language and are perhaps not so readily accepted as
being important--because they are
not visualized, and because they em-
body relations rather than references.
But the tenses glide too (from "sang"
through the ambiguous "by and by...
doth take away,...seals up all"--
these hovering between present and
future--to "must expire"); without
this glide we could not be disposed
to grasp in the last quatrain the
simultaneous annulling of tense (for
the fire is made to symbolize continuous process) and the irradiation
of the one remaining moment of un-
extinguished vitality with passionate
importance and concern. More important still, the second quatrain
increases the degree of figuration
superimposed upon the basic metaphor.
In the first quatrain extra figuration
was applied only to one distinct element of the time of year, that is to
the boughs, which were metaphorized
as "Bare ruin'd choirs." In the second
quatrain it is "black night," swamping
all the afterglow in the west, that is

75

given extra figuration--not only
as "Death's second self" but also
as that which "seals up all":   this
extra load of figuration prepares
the way for the almost unanalyzable
intricacy of

                                such fire
That on the ashes of his youth doth lie,
As on the death-bed whereon it must expire
Consum'd with that which it was nourish'd by.[4]

The critic concludes, therefore, that while the major
parts give the poem some structure, it is perhaps
not the most important, for within the similar and
contrasting images there is a rich "continuous process of change, of multiple relationships undergoing
multiple transformation."

    Given this multiplicity of relationships, it is
all the more striking that our basic impression of
the poem is one of cohesiveness and unity. But while
the work, and indeed our impression of it, have this
sense of overall unity about them, our analysis rarely does. The basic relations of the poetic structure
are not always easily perceived nor being sensed can
they be easily described. Thus, we typically suggest
general impressions of the work and attempt to relate
them to the complex unity of its structure. We make
probings into that complexity and hope finally to
convey some insight into the final unity.

Structure in the Lyric: Blake's Tyger

    Reversing the usual order for treating our two
basic texts, let us proceed here to further analysis
of Blake's "Tyger." But how do we begin to unravel
such mysterious and complex meanings, such deceptively simple structures? Perhaps, if we look first at
the essentials of the natural structure, we can move
to particularities in the poetic structure, to details
that seem relevant to our sense that this is an extraordinary speech.

    The rhetorical shaping of this speech affects,
as we have seen, some inevitable and basic meanings:
there is a speaker, speaking to someone, about something, to achieve some purpose. The speaker in our

poem, whether or not he is the prophetic bard who opens the Songs of Experience and who contrasts with the piper of Songs of Innocence who sings about the contrary state of soul--the speaker here is a thinker and his speech is essentially speculation about ultimate significance, of the Tiger as symbol, of his creator, of reactions to him. The speaker is not, however, an analyzer of generalities and abstractions, at least immediately, nor is he philosophically detached from his musings. Rather he is deeply and emotionally involved in the vision which clothes his problem; he presents his emotional reaction to, as much as any cognitive intuition about, the mysterious tiger and his creator. He is in a word presented as a mystic--as Coleridge said of Blake in one of his letters "a mystic emphatically." Compared with Mr. Blake, he went on "I am in the very mire of commonplace common-sense" (Letter to H.F. Cary, 6 February 1818).

What comes through strongest about the speaker created for the poem, therefore, are his attitudes and purposes. No references in the speech flesh out the character and personality of one who speaks in a definite, an authoritative, but an impersonal voice. The attitudes themselves are somewhat ambivalent-- perhaps a touch of admiration and positive wonder, but a large measure of fearful concern and awe. It is a matter of astonishment and astonishment says Edmund Burke, "is that state of the soul, in which all its motions are suspended, with some degree of horror. In this case the mind is so entirely filled with its object, that it cannot entertain any other, nor by consequence reason on that object which employs it."[5]

How we interpret the tiger will, of course, affect our interpretation of the speaker's attitude. There is much in the poem, however, to suggest that the attitude is one of astonishment, in Burke's sense of the term: the opening exclamations (followed by what 18th century grammars called "admiration points"); the insistent questions; the broken sentences suggesting incoherence; the direct references to fearful symmetry, sinews of the heart, dread hand, deadly terrors and so forth. This excitement indeed establishes one of the strongest relations in the speech--that between the speaker and what he is speaking about. From the rhetorical point of view--of one, say, who is simply celebrating the tiger and what he stands for or

77

of one moving us to judge these things as he does--
this emotion is, perhaps, excessive. But in the poetic structure, this excess becomes a matter of good
balance with the extreme affectivity of what is objectively described.

     Much of what is being described is, of course,
the Tiger. In that pseudo-address we call apostrophe,
it is he who is questioned by the speaker. There are
many interpretations of what he symbolizes, in fact
several large and growing forests of differing opinion
where, fortunately, he still burns brightly and free.
We might offer here, however, three broad interpreta-
tions--that he is simply evil in the orthodox view
and so something negative, something opposed to the
innocent Lamb; that he is the admirable force of human passion and creativity, for which the Creator is
as much responsible as for innocence; that he is a
composite, a fearful symmetry, of good and evil forces.
Among recent Blake scholars such interpretations are
given extensive support from the symbolism developed
by the poet in his later work. If any of these or
similar interpretation is held exclusively, however,
the poem then becomes, from the rhetorical point of
view, a meditative argument to persuade others to this
view of the tiger and what he and his creator stand
for. But another possibility is suggested by Northrop
Frye:

               Scholars will assert that the question
               in "The Tyger," "Did he who made the
               Lamb make thee?" is to be answered
               with a confident yes or no; Yes if
               Blake is believed to be a pantheist,
               no if he is believed to be a Gnostic.
               Most of those who love the poem are
               content to leave it a question, and
               they are right.[6]

I would take this approach, too, but I would add that
the basic question is the opening one--who could frame
the fearful symmetry. The questions following explore
the implications of the opening question.

     What is in doubt at the beginning of the ques-
tions is somewhat ambiguous. It could be the ability
or capability of any imagined creator of the Tiger;
on the other hand, it could be his prudence in deciding

to create the Tiger which is questioned. As the potential subjunctive <u>could</u> creates this ambiguity, the
auxiliary <u>dare</u> (dare he aspire; dare seize the fire)
raises doubt not only about wisdom but also courage.
By the time we reach the more detached reflection on
the dilemma in the fifth stanza, however, this ambiguity is being resolved. It is not capability which
is being questioned but prudence, wisdom. The final
contrast of <u>dare</u> <u>frame</u> with <u>could</u> <u>frame</u> makes the
point clear. The questioning of the poem, therefore,
does not simply return upon itself and end where it
began. Rather it spirals to a more intense and awful
question about the Maker.

It is the Maker, indeed, who is the other primary concern of speculation. While the speaker attempts to summarize the mystery of the Tiger in the
phrase about his "fearful symmetry," he makes no similar attempt for the Creator. Instead he presents
him in his mysterious creative activity, a fiery and
somewhat sinister blacksmith who flashes into the
speaker's vision only in terms of hand, eye, wings,
shoulder, and of his heavy metallic tools. In some
primordial or eternal past, this maker engages in the
fierce labor of hammering together a Frankenstein
monster out of fiery eyes, sinewy heart, and flamming
brain. Then, as the "stars" of heaven (most immediately, Satan's angels defeated by the original evil of
their own disobedience--Apocalypse XII, 7ff.) make
clear their reaction to the Tiger, the question is
raised about the creator's reaction. And at this
point, there seems to be no question about the creator's responsibility for actually making the Tiger,
for "his work." But even this certainty falls immediately before the paradox of the Tiger and the Lamb
and the repetition of the opening question--still unresolved and even further complicated and more awe-
some.

Doubtless there is much more that could and should
be said about the depth and complexity of the implication in these visionary accounts and questions. I
have been mainly concerned, however, with indicating
the rhetorical shaping of these meanings as the speaker
sets about to impress us, as he does so successfully,
with the awfulness of the mystery he contemplates.
However, if we move beyond individual meanings, grammatical and rhetorical structures, to the ways they

balance and contrast, to the consistencies of their interactions, our problems are different.

Many of the smaller details of the poem are so fine that it is worth recalling, as we begin the next stage of analysis, how admirable are some of its more pervasive qualities. These characteristics are strong in themselves, and they are in strong contrasts that run through the whole poem. We have noted already that the poem is deep and mysterious, yet very simple and straightforward. We can add that it is unrelenting and insistent as it develops its basic ideas but that it escapes any sense of repetitiousness, indeed that it is filled with continual surprise; that, in the cosmic sweep of its questions, it makes absolute separations between the tiger and his maker, between the tiger and the lamb, between the speaker and the objects he contemplates, but it also hints at puzzling identifications between them all; that it is pitched at once to a high level of intensity, but that it proceeds to still higher levels.

Some of these contrasts are apparent in the first quatrain. The double exclamation (Tiger! Tiger!) which opens the poem initiates immediately the dense patterns of recurrence which, some would say, are incantatory and hypnotic in their effect. Be that as it may, what we have seen already in the sound structure is true of other structures in the poem: Blake comes extremely close to annoying repetition of a simple item but has sufficient variation to avoid that fault. The most striking grammatical feature of the poem, for example, is that every sentence is a question. Fifteen questions in twenty-four lines could be a problem. But Blake manages sufficient variation in the length of the questions themselves and in the openings--the involved openings of the first, fifth, and final stanzas, shorter prepositional phrases (In what distant, On what wings, In what furnace), and the simple and most frequently repeated what. On the other hand, when he wants a staccato flurry of questions in the fourth stanza, he rolls four of them off with the same opening. Even here, though, he varies them in length and interrupts them with a fifth which begins differently.

In another aspect of the grammatical structure, we can see Blake bind himself to a norm of plainness

but achieve sufficient complexity with minimal variation. As in the other <u>Songs</u>, the poet's vocabulary
here is about 80% monosyllabic.[7] While we have the
overall impression of simple speech, however, we find
polysyllables concentrated in the key first and final
stanzas and also in the fourth, a climax in a series
of three quite similar quatrains.

   Part of the economy, therefore, that contrasts
so strongly with the intensity and pregnancy of the
poem depends on restricting the number and the complexity of the elements being used and using them
with minimal variation. Another aspect of the same
economy is the multiple functioning in individual
elements, something typical of any concentrated lyric,
of course, but especially true of "Tyger." "Burning
bright" in the first line, for instance, not only
presents what Kathleen Raine calls "the flaming beauty of the living creature" but the phrase starts the
metaphorical development of the tiger, it takes the
first step in a chain of fire and light images, becomes a contrastive pole for the imagery of darkness
in the next line, and figures in the intricate pho-
netic play of <u>i</u>, <u>r</u>, and <u>t</u> sounds which were alluded
to earlier here.

   We have alluded, also, to the effective combination of positive (beauty, order) and negative (evil,
fear) elements in <u>forests of the night</u>. We need add
here only that the <u>plural form of forests</u> begins
the emphasis on the more universal significance of
the tiger. The phrase also completes the first couplet, and a series of couplets such as we have here
presents the closest and densest possible end rime.

   The significant achievement of the first stanza,
however, is that it does not decline after this brilliant opening. For now the maker is introduced, the
central figure of the poem actually. He is introduced with the synecdoche of eye and hand, of wisdom
and skill, and the basic question about him is posed:
could the tiger have been made even by an immortal
creator? The question concludes, however, with a
trope that contends with "forests of the night" as
the most effective and concentrated of the poem--<u>fear-
ful</u> gathering for immediate projection again the awe
and horror already stated, <u>symmetry</u> repeating the contrary elements of beauty and admiration. And again,

there are interesting semantic and phonetic tie-in's of <u>could frame</u> with <u>fearful</u> symmetry: the possible-impossibility suggestion of <u>could</u> relating to <u>fearful</u> and the craft of <u>frame</u> connecting with <u>symmetry</u>; the <u>fr</u> of <u>frame</u> with the <u>f-r</u> of <u>fearful</u> and so on.

It is not too much to say that the first stanza contains all the themes of the poem, that is, the major meanings that will be repeated and varied in later parts of the poem. They are: the tiger; a setting (time, place); the maker; the process of making (specifically, the possibility of making); the speaker (questioning and reacting). Three meanings are combined in the basic question, what maker could make the tiger? In some fashion, that question seems to be repeated in every quatrain, for a while in every couplet. It becomes the normal element of repetition in the meaning structure (much as the opening line is the norm of the metrical structure)--to be played against by other combinations of meaning, as in the second quatrain, to be departed from in minor and major ways, especially in the fifth stanza.

But there is considerable variation in the elements of the basic question itself as they are repeated. The method Blake chooses for variation is represented in the change from <u>tiger</u> to <u>fearful</u> symmetry in the first stanza. Not only does the poet avoid discussing the significance of the tiger (or of the maker), but after presenting the tiger he avoids anything like a wholistic description. He gives his symbolic action, <u>burning bright</u> and his general quality, <u>fearful</u> symmetry, but then only the parts and aspects that separately enter his creation: fire of eyes, sinews of heart, the brain and its terrors. Similarly, the maker appears as an eye or hand, wings, shoulder, feet, a grasp as he frames, dares to aspire, dares to seize, twists, dares to clasp--and smiles. This substitution of part for whole would seem to be an aspect of the poem's mysteriousness. For as it is used with both, it seems to hint at an identification of creator and creature. And across the gulf of their difference, there are also at times flashes of aversion and attraction, not unlike the ambivalent astonishment of the speaker: the maker's hand daring to seize the fire, daring to clasp the terrors of the brain, and again, smiling.

After the basic question is first posed, the next three stanzas ring variations on maker-making-tiger with the synecdoches just described. The fifth stanza then explores possible reactions to the tiger more completely, as it repeats the question in still another form and before the question is reformulated in the final stanza. Let us now consider the matter of tempo and emphasis in this development and consider an earlier assertion that the poem begins at a high level of intensity and proceeds to a still higher.

It should be observed that, in its initial presentation, the basic question extends over two couplets and fills the first quatrain. As intense and pregnant as the question is here, it is also solemn and rather measured. By comparison, the next three stanzas are frantic, and, in that sense, even more intense. There is a flurry of questions in rapid succession and the couplet now becomes a more distinct unit, though the questions are frequently more brief than the couplet itself. In each of the questions, the questioner darts off in a different direction, seeking his answer and raising the basic question in the form of more specific problems about place (what forbidden place, accessible only to Icarus wings or Promethean hand, held the fire of the tiger's eyes); about strength and skill (what superhuman body and intelligence were capable of producing the heart); about instruments (what cosmic blacksmith's tools could be used to create the brain).

This series of three stanzas has a small climax, perhaps effected by the concentration of polysyllables already noted; the forceful images of the smithy with their suggestion of strong noise; and the approach to a run-on line (as in the opening and closing stanzas) in the second couplet which itself seems rather clotted with its d alliteration, the free patterns of d-t and r-s, and the complicated asp syllable of the rime:

> What the hammer? what the chain?
> In what furnace was thy brain?
> What the anvil? what dread grasp?
> Dare its deadly terrors clasp?

The next stanza provides a different contrast: it is more relaxed, a slight pause before the ascent to the intensity of the final reprise. Again, the couplets combine in a sentence for the whole question, and the themes of setting and of reaction to the (newly made) tiger are developed more extensively and variously with totally new items of meaning (the stars with their spears and tears, the Lamb) are introduced.

And how is it that the final stanza is a new and ultimate climax of meaning and intensity, since it only repeats the first stanza with the slightest of variations? The return to the beginning, while it constitutes a frame for the intervening variations, also provides definite closure, a sense that there will be nothing further.[8] What is heightened and emphasized, however, are the implications of the basic question as even greater reasons for the astonishment, the new intensity crystallized in the shift of <u>could</u> to <u>dare</u>.

There are series of smaller meanings than those which we have been discussing as themes. They help to modulate and articulate the major meanings at specific points, extend their continuities and contrasts in more subtle ways in the poem, and so contribute to the unity of the whole. Supporting and mirroring the troubled affectivity of reactions, of astonishment, aversion and admiration, the disappointment of the stars, for example, are the sememes of violence connected with the actions of the tiger, the maker, and the stars: burning, seizing, twisting, throwing down. While the stars may throw down their spears, however, they also water heaven with their tears before the Lamb is introduced to the generally less violent setting of the fifth stanza; this is another of the careful modulations we come to expect in "Tyger." Again, and perhaps less conspicuously, there is a contrastive series of large and small--in <u>immortal</u> and <u>hand</u> <u>and</u> <u>eye</u>, or in <u>distant</u> deeps <u>and</u> <u>skies</u> and <u>fire</u> <u>of</u> <u>thine</u> <u>eyes</u>. It is, perhaps, this loose series that relates the extreme deviation of the fifth stanza to the rest of the poem and supports its unity at this point--hence, <u>stars</u> versus <u>spears</u>, <u>heavens</u> versus <u>tears</u>; <u>he</u> versus <u>his</u> <u>work</u>, and, perhaps, <u>Lamb</u> versus <u>thee</u>, with a reversal of the usual order. There are also patterns of light and dark and of fire and heat throughout the poem, and these anchor in the whole the shorter and more unusual series of blacksmith images--as they echo and contrast in various ways with patterns of violence, troubled affectivity or, on the other hand, with admiration and the positive aspects of _burning_ _bright_, _symmetry_, _Lamb_, and _smile_.

Let us now turn from such micro-analysis to the larger parts and their articulations. What we have suggested here is that "The Tyger" is developed in three large parts. The first posits a question, a set number of themes; the middle section of four stanzas develops these themes; the conclusion restates the original set of themes with a significant change and significant increase of the mystery and intensity so central to the poem. The structure is tri-partite, but played against it are other obvious divisions into six quatrains and twelve couplet units--and we have seen some of the interactions between couplets and quatrains.

There are other patterns corresponding to and crossing these parts, for example, the division between the present time at the opening and closing and the primordial past of the middle section describing the creation of the tiger and initial reactions to it.[9] But it is a difficult and delicate task to describe just precisely the way patterns are repeated and contrasted or are articulated in a whole work which impresses us with its coherence.

The most basic principle which relates one part to another in a structure is simply one of sameness and difference, balance and contrast, repetition and variation. At its most basic, structure, as has been intimated already, can be reduced to the elementary principle that similar and different parts are being related--light stress and heavy stress to form a meter; partially similar and dissimilar syllables to form a rime; similar and dissimilar incidents to form a plot; similar and dissimilar traits to develop a character; similar and dissimilar plot, character, setting, and "themes" to form a narrative.

All structures combine both similar and different parts. But as the structure is built of these parts, it may emphasize similarity by repeating identical or slightly varied parts. Thus, it creates a _serial_ structure--a loosely episodic story, for example, or a highly repetitive lyric like Ned O'Gorman's "The Rose and the Body of the Rose":

THE ROSE AND THE BODY OF THE ROSE

The rose and the body of the rose
the stem, and the balustrade of air
the pith of darkness in the fist
the rose and the body of the rose.

The wolf and the body of the wolf
the jaw and the marrow in the skull
the furnace fastened in the eye
the wolf and the body of the wolf.

The wren and the body of the wren
the wing and the vessel of its flight
the lyre in its runic throat
the wren and the body of the wren.

The shark and the body of the shark
the sudden mouth and fix of knife
the panic shackled to the fin
the shark and the body of the shark.

The snake and the body of the snake
the twist of choking in the grass
the feet of scorpion on the tongue
the snake and the body of the snake.

The bat and the body of the bat
the flash of demi-bird and slap
the divination of the chin
the bat and the body of the bat.[10]

On the other hand, the total meaning structure can be built by balancing or contrasting distinct parts or by subordinating one to another in a tight construction. Hence, we can get a systematic structure--the meaning structure of Oedipus Rex or even of Blake's "Lamb," which plays definite question against definite answer to make a complete structure.

In Ted Hughes' poem "The Thought Fox" there is a definite step-by-step progression to a climax, an ordering of the middle section that seems quite different from the recurrent similarity of "Tyger"-- though like "Tyger" it has a frame with a final significant difference:

The Thought Fox

I imagine this midnight moment's forest:
Something else is alive
Beside the clock's loneliness
And this blank page where my fingers move.

Through the window I see no star:
Something more near
Though deeper within darkness
Is entering the loneliness:

Cold delicately as the dark snow, /
A fox's nose touches twig, leaf:
Two eyes serve a movement, that now
And again now, and now, and now

Sets neat prints into the snow
Between trees, and warily a lame
Shadow lags by stump and in hollow
Of a body that is bold to come

Across clearings, an eye,
A widening deepening greenness,
Brilliantly, concentratedly,
Coming about its own business

Till, with a sudden sharp hot stink of fox
It enters the dark hole of the head.
The window is starless still; the clock ticks,
The page is printed.[11]

The most difficult feature of the interplay of sameness and difference, however, is not the fact that
one or the other may finally dominate the structure,
but rather that the two principles are in such constant interaction:

> Serial organization is the order
> of recurrence of some identity;
> such organization operates to dif-
> fuse an established identity: it
> is exemplified typically by metrical
> rhythm. Systematic organization,
> on the other hand, operates to es-
> tablish new identities by concentra-

tion, or cumulation, of elements
into relatively discrete unitary
entities. To take an example
again from rhythmic structure, the
foot is a small system; the strophe
a larger system. The normal interaction of the two types of organization is illustrated in these examples. You must have some systematic
unit, which may be repeated, before
you can have a series: you must have
a foot if you are to have a meter.
But you can constitute a larger system serially, simply by "marking off"
a certain number of repetitions of
the smaller system: so lines and stanzas may be constructed, by serial
organization of small units (feet) into
cumulative systems of a larger order;
and then these larger systems in turn
may be repeated serially again, or
ordered into yet larger systems. The
interaction, or interinvolvement, of
the two types of order occurs at all
levels and tends always to be complementary.[12]

The outline of the poem's structure in the accompanying
Note A attempts to trace some of this interinvolvement
in Blake's "Tyger."

Our lengthy examination of Blake's lyric suggests
that several larger structures of meaning and sound
are operating in the poem, developing simultaneously,
at times independent of one another, at other times
touching and mutually supporting one another. One is
reminded of the atomic model used a few years ago with
several particles orbiting around a nucleus. While
there is no nucleus here, there are distinct melodic
and metrical structures, structures of the qualities
and the quantities of sound. On the side of meaning,
there are two similar structures--of the kinds of
meanings and of their intensities or quantities.

Our final concern, however, has been that there
are not four structures, but, in a very important
sense, one structure. We felt that the poem had a
special radiance of structure, of coherence and unity,

of relationships that were peculiarly fitting. Its
coherence, we saw, resulted from the way several of
its general qualities and the development of its parts
were sustained--the excitement, astonishment, and per-
plexity of the speaker, for example, or the dense repetition of the sound structures with just sufficient
variation. The poem's coherence seems related, also,
to the expectation raised by its highly emotional
opening and its successful conclusion on an even
higher note--again, with just sufficient variation in
the fifth stanza. But, perhaps, the most striking
aspect of the coherence is this welding of such strong
contrasts--the simplicities of idiom and sound pattern
with the deep complexities of the symbolic actions
and the mysterious question they raise.

We have been probing from one side or another
to get a sense of total structure in some particular
ways. And naturally when we find some special relation of meanings or of meanings and sound, we would
like to offer some "proof" for our sense that they
are indeed special, that they are part of a poetic
structure. But it is unfortunately easier to point
up mistakes than to prove successes--to show that
the constant iambic meter of Kilmer's Trees becomes
an objectionable drone than that Sonnet 73 has perfectly wrought images.

But the critic does have a few tools, rather simple and elementary, at his disposal. One of them is
to compare or contrast works, perhaps of the same
author, to show that one is more successful than another in a particular respect. Another frequently
used gambit, we have seen, is to change structures
at some point where the construction seems particularly fit--and to suggest alternatives. The critic typically does the reverse: he suggests improvements
for what he considers flaws. But he could also take
a striking phrase like fearful symmetry and suggest
that shocking symmetry or frightful, or startling,
or awful, direful, haunting, ghastly symmetry is too
much or too little for what is required in the context
at that point. Or the critic may suggest alternatives
which the poet himself tried in earlier versions of
his work. We have, fortunately, three earlier versions of "The Tyger" and while I will not even allude
to the many insights they afford into the final form
of the poem, I would suggest that Blake's art con-

89

sciously or unconsciously intervened at several crucial points to cancel out his first tries.[13] Had it not we would have had lines like

> And when thy heart began to beat
> What dread hand and what dread feet

> Could fetch it from the furnace deep
> And in thy horrid ribs dare steep.

And again,

> In what clay and in what mould
> Were thy eyes of fury rolled.

I think in both cases it will be agreed that the lines would represent an excess in the present context.

Aside from such simple experiments, the basic recourse of the critic is to return to the work with his hypothesis and to check his reaction against the intuition of others. And this indeed is our situation with the poem and our analysis here: we have attemted to show that there is sturcture in the poem where there might not have appeared to be, to show that various elements do connect, and that in connecting as well as they do, that they radiate that special sense of fitness we call the literary quality. What we have also demonstrated, perhaps, is that the total structure of even such a small work is fantastically complex and that it cannot be fully encompassed by rational analysis. In pointing to some aspects of the structure, however, we have enhanced our sense of the perfection that is still there to be enjoyed-- and is still free.

Narrative Structure: Salinger's "Esmé"

As we return to the Salinger short story, we may note that our focus in analysis rather automatically adjusts to other interests. In particular, we become concerned with other kinds of units that seem more relevant to the total structure of a story as opposed to that of a lyric. We are certainly no longer concerned with metrical or melodic structure in the consistent way we were with "Tyger." On the other hand, we did examine one small structure and saw that relations among very small bits of meaning and sound

were crucial to its success--and there are a number
of similar structures in the story. But as we moved
to consider a character, we began to see that the
most important relations for the way the whole story
worked successfully were those among larger parts.
What might be of value now will be to consider the
very largest divisions of the story as an approach
to the interaction of characters, plot, setting, and
thematic structure.

In its largest outlines, the story of Esmé is
rather obviously and emphatically structured into two
major parts. Each part has a small but important
introduction in which the narrator speaks in the present and describes his relationship to the story.
Thus, we are told in the introduction to the first
part that the story has been prompted by an invitation
to a wedding which the writer, though he would have
liked to, will not be able to attend. The story is,
therefore, something of a wedding gift to make up for
his absence, a prose narrative epithalamium for Esmé.
In more practical terms, it also represents a reply
to the wedding invitation and hence the inclusive
letter-narrative in which letters, from the initial
invitation to the final letter of the story, have
important functions. Later in the narrative itself,
we learn that it also represents a belated fulfillment
of a promise made by the author to write a story about
"squalor" just for Esme. From these facts derives
the significance of the title.

Each part with its (1) brief introduction is
further developed in three stages. There is next (2)
a stretch of summary and panoramic narration (the sequence of barracks, town, church and civilian tea-
room in the first part; the second-floor room in the
civilian home in the second part); then (3) a scene,
the major section in each part, with extensive dialogue between Sergeant X and another main character;
and finally (4) a brief appendix and closing. These
divisions seem to be intended by Salinger, for most
of them have additional spacing to set them off.
Thus, while the narrator proposes and actually works
out a strong contrast between the two major parts of
the story (changing even his mode of narration), there
is much similarity in the way the large blocking of
story is presented. There are, too, a number of balances among thematic and other strands of the story--they

will be pursued here--that cut across the basic contrast, as well as echoes of specific situations and
images. In the first part, for example, X reads
widely, but in the second he is "triple-reading paragraphs"; in the first part, he is charmed by Esmé's
crossed feet, in the second, repelled by Clay's feet
on his bed. Again, the whole squalid story of American soldiers in the second part recalls Esmé's remark in the first part, "Most of the Americans I've
seen act like animals"--and it raises again the issue
of compassion.

But the fundamental unit which is repeated and
varied in the story's structure, more specifically
in the plot, could be called "the attempt to communicate." (See Note B to this chapter.) And this small
unit has both a positive and negative form, as the
attempt succeeds or doesn't. The opening section,
for example, contrasts the success of Esmé's invitation in evoking a warm response from X with the failure
of X to get a sympathetic response from his wife. In
the following section, the summary iterations of
failed communication in the barracks and of X's solitary walks, the particular walk in the rain, and the
cold reception by the tea-room waitress are contrasted
with the moment of communing in the church as Esmé
is introduced (in turn contrasted with the choir director's failure to communicate with the children)
and finally, with Esmé's entrance in the tea-room.
The conversation which follows is built with succes-
ses in finding common ground or expressing sympathy,
varied by occasional slips and miscues that cause
temporary embarrassment (or anger, with Charles), as
one or another topic is attempted. The coda is then
patterned with these successful communications: Esmé's expression of affection, forced through Charles;
X's setting up Charles for his punch-line; the reite-
ration of the promise to write a story for Esmé.

This sequence, and its reversal in the second
large block of the story, has its roots, of course,
in the characterizations. For this is a story of
character rather than incident, sitting and talking
constituting the bulk of the action; it is a story
of illuminations rather than passions or even suf-
fering.

What the title may somewhat distract from is the

fact that the story has its basic unity in X. It is
his story rather than Esmé's, and the introduction
serves to characterize X in important ways. First,
and most crucially, it suggests a relationship with
Esmé in his response to the invitation and then contrasts this relationship with those X has with members of his own family. Secondly, it presents X as
a writer. Hence he has "gone ahead and jotted down
a few notes" which he presents with a twist on the
traditional Horatian formula: not to please but to
instruct. The fact that he is a writer (with little
success) will provide the last climax in his own
development. There is, thirdly, a note of self-consciousness struck in these few remarks as also in his
observation that "I don't think I'm the type..." and
again in the intelligence hocus-pocus as he introduces the second part. As the narrative itself develops, it soon becomes evident that the main characters are extremely self-conscious, that they are,
moreover, pre-occupied with self-analysis and the
analysis of each other, and that others are prone to
analyze them, too much of this in explicitly psychological but rather inaccurate fashion. Finally, the
introduction establishes in the narrator's voice the
note of an ironic, detached, but not intolerant humor.

As X's character is developed the stress is on
his introversion and his progressive isolation from
country, relatives, soldier companions, the war effort itself, his isolation being effected as often
as not by letters and letter writing. But as Esmé
is introduced, we see that she complements positive
traits of X's character that then emerge more fully
--his intelligence, sympathy, sensitivity. But their
meeting also develops contrasts between their traits.
Such contrasts, some rather obvious, are those between
female and male--or between the stereotypes of feminine illogicality and intuitiveness, and masculine,
sober reasonableness--youth and age, naivete and experience, civilian and military. These contrasts
counterpoint and to some extent limit the happy communing between X and Esmé that is made possible when
he speaks to her condition in a way that he could
not with his companions and will not later with Clay,
and addresses her level in a way that contrasts strongly with the choir coach's talk to the children.

As the main characters are isolated and brought together in this fashion, it becomes clearer that this very relationship between characters is pivotal in the structure of the story. The story is not about abstract ideas of love and squalor; it does not have a complicated thematic structure. It is about characters who find themselves in loving communication--or, squalidly, without such communication.

If the first confrontation of X and another has developed the positive qualities of his character, therefore, the second develops some of his liabilities. The exploration of his mental breakdown, the anguish of his isolation especially, develop X as a pathetic figure. The contrasts with Clay's insensitivity redefine the first stage of X's development, adding now a touch of bitterness and more than a touch of smugness. The method again is to isolate X in the opening section of the part but now to deepen that isolation in another lengthy conversation that lacks anything like communication, even though the other character is now a military man of similar age and experience. And the second conversation also lacks some of the complexity and variation of the first.

The contrast with the first part of the story is indeed obvious enough. What is not so obvious, perhaps, is that the development of X's character is through several moments of special emotion and illumination. In each of the major parts, these moments are placed rather symmetrically, the first coming at the end of the summary narration, the second after the lengthy conversation. The first moment of heightened experience comes for X as he listens to the children's choir: their "voices were melodious and unsentimental, almost to the point where a somewhat more denominational man than myself might, without straining, have experienced levitation." He leaves the church under "the spell the children's singing had cast." The second moment comes in parting with Esmé at the end of their conversation: "It was a strangely emotional moment for me." In the squalid part of the story, the first point comes with X's response to the "hopelessly sincere" inscription written by the Nazi woman--"Dear God, life is hell" --an exclamation which for X "appeared to have the stature of an uncontestable, even classic indictment." The second comes when X is driven to nausea by the conversation with Clay and especially, it would seem, by Clay's accusing question "Can't you ever be sincere?"

It might be argued that after each of these moments X makes some special effort to communicate-- his entering the dialogue with Esmé with proper seriousness; setting up Charles to answer his riddle the first time around; attempting to write the counter-inscription from Dostoievski "with more zeal than he had done anything in weeks; answering "with great effort" the remark of Clay's mother in her letter, that she was glad X and Clay have been together. Again, there appears to be more patterned complexity in one of the story's elements than might first appear.

The climax in the way of epiphanies, however, is in the closing of the second part as X responds to Esmé's letter. Like the addendum to the first section, in which Esmé drags Charles back to the tearoom, this part is devoted to a more particular expression of Esmé's affection and the indirect expression of that love forced through Charles--his wet smacker in the first section, his note at the end of Esmé's letter in the second. The letter is a vivid re-introduction of Esmé, capturing all of her mannerisms with statistics, her charming dislocations of vocabulary, her competence in managing a situation and teaching Charles. The evocation is so good, in fact, that X addresses her directly, switching appropriately into the speaking which symbolizes their earlier communing.

The letter and the gift of her father's watch are high points of Esmé's generosity and of her beneficial effect upon X. But there is some implication that this effect goes beyond the inner narrative to the time of narrative frame. One need not infer further association or even further correspondence between the hero and heroine (though Esmé apparently does have X'x current address for the wedding invitation), but the final salutary effect of the encounter must be described in terms of X's writing at last a story for someone, something he had never done before. (Conversely, the announcement of Esmé's wedding at least suggests that X's assurances about Esmé's lack of humor, her coldness, and lack of compassion have

not been without effect in her growing up.) In the
end, therefore, it can be argued that X develops,
that he has not simply recovered his faculties as a
result of Esmé's love but has achieved a sympathetic,
if still ironic, tolerance--a spirit more akin to the
mood of the Esmé dialogue with X's defense of the
American soldier than to his sarcasm and condescen-
sion in the Clay dialogue. And this former is the
tone of the introduction. Nevertheless, X remains
something of a flawed character: his failure to cope
more successfully with life's problems contrasts un-
favorably with Esmé's energy and initiative, perhaps
mainly because he is cast in the role of adult, father-
image, and advisor.

    If X as a character has some liabilities, he is
a narrator much better. Even the radical shift in
his point of view does come off. As one looks back
on it, the personal speaker is appropriate for the
love section and the use of indirect discourse typically to report his own side of the dialogue does
highlight Esmé in her one big scene. And the switch
to impersonality in the next section reduces the sentimental possibilities of a narrator reporting his
own breakdown.

    We have come to appreciate the importance of
voice in all works of literature, to understand that
it is as much a creation of the author as the characters or settings which he invents. It is of great
importance in "Esmé"--a structure which frames and
mediates the more serious, and at times, sentimental
possibilities of isolated soldier and girl responding
to each in the balanced dialogues and illuminations
of their story. It makes the story the humorous-
serious, bitter-sweet mixture that it is.

    Once again we have been probing at some of the
interrelations important to our sense that the story
is good, that it hangs together. In itself, for instance, to divide a story into two major parts is a
matter of indifference for literary value. However,
once the author has chosen to write about communication and non-communication, about love and squalor,
then the marked division and the balancing of smaller
sections within the parts assume more importance.
When the largest parts further mirror one another in
similar and contrasting details (e.g., letters that

isolate or unite) or in important moments of the story
line (e.g., the epiphanies), the appropriateness of
the bipartite design has more to be said for it.

At the other end of the scale, the smallest structures of the story continually impress us as successful flashes of ironic humor, convincing suggestions
of speech and gesture, freshly observed reports on
reality. One thinks, for instance, of the parents
in church "bearing pairs of small-size rubbers, soles
up, in their laps," of the children "like so many un-
derage weight-lifters" raising their hymn books, of
the waitress who looked "as if she would have preferred
a customer with a dry raincoat," of the defining pos-
ture, phrase, and tone in Esme, Charles, and Clay.
And one is further impressed with the fact that these
brief flashes don't distract but also serve the function at hand.

Between the extremes of largest and smallest
structures, there is something to be said, too, for
consistency--of choosing a tone and maintaining it
at the right level in the narrator's voice; of repeating an interesting quirk in a character, but varying it successfully--and not trying it too often; of
constructing a series of similar situations and moments in each major part, but in due measure, with
interesting changes, reversals, and results.

What is being said here, finally, is that these
are reasons that the story works, though not without
flaws. They are not reasons that we necessarily
are conscious of as we first encounter the story. But
they are things that we seem to respond to as we read
and enjoy the story--and that we make clearer to ourselves in analysis. These are the kinds of reasons
that we would discover in analogus ways in larger
works--plays, novels, epics--where the possibility of
encompassing all the complexity of a total structure
is even more remote, but where the same kind of analysis can yield important insights into the way something does or does not work well.

Notes

[1] A. Willem DeGroot, "The Description of a Poem," in _Proceedings of the Ninth International Congress of Linguistics_ (The Hague: Mouton, 1964), p. 295.

[2] For a discussion of the nature of forms and genres and how they can be related, see Daniel Burke, FSC, "Classifying Forms and Genres." (Appendix V)

[3] John Dewey, _Art as Experience_ (New York: Minton Press, 1934), p. 45.

[4] Nowottny, pp. 78-79.

[5] The quotation from Burke's _Enquiry_ I came upon several years ago in an article by Monroe Beardsley, "The Discrimination of Aesthetic Enjoyment," _British Journal of Aesthetics_ 3 (1963), p. 295. Its appositeness to the speaker in "Tyger" has been noted by, among others, Morton D. Paley, "Tyger of Wrath," _PMLA_ 81 (1966), 540 ff., who also provides references to the abundant scholarship and different views on the poem. Among discussions since Paley, see especially Mary R. and Rodney M. Baine, "Blake's Other Tigers and 'The Tyger,'" _Studies in English Literature_, 15 (1975), 563-578, who argue from Blake's illustration and from other use of tigers in his work that the Tyger represents the "perennial problem of believing in a benign universe...the most agonizing of all moral dilemmas" (576), and Nick Shrimpton, "Hell's Hymnbook: Blake's _Songs of Innocence and of Experience_ and Their Models," in _Literature of the Romantic Period 1750-1850_, ed. R.T. Davies and B.G. Beatty (Liverpool: Liverpool University Press, 1976), pp. 19-35.

[6] "Blake After Two Centuries," _University of Toronto Quarterly_, 27 (1957), p. 12.

[7] See Joseph Wicksteed, _Blake's Innocence and Experience_ (New York: Dutton, 1928), pp. 62ff.; see also Josephine Miles, _Eras and Modes in English Poetry_ (Berkeley: University of California Press, 1964), pp. 78-99, and cf. J. Walter Nelson, "Blake's Diction --An Amendatory Note," _Blake Studies_, 7 (1975), 167-175.

[8] On framing devices for closure, see Smith, pp. 64-67.

[9] I remain unconvinced by some discussion that construes the final _dare_ of the poem to be in the past tense: see John E. Grant and Fred C. Robinson, "Tense and the Sense of Blake's 'The Tyger,'" _PMLA_, 81 (1966), 596-603.

[10] Ned O'Gorman, _The Night of the Hammer_ (New York: Harcourt, 1959), p. 24.

[11] Ted Hughes, _The Hawk in the Rain_ (London: Faber and Faber, 1959), p. 14.

[12] J. Craig La Drière, "Literary Form and Form in the Other Arts," in Paul Bockman, ed., _Stil und Form Probleme in der Literatur_ (Heidelberg: Winter, 1959), p. 34.

[13] See, for example, Martin K. Nurmi, "Blake's Revisions of _The Tyger_," _PMLA_ 81 (1956), 669-685.

Suggested Readings

Brooks, Cleanth. _The Well-Wrought Urn_. New York: Harcourt Brace, 1947, pp. 192-214.

Ciardi, John. _How Does a Poem Mean?_ Boston: Houghton Mifflin, 1954.

Weidlé, Wladimir. "Biology of Art." _Diogenes_, 17 (1957), 3-8.

Wellek, René and Austin Warren. _Theory of Literature_. New York: Harcourt Brace, 1949, pp. 139-158.

NOTE A

"The Tyger":   A System Constituted Serially

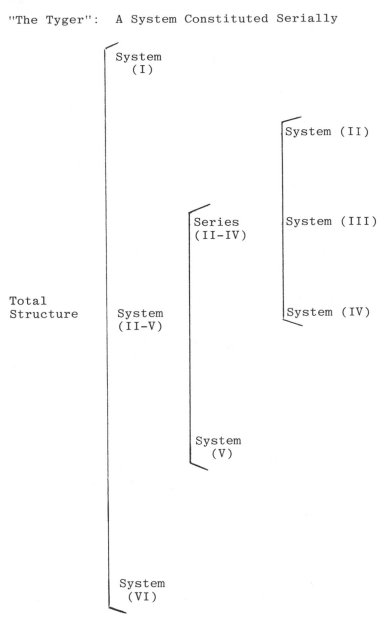

I
  System (1-2)
  System (3-4)

II
  System (5-6)
  Series (7-8)

Series   Tiger! Tiger!
System   burning bright

System   In the forests of the night,

System   What immortal hand or eye

Series   Could frame thy fearful symmetry?

System   In what distant deeps or skies

System   Burnt the fire of thine eyes?

System   On what wings dare he aspire?

System   What the hand dare seize the fire?

Series   And what shoulder, and what art,

III

System (9-10)   System   Could twist the sinews of thy heart?

System (11-12)   System   And when thy heart began to beat,

                 Series   What dread hand? and what dread feet?

IV

System (13-14)   Series   What the hammer? what the chain?

System (15-16)   System   In what furnace was thy brain?

                 Series   What the anvil? what dread grasp?

                 System   Dare its deadly terrors clasp?

Series (17-18)   System   When the stars threw down their spears,

                 System   And water'd heaven with their tears,

Series (19-20)   System   Did he smile his work to see?

V   System   Did he who made the Lamb make thee?

102

VI

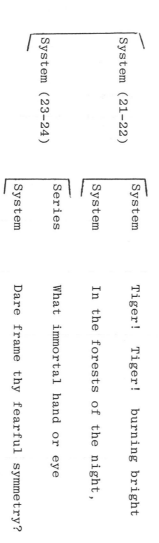

System (21-22) ⎰ System — Tiger! Tiger! burning bright

System (23-24) ⎱ System — In the forests of the night,

Series — What immortal hand or eye

System — Dare frame thy fearful symmetry?

NOTE B

"Esmé": A System Constituted Systematically

```
                              ┌───System:  Introduction
                              │
                              │   System:  Barracks
              System          │            Church
              (Part I)        │            Tea-room
                              │
                              │   System:  Conversation
                              │
                              │   System:  Return
  Total                       └
  Structure                   ┌───System:  Introduction
                              │
                              │   System:  X's room
              System          │
              (Part II)       │   Series:  Conversation
                              │
                              └───System:  Return and
                                           Close
```

The total structure of "Esmé" is only sketched here, since it is obviously much more complex than that of "The Tyger." The diagram does indicate the division of each major part into the four parts discussed in this chapter: dotted lines indicate the narrator's speech in "present" narrative time, the few sentences, that is, that create the frame for the past events recounted. The basic element of repetition is, again, the attempt to communicate. The introduction in the first part, for example, suggests the unsuccessful communication of Esmé's invitation and contrasts it with the failure in the discussion between X and his wife. The second part has at least three systems that could be analyzed as

```
  ┌  System:  Non-communication in the barracks
  │           and walk
  │
  │  System:  System: ┌Non-communication by
  │                   │choir director
  └
```

104

NOTE B (continued)

		System:	Communication by choir
		System:	Non-communication by choir director
System	Series	System:	Non-communication by waitress
		System:	Non-communication by letter

    The major section which follows is constituted by the series of exchanges by X and Esmé in their successful communication: 1) these are on a variety of topics; 2) they proceed in assertions, inquiries, observations in many of which is agreement, though often not (but the communication is not undermined); 3) they are interrupted by the nurse and Charles, the interruptions also involving successful and unsuccessful communications. The major section of the second part is, by contrast, a rather unrelieved and uninterrupted series of non-communication with Clay.

VI LITERARY AND OTHER VALUES OF LITERATURE

The "greatness" of literature cannot be
determined solely by literary standards;
though we must remember that whether it
is literature or not can be determined
only by literary standards.

> T.S. Eliot
> "Religion and Literature"
> (1935)

The first task of critical analysis is to establish the fact that a particular object is a work of art, to present whatever evidence is available, that is, to show that it is an art object and not a technical object, a literary speech and not a simply rhetorical speech. Even this initial task is fraught with some difficulty, for there is (1) much disagreement about what makes the essential difference and (2) no consensus about how this factor is related to other values obviously presented by the literary work. A.E. Housman explains the situation this way:

> If a man is insensible to poetry, it does not follow that he gets no pleasure from poems. Poems very seldom consist of poetry and nothing else; and pleasure can be derived also from their other ingredients. I am convinced that most readers, when they think that they are admiring poetry, are deceived by inability to analyse their sensations, and that they are really admiring, not the poetry of the passage before them, but something else in it, which they like better than poetry.[1]

In the present discussion, it has been assumed quite explicitly that the literary quality of a work is an aesthetic value, a special sense of relationship that makes a structure interesting for its own sake, that gives it a compelling and pleasurable sense of unity. What has not been assumed here, however, is that this aesthetic value is the only value of the literary work. What these other values are, what their relation is to the aesthetic value, and what special problems are posed by the ensemble of values, will be the questions pursued here. The pursuit, it should be noted immediately, will be sketchy. The attempt will not be to offer definitive answers to any of the questions, but rather to suggest the place of the problem in the general theory being developed here and to outline its possible solution.

Fitness

To begin with, it may be well to recapitulate

and refine the notion of relational or structural fitness which we have been identifying with the aesthetic value. Our basic definition is from the accompanying reading by La Drière (Appendix VI), that it is the "coincidence, in matters of relatedness, of what is with what ought to be." As the article thereafter suggests, the concept is one with extremely wide application. It applies to grammar and law, to rhetoric and etiquette; it is as wide as the possibility of relating different things well or badly; it is limited only by its basis in nature and convention.

What distinguishes aesthetic fitness from a variety of other kinds is ultimately difficult to define precisely. But we have stressed here the complex and sometimes rather minute nature of the relationship involved (in, say, "breathtakingly levelheaded"); the development of norms for what is fit completely within the work, contextually, not from an external standard; the final dependence, therefore, despite the involvement of general or conventional patterns, of the work's unity and fitness on norms which are entirely unique to itself.

The closer the work approaches to the fit structure demanded by its own logic, the more difficult, in a way, is it to assess or to demonstrate its achievement. Mistakes, failures to meet a demand the work has obviously generated for itself are usually easier to detect. What one does, though, to assess positive value is to gather support for his initial impression that fit relation does exist by showing that structure itself does exist where at first it might not have seemed to; by contrasting or comparing to grasp better what the uniqueness of the structure is; by checking one's impression with that of others. In such processes, conclusive demonstration is not possible, of course. One returns to the impression that he had to begin with. But critical analysis is not circular. Rather it is spiral; it strengthens or weakens, perhaps displaces one's first impression; it leads, hopefully, to corroboration by others.

The creator of a literary piece has previously engaged in a similar exploratory work as the structure of the piece has developed under his hand. The poem is an organism, said Coleridge. But it is not one that grows automatically to its inherent goal as does a plant. That goal, as a recent theorist has put it well,

> if it must be located, is in the
> interplay between the maker's mind
> and the developing structure. As
> relationships occur to the inven-
> ting poet in the presence of his
> shaping poem, he is rejecting and
> selecting, exploring potencies;
> he is reader of what has already
> emerged as form, or, to use Leonard
> Meyer's term, of "antecedents," and
> he himself experiences the "expec-
> tation" of the "consequents." In
> his choosing of this consequent ra-
> ther than that, he specifies new
> relationships, the form is actualized
> more, norms are more traceable, the
> probability of a new particular con-
> sequent is increased. To this the
> poet defers, regardless of his ini-
> tial plans, regardless of himself.
> This is what Eliot refers to as the
> poet's "surrender of himself" to
> something "more valuable." He does
> not mean that a poem is more valuable
> than a man, but that to the new and
> unexpected demand of a fitness (to
> what is just coming to existence) a
> new and previously unthought of answer
> must be given, having nothing to do
> with demands made on the poet because
> he is a man.[2]

Under what necessity is the artist in making any
particular choice? Or, from another point of view,
how necessary is any one relationship, any one part
or another to the organic unity of the whole? To
answer the second form of the question briefly, it
can be said that any one part is absolutely necessary
and is relatively necessary. It is absolutely necessary, if the work is to be this particular work; the
slightest change will necessarily alter the absolute
uniqueness of any work--as it does frequently in the
process of the author's revisions. On the other hand,
the part or relationship may be only relatively necessary for the general or acceptable unity and fit-

ness of the final work, for its goodness. "Breath-takingly commonsense" is pretty good--in terms of the whole story; "breathtakingly levelheaded" is better. Conceivably something else is even better. But there is a certain range of what will, at least, work at that spot. And beyond that range, there are many things that won't do at all. Our cherished phrase here is necessary, relatively speaking.

Fitness and Unity

The correlative concepts of unity and fitness have had a long history, though they may have not always been as explicitly connected as they are here.[3] Unity, for example, was a concern for Aristotle as he distinguished between aggregates in which "the position of the parts in relation to each other makes no difference" in the object--and wholes, in which the position and character of the parts depends on the total structure (Metaphysics, 1024a). In wholes, parts cannot be removed or transposed without changing the character of the total structure or of the other parts. Plato had earlier suggested (Phaedrus, 264c), and Aristotle later applied to plots, the idea that whole speeches must have a beginning, middle, and end: "A 'beginning' is that which does not itself necessarily follow something else, but after which something else naturally exists or happens..." (Poetics, 50b26). Thus, the required and developing nature of relations between parts of a whole was emphasized. St. Augustine and other late classical and medieval thinkers spoke with a somewhat different emphasis. They were impressed with the contrast between the variety of parts and the unity which had, nevertheless, been achieved. The unified whole was thus seen as dominating a multiplicity, as a congruity of sameness and difference. In a similar fashion, modern theorists speak of a "balance of tensions," a "unified diversity," or a "dynamic order." Trygeve Emond, for example, speaks of structural balance in art as a kind of order, to which asymmetry gives a dynamic quality. Mutual adaptation of shapes and colors to one another makes for order in a composition; introduction of contrasts integrated in that order animates it. Repetition represents order; variation adds vitality.[4]

In the last two centuries, the term "organic unity" has also been used frequently by writers,

though the analogy of works of art to living creatures
was begun by Plato. Coleridge, for example, speaks
of "the balance or reconciliation of opposite or
discordant qualities" achieved by the imagination of
a complex of indeterminate and constantly changing
components not unlike that found in living things.
Borrowing from contemporary German theorists, he also
spoke of form as

> mechanic, when on any given ma-
> terial we impress a pre-deter-
> mined form not necessarily arising
> out of the properties of the ma-
> terial; as when to a mass of wet
> clay we give whatever shape we
> wish to retain when hardened. The
> organic form, on the other hand,
> is innate; it shapes as it develops
> itself from within, and the fulness
> of its development is one and the
> same with the perfection of its out-
> ward form.[5]

The dependence of parts on the whole has been
treated in modern psychology in terms of a gestalt,
a set or quality belonging specifically to the whole
as such and not to the simple addition of its parts.
In a sense, then, the whole is more than the sum of
its parts, a melody, for example, having a character
distinct from the sum of individual notes. Hence,
one can recognize a short group of notes as belonging
to a specific melody.

A frequent objection to such accounts of unity
in artistic structures is that the same idea can be
applied to non-artistic structures. Indeed, parts
are related to form unified wholes in any kind of
structure. But artistic unity clearly has special
effects. Our thrust here has been to connect these
effects with the appropriateness or fitness of the
relations between parts. Thus, the relations themselves become primary, something worth contemplating
in themselves and for themselves.

The concept of fitness has had as continuous a
history as that of unity. While it was a fundamental
principle for ancient theorists concerned with poetic
structure, it was later, as rhetorical decorum, often

narrowed in its applications: diction, for example, should be appropriate to the social status of a speaker, said the rhetorician. But whether as "consistency" or "appropriateness," fitness is a concept to which theorists and critics constantly return, for as La Drière indicates, it

> seems to be prior to unity; it is
> rather because its internal rela-
> tions are fit that a structure
> presents itself as unified than
> because it is unified that its re-
> lations seem fit.[6]

Other Values of Literature: The Classic

To make the minimal determination of whether this short-story or poem is a work of literature, we need not leave the work itself. We can seek more light on particular meanings, of course, in a study of the work's background, the biography of its author, and so forth. But once the work has been understood, the aesthetic question can be answered within.

Given a basic aesthetic value, the critic will frequently enough make assertions about a "degree" of aesthetic value and, indeed, of other values the work may involve. In making such assertions, the critic will implicitly or explicitly compare the work in hand with others. "This," he may say, "is Salinger's best short-story"; or, "this is the best American short-story, a classic, a masterpiece." As the critic ascends this ladder of praise, the grounds of his assertion usually get thinner and thinner. If he says, this is Salinger's best, it may be that he has carefully analyzed all of the short stories and can back up his assertion with some enlightening comparisions and contrasts. The further up he goes, however, the less control he is able to exert over the materials being compared; in the upper levels, he rarely goes beyond his impressions, as reliable as they may in some cases be.

The further reaches of this ascent bring us to another element implied in the comparisons. The "masterpiece," the "classic" has obviously a superiority, a magnitude, a surplus of values--and this surplus belongs as much to the non-aesthetic values of the

work as to the aesthetic, perhaps more so. In any
event, the classic offers a good perspective from
which to consider the mixture of values in any work.

If we begin with a secondary note, it is interesting to observe that a classic is usually thought of
as a work of a magnitude simply in terms of its size
or bulk. We do not ordinarily think of a sonnet, or
a couplet, or perhaps even a short story as a classic.
This prejudice is unfortunate, perhaps, since splendid
achievements are possible in the smaller forms. What
our usual way of thinking does emphasize again, however, is that the classic must have magnitude, not
simply of size but of value, quality, impact, development, sweep.

There are several distinct aspects that we seem
to prize in such magnitude--and prize indeed when we
find them in smaller measure in more ordinary works
of literature. There is depth; Dostoievski's or
Shakespeare's treatment of isolation and of love are
certainly more pregnant than are Salinger's. As a
result, their works are more universal; they appeal
not to one time or place or nationality, but to many,
perhaps so many that one can say, to humanity. Thus,
their work has permanence, tested for several centuries for Shakespeare, even longer for others; their
meaning and value have a certain inexhaustibility,
as one generation after another finds something that
speaks to its condition. And in other directions
there are achievements in the classic which contribute
to its permanence, too: a range and variety in the
human types and situations it treats, subtlety in
analyzing them, maturity in moral judgment about them.

Given the total production of works classified
as literature, those that achieve the plenitude of
value we are talking about here are relatively rare.
But that fulness is certainly an ideal every serious
writer aims for. And in whatever measure he achieves
the ideal, he usually finds responsive readers. What,
again, are the readers responding to? The hypothesis
suggested here is that readers respond to a mixture
of values. Even in the aesthetic experience of a
literary work, an experience marked by great intensity,
by a sense of detachment from practical concerns, and
contemplative absorption, by a sense of great unity
--there seems to be to some extent a complex of re-

sponses which are, however, definitely hierarchized. When our response to a work is <u>primarily</u> aesthetic, it is the aesthetic value, the structural fitness of the work, that we are reacting to, that we have in "focus." We respond to the other values subordinately; they are present to us but out of focus, peripherally. We can, however, on another occasion and even with the same work, reverse this approach and pursue our interest in the non-aesthetic values so that they are in focus and not merely present. In pursuing this course, however, we are not using the work for its primary purpose--to be enjoyed at a high level of human response to its aesthetic value, to the value it has in itself. On the other hand, our effort is rather misplaced when we attempt to purge our response of all non-aesthetic involvement--any pity for the "person" in that situation, any concern for the relevance of the treatment to my own situation. Our effort, rather, should be to discriminate, to try to learn in reading what we are responding to and why. The emphasis throughout the discussion here has obviously been on the question of the aesthetic value and on the minimal question of what it is that makes a work literary, not necessarily great. Both emphases are necessary because they are about issues frequently lost in discussions of grander and vaguer generalities or avoided because of their difficulty.

Some Problems of Mixed Values

We have already implied a simple fact about human sight: we see many things simultaneously but normally focus on only one area in the field of vision. While we automatically adjust to this fact, we have some difficulty with the similar though more complex situation in which we apprehend literary works. These, too, present a mix of values and meanings--and normally it seems possible to have only one "focus" on them, one set to our reaction that keeps one type of value in focus, others present but out of focus. What is, perhaps, lacking for many in this process is a clear conviction about what the aesthetic value is and what its general role is in human life.

That aesthetic value exists and that man and society have a need for it is generally acknowledged. While there is much disagreement about what aesthetic value is, there is much more agreement about its be-

nefits for the individual and the community--in con-
tributing to the fulness of the human personality,
developing imagination and sensibility, giving a fuller appreciation of the variety of human experience,
making one sensitive to the crucial difference between ends and means in human life and so forth.[7]

There is also the "escape" value of literature.
But the caution here is that the "re-creation" of
the human spirit is a better way of conceiving this
function of respite from ordinary duties. For the
initial demands made upon a reader by a real work of
literature are rather removed from the limp passivity
or the excited involvement in crude suspense offered
typically by television and other popular forms of
entertainment. There may be a need for such forms
of escape, but we should not confuse them with art.

Good literature itself has, unfortunately, sometimes been approached as pure or total escape from
the various demands life makes upon us. This is the
basic mistake of art-for-art's-sake philosophies in
some periods, as it is, perhaps, of the bohemianism
which tries to convert all of life into role-playing
and dramatic gesture. The error of the art-for-art's-
sake advocate is not that he thinks art is a value
to itself (structuralism shares the same notion), a
human value distinct from other human values. Nor is
it that art is an end in itself, something to be enjoyed for its own sake. Rather, it is that this advocate gives such a high priority to the artistic
value among all values ("What care I," said George
Moore, "that millions of wretched Israelites died
under Pharoah's lash or Egypt's sun? It was well
that they died that I might have the pyramids to look
on...")--or that he indeed makes it the only value
a human life can properly be dedicated to. The feast
of life is for him all dessert; the complete aesthete
can enjoy, can be serious about only what art has to
offer. For the truly human person, however, the feast
of life has many courses. When he comes to the dessert, he will want it to taste like dessert, he will
take his art for the sake of art. But he will have
also done justice already to the main course.

If we have difficulty understanding the role of
aesthetic value and placing its positive pleasure in
the total context of human values, we may also have

difficulty in harmonizing apparent conflicts in the values presented by the literary work. There are many problems here, but we will consider three principally.

There is first the problem of <u>poetry and belief</u> --of whether I can enjoy Milton's poetry although I find myself at odds with his Protestant theology or Dante's <u>Divine Comedy</u>, if I am a Protestant. From the opposite point of view, there is the problem of how much I enjoy in Dante simply because I am a Catholic. The hypothesis advanced here for a mixture of value and a mixed response--in both cases with a hierarchy and unity that gives dominance to the aesthetic--provides some obvious lines for a solution to these difficulties. A structuralist interpretation has been offered, for instance, for the beautiful line of Dante, "In His Will is our peace":

> The meaning of <u>la sua voluntade</u>
> <u>e nostra pace</u> in Dante's poem
> and the meaning of the statement
> in a treatise of Père de Caus-
> sade on <u>Abandonment to Divine</u>
> <u>Providence</u> is the same meaning.
> The function of de Caussade's
> statement is to communicate a
> truth to the reader. Dante's sen-
> tence fulfills this function, too;
> but it has another function as
> well, one not more primary in
> itself, but more primary to its
> present context--the function of
> acting as part of the structure
> of a beautiful object, an object
> of independent value, to be ad-
> mired in and for itself, part, that
> is, of the structure of meaning
> and part of the structure of sound
> of this poem. And it is in this
> latter function that it is a peculiar-
> ly literary phenomenon, and not in
> the function that it shares with
> de Caussade's statement. It is this
> that distinguishes it as poetry
> from the statement of identical meaning
> that is not poetry. And it is our
> response to it in this function that

> constitutes specifically literary
> appreciation. So far as the re-
> sponse to it is concerned, belief
> seems irrelevant, whereas to the
> response to it in its other func-
> tion, belief is highly relevant.[8]

And again,

> The communicative aspect of the
> statement is subordinated to the
> structural. It remains a communi-
> cative statement..., and yet at the
> same time it ceases to be communi-
> cative, just as the sword in the
> hands of St. George in the bronze
> statuary group before me at the
> same time is, and is not, a sword.
> It has all the appearances of a
> weapon of destruction, it is a
> weapon of destruction, and yet, only
> in so far as, in a sense, it ceases
> to be a weapon of destruction, can
> it find its place as a part in the
> statue. To the extent that the sword
> should actually be thrust at the
> dragon in an actual killing process,
> to that extent it would cease being
> a part in a beautiful statue and de-
> stroy the pattern, the order, the
> arrangement which is the source of
> our pleasure.[9]

The problem with works that support, as well as with
those that differ from, my own beliefs is to know
what I am reacting to. A different faith, even a
conflict with my own faith, won't necessarily preclude
a "willing suspension of disbelief"--for the purposes
of the aesthetic situation.

There are similar difficulties for the reader
with issues of art and prudence. To some extent,
this is the problem of shoddy, lazy, and cheap art
itself, that fails to achieve the ends it proposes
to itself, that fails to concern itself with significant issues in an honest view of reality. The
problem arises, too, when the literary work offers notions, dramatic situations, and especially attitudes

repugnant not to my faith but to a related sense of
morality, my sense of what is right or wrong human
action. This might involve a matter of hatred between races, of divorce or abortion, of unadulterated
materialism; most frequently, of course, it is a matter of sex, the mystery that man is so strongly and
constantly attracted to.

In the traditional view of ethics and morality,
the problem here is actually not when the attitudes
about, the treatment of, any of these matters is repugnant. It is rather when they are superficially
and speciously attractive, so that man in the ordinary
weakness of his human condition may be influenced to
evil thought, intention, or deed. The problem is not
typically, either, with the work that is consistently,
obviously immoral. Here the ethical choice is clear-
cut. Rather it is with the work with a questionable
chapter, a vividly realistic scene, an ambiguity of
attitude at the conclusion and so forth. Out of context, the part would be objectionable; but it appears
to be integrated into a real literary structure, to
be justified by norms authentically developed within
the work. Is the reader to choose in terms of his
moral safety and reject all because of the part--or
is he to choose the aesthetic value of the whole and
risk the possible effects of the part?

By what standards is he to choose? There are
several standards of art that demand the good of the
work above all--and that assume that for readers
the aesthetic response will be the normal one to a
real work of art. There are general standards of
ethics that require the integrity of the person above
all other values. There are norms of revealed morality that put love of neighbor and God above all other
values.

As in any moral decison, however, the final
judgment has to be made in terms of the individual
and his experience; he applies general principles
but to himself, in this situation; as far as I am
concerned, will this work be good or bad for me in
these circumstances? The response to a work which
is really art should be aesthetic. But such a response is not automatic for all nor is it ever purely aesthetic. And some do not have the maturity, the
sensibility or the experience to insure the dominant-

ly aesthetic effect we have discussed. The deficiency is, then, not so much in the work, perhaps, as in the immature person. This is unfortunate from an aesthetic point of view; from a moral point of view, the fact must be faced honestly by the individual.

On a wider scale, there is a problem similar to that of art and prudence in censorship. This is not the problem of military censorship a government might legitimately invoke in war-time to restrict information valuable to an enemy, nor the problem of the ideological censorship a tyrannical government might employ to control thought. Rather it is a question again of moral censorship when the state feels printed material will be harmful to a significant part of the community, ultimately to the community as a whole. The scope of the problem is now obviously beyond individual morality; it is one of social morality and ultimately one of politics, as a governing body concerned with the common good comes to make judgments for a group who profess differing standards of ethics.

Two opposed positions on the problem might be sketched briefly. The first objects to any censorship whatever on moral grounds. At the theoretical level, people here argue that what is endangered by censorship is the high human value of freedom. It is especially endangered by any attempt to confine man's intellectual and creative endeavor, for man exercises his highest faculties in such work and he should have the freedom to roam where he will. Since artistic value is its own justification, moreover, art can be judged only by the art critic, not by policeman or jury. At the practical level, too, people argue that censorship has been eminently ineffective --even in dealing with material of little or no artistic interest like hard-core pornography for which the fulminating censors simply get more attention. It is even argued that such material can be considered a safety-valve for society, a catharsis for man's "baser passions." Finally, it is argued that any attempt to control the misuse of free speech is a dangerous wedge for control over what is good and legitimate--and so not worth the potential price.

On the other hand, the advocates of censorship argue that complete freedom of expression is a false goal. One cannot have simply absolute freedom to

direct any way he chooses; it must finally be directed
to something human, good--or it ceases to be freedom.
Art, moreover, involves not only thought but emotion,
impulse--and it can arouse desire. Not all of man's
impulses and desires can be indiscriminately stimula-
ted, if he is to remain fully human. It is precisely
the license of such stimulation and expression today
that damages the moral fabric of society; in any commonsense view, it has to be related to increases in
illegitimacy, rape, divorce. Hence, it is a clear
duty of government to promote a healthier moral atmosphere in society by restricting the circulation
of harmful material. If what has been said of art is
valid to any extent, it is all the more true of pornography, above all when it is a question of immature
readers. Here censorship can be effective, but more
severe laws are required to curb the criminal exploi-
tation of man's "basest passions" and the corruption
of innocence.

It would be difficult to sift out the elements
of truth and of sensible policy from these positions
very exactly; neither side has a monopoly on these
commodities. What can be said is that there is scant
reason for censoring of literary works like those of
Joyce or D.H. Lawrence banned until recent years. If
the young, uneducated, or morally unsophisticated are
to be directed away from such work for a time, it
should be by home, school, or church, rather than by
the state. Again, the deficiency here is not so much
with the work as with the particular audience. The
case for the control of pornography--which, say the
courts, is without redeeming social merit--has more
to be said for it--or perhaps will have, when more
efficient means of control are devised.

The intention of the present chapter, however,
was not to dwell simply on the difficulties presented
by the mix of values in literature. Rather it was
to stress the complexity of the mix and more especially its richness. The good literary structure itself
is a treasury of surprise, of new attraction at every
turn and twist in its unfolding and building. The
many values of the materials themselves invite in
many other directions. One can agree warmly with
Charles Wheeler who put it that

Poetry is refractory, opaque,

durable. Using materials selected
from the verbal traffic of everyday
life, poetry manages to secure for
them exemption from the common fate
of language. It is not even defeated
by our lack of complete understanding;
it knows, so to speak, that our habit
is to take the contents if we can
and then throw away the package.
Thus it prevents this easy transaction
by perpetually withholding some
undefinable remainder of its meaning,
forcing us to come back to the language itself again and again. And
when we do so, with full attention
to the texture as well as the import
of what we read, we discover that even
the areas of meaning supposedly familiar
appear fresh and new, miraculously
reanimated. This experience is freely
available; it is not reserved for the
few. But it demands as a primary
condition that we respect the inherent
right of language to aim at a state
of achievement, even though we are in
some sense the victims. For language
is a human achievement, and poetry is
language triumphant.[10]

Notes

1 A.E. Housman, Selected Prose (Cambridge: Cambridge University Press, 1961), p. 185.

2 Sister Mary Francis Slattery, "Formal Specification," Journal of Aesthetics and Art Criticism, 25 (1966), 86; on the fulfillment of expectations in music, see Leonard B. Meyer, Explaining Music (Berkeley: University of California Press, 1973), pp. 18 ff.

3 The discussion here draws upon Trygeve Emond, On Art and Unity (Lund: Gleerups, 1964); G.S. Rousseau, Organic Form: The Life of an Idea (London: Routledge and Kegan Paul, 1972); and G.N. Giordano-Orsini, Organic Unity (Carbondale: Southern Illinois University Press, 1975).

4 Emond, p. 118.

5 Shakespearean Criticism, ed. T.M. Rayson (London: Kent, 1960), I, 223-224.

6 See the article on fitness, Appendix VI.

7 See, especially, Monroe C. Beardsley, Aesthetics (New York: Harcourt Brace, 1958), pp. 557 ff. and William J. Rooney, "Discrimination Among Values," The Journal of General Education, 13 (1961), 40-52.

8 William J. Rooney, The Problem of "Poetry and Belief" in Contemporary Criticism (Washington: Catholic University Press, 1949), pp. 115-116.

9 Rooney, pp. 117-118.

10 Charles B. Wheeler, The Design of Poetry (New York: Norton, 1966), p. 31.

Suggested Readings

Forster, E.M. Two Cheers for Democracy. New York: Harcourt Brace, 1951, pp. 88-95.

La Drière, Craig. "Structure, Sound, and Meaning,"
    in Sound and Poetry, ed. Northrop Frye. New
    York: Columbia University Press, 1957, pp.
    85-108.

Santayana, George. Reason in Art. New York: Scrib-
    ner's, 1965, pp. 166-190.

APPENDIX I: APPROACHES TO LITERATURE

A.   Yury Lotman, "The Reader and the Scholar"

In the final reckoning, all investigative analysis rests upon the reader's direct perception. This perception underlies that intuition which enables the scholar to avoid sifting through all the logically possible combinations of structural elements and immediately to set aside a certain minimum number for further consideration. Consequently, the absence of a reader's direct reaction, as when, for example, the object of study is from a remote epoch or an alien culture, drastically reduces the economy of the investigation. Very frequently a conception whose refutation would be most difficult can be rejected out of hand for the simple reason that it sharply diverges from a direct experiencing of the text. Also connected with this general phenomenon are those difficulties, common in the history of scholarship, which often arise when an investigator richly endowed with erudition is deprived of intuitive contact with the text and of the capability to perceive it directly.

However, the reader's feeling that constitutes the basis of scientific knowledge can also be a source of error; within certain limits surmounting it is just as much a necessity as adherence to it. The reader's feeling and the investigator's analysis are two principally different types of activity. They come into contact in no greater degree than do the "common sense" of everyday experience and the principles of contemporary physics. Meanwhile the reader's perception aggressively and partially gauges the truth of scientific conclusions by their coincidence with its own ideas. No matter how conditional or relative the judgment stemming from the reader's impression, their formulators are most frequently inclined to accept them as absolute truth. If scientific thinking is critical, the reader's is "mythological," that is, gravitates toward the creation of "myths" and regards their criticism with extreme irritation.

Another distinction between the reader's approach to a text and a scholarly approach is that the former

is synthetic. The reader perceives all of a work's
aspects in their unity. Indeed, he must not perceive
them otherwise for the author reckons on just such
an attitude. The danger comes when the reader, seeing
analysis as the "murder" of art and an infringement
on its organic integrity, begins to demand such a synthetic view on the part of the investigator. However,
the integrity of a work cannot be conveyed in an investigative study given that feeling of direct unanalyzable integration which remains both the superiority
and inadequacy of the reader's perception. Science
attains its goals through preliminary analysis and
subsequent synthesis.

One must note still one further important difference in the approaches of a reader and a scholar
to a text; they make different demands with regard
to the exhaustiveness of the conclusions. The reader
prefers definitive conclusions even if doubtful; the
scholar, conclusions that submit to scientific verification even if incomplete. Each of these positions
is completely justified so long as it remains within
the limits set aside for it in the general scheme of
the culture. To replace the reader by the researcher
would be ruinous for literature just as would be the
replacement of the investigator by the reader.

from Yury Lotman, Analysis of the Poetic Text, ed. &
    trans. D. Barton Johnson (Ann Arbor: Ardis,
    1976), pp. 137-138.

B. M.H. Abrams, "Orientation of Critical Theories"

Four elements in the total situation of a work
of art are discriminated and made salient, by one or
another synonym, in almost all theories which aim to
be comprehensive. First, there is the work, the artistic product itself. And since this is a human
product, an artifact, the second common element is the
artificer, the artist. Third, the work is taken to
have a subject which directly or deviously, is derived
from existing things--to be about, or signify, or reflect something which either is, or bears some relation to, an objective state of affairs. This third
element, whether held to consist of people and actions,

126

ideas and feelings, material things and events, or
super-sensible essences, has frequently been denoted
by that word-of-all-work, "nature"; but let us use
the more neutral and comprehensive term, universe,
instead. For the final element we have the audience:
the listeners, spectators, or readers to whom the work
is addressed, or to whose attention, at any rate, it
becomes available....

     Although any reasonably adequate theory takes
some account of all four elements, almost all theories,
as we shall see, exhibit a discernible orientation
toward one only. That is, a critic tends to derive
from one of these terms his principle categories for
defining, classifying, and analyzing a work of art,
as well as the major criteria by which he judges its
value. Application of this analytic scheme, therefore,
will sort attempts to explain the nature and worth of
a work of art into four broad classes. Three will
explain the work of art principally by relating it to
another thing: the universe, the audience, or the
artist. The fourth will explain the work by considering it in isolation, as an autonomous whole, whose
significance and value are determined without any reference beyond self.

     To find the major orientation of a critical
theory, however, is only the beginning of an adequate
analysis. For one thing, these four co-ordinates are
not constants, but variables; they differ in significance according to the theory in which they occur.
Take what I have called the universe as an example.
In any one theory, the aspects of nature which an artist is said to imitate, or is exhorted to imitate,
may be either particulars or types, and they may be
only the beautiful or the moral aspects of the world,
or else any aspect without discrimination. It may
be maintained that the artist's world is that of
imaginative intuition, or of common sense, or of natural science; and this world may be held to include,
or not to include, gods, witches, chimeras, and Platonic Ideas. Consequently, theories which agree in
assigning to the represented universe the primary control over a legitimate work of art may vary from re-
commending the most uncompromising realism to the
most remote idealism. Each of our other terms, as we
shall see, also varies, both in meaning and functioning, according to the critical theory in which it oc-

127

curs, the method of reasoning which the theorist cha-
racteristically uses, and the explicit or implicit
"world-view" of which these theories are an integral
part.

---

from M.H. Abrams, The Mirror and the Lamp (New York:
    Oxford University Press, 1953), pp. 6-7.

C. Craig La Drière, "The Role of the Critic"

    There is certainly plenty of criticism which
torments poetry, and poets; it should comfort tormen-
ted poets to consider that the most exquisite torments
in this kind are probably, however, those which critics inflict upon each other. In any case, if we
provisionally concede that the critic need not invariably be a tormentor, it may yet be argued that he is
always an interpreter. To say this has in fact become one of the stock preliminaries in the usual account of the critic's function; critics themselves,
from Plato's Ion to our own time, have accepted this
designation, and many of them have very explicitly
disclaimed any other.

    The critic must interpret, of course; but inter-
pretation does not make criticism. There are many
kinds of interpretation, and the critic's is only one
of these; rather, the critic has no interpretation
which is particularly his own, and we may find that
he is not performing a work specifically his own when
he interprets, but using the instruments and the procedures of other workers to perform an operation which
for criticism is only preliminary or accessory, at
most accidental. So with torment. The critic may
torment; it is not the least useful function of the
critic to torment upon occasion. But it is not a specifically critical function; it is indeed legitimately possible only when the critical operation has been
performed, and is done. The critic's proper work is
to show that torment in merited--torment of poem, of
poet, of reader perhaps especially often--and possibly
to indicate the effective method for it; but strictly,
when he has done this, the critic should turn his
victim over for the actual execution of his sentence
to some extra-critical arm.

I have spoken of "the critical operation," and of "the critic's proper work." What are these, precisely? It is not our primary purpose here, as I understand it, to define criticism. We are to discuss the <u>role</u> of the critic. I take this to mean not so much an analysis of the work of the critic as some account of the utility of that work and the conditions of its effective performance; not an analytical investigation of the procedures of criticism, but an assessment of their results and an inquiry into their value for the community of writers and readers of poetry and into the responsibilities of critics to society and to themselves. This is what I have in view, and shall keep in mind, as the end of our discussion. But we cannot achieve this end without a clear notion of the nature of criticism. Unless we know what criticism is, we cannot assign it a use; unless we know what a critic is doing, we can hardly say what is required of him in doing it. To settle what the role of a critic is, we must first decide what a critic is.

This is not the place, and there is not time, for a cautious balance of all the elements involved in all the answers that have been made in the past to such a question. Not that these have been so many; the question has usually been avoided. It has usually been assumed that everybody knows what a critic is. I am so far from making that assumption that I am not sure that I know; but I welcome this occasion for dogmatic statement. A critic is one who judges judgments. Criticism is evaluation of evaluations.

The virtue I should claim for this definition is that it assigns to the critic a work which he invariably performs, whether openly or surreptitiously; that this is the only work which the critic does invariably perform whatever else he may do, nobody but a critic ever performs, or perhaps wants to perform. It is therefore a true <u>differentia</u> such as we need for an exact definition. But even in so dogmatizing a context as this, we cannot be content with mere statement of this <u>differentia</u>. In expanding it a little I am concerned not so much to justify as to clarify it by indicating some of its implications. Rather, by indicating two of its implications; for upon two points I think it sufficient to insist.

The first of these is that the critic is indeed

a judge, an evaluator. Where there is no evaluation,
no estimate of worth, there is no criticism. No amount
of pure description, or classification, which is merely descriptive, will produce criticism. Let me note,
though, that description and classification may serve
as the means of presentation, so that the judgment
is nowhere explicitly made. If a clear implication
of judgment appears in such description, it is criticism, but, unless there is judgment of worth, explicit
or implicit, there is no criticism. It is necessary
to emphasize this, because many different kinds of
influence have operated in recent times to make critics a little ashamed of this essential part of their
office.

What is now called "value" has been through rather a bad period with the epistemologists, and the
critics have not all been willing to go along with it.
In general, of course, their expedient in this emer-
gency has been to profess some kind of scientism, to
insist that their concern was not after all with value
but with some category of fact, and to suggest that
all the values in the world might vanish without putting critics out of their jobs. They were safe, of
course; anybody who knows the world at all knows that
critics are more likely than values to vanish out of
it--that, indeed, values will be the last things to
go. This was not a very serious crisis, I think,
though it had great importance especially in forcing
criticism to consider its foundations. Its service
in that respect is not yet over. But we need not here
delay over the perhaps vain question whether value is
distinct from fact, or attempt to settle the relations
between the two--if we think them two. This allusion
to the problem suffices for the present purpose, for
it has pointed up two relevant facts: criticism is
not science or simple knowledge of fact, and values
are not created by or dependent upon criticism.

These lead to the second of the two implications
in the definition upon which I want to insist. I have
said that the critic is a judge, an evaluator. But
he is more than this. To say that he is an evaluator
is not to differentiate the critic from men in general
or to assign him any specifying task. For men in general are evaluators; every man is constantly engaged
in evaluating. Evaluation of all kinds, moral or
practical, philosophic, aesthetic, is as natural and

inevitable to man as breathing. And nobody conceives that every evaluation man makes thus inevitably in the normal conduct of life is criticism. Such evaluation is merely the ground and the occasion of criticism. Its presence and its necessity is the provocation to criticism and the basis of criticism's claim to the vast importance it has in man's life, but it is not criticism.

It is not criticism to say that you prefer Beethoven to Brahms, or that the roast is overdone. Criticism begins when, having drawn tears by your judgment that the roast is overdone, you undertake to explore alternative possibilities with a view to displacing the opinion you originally embraced. Let it be noted in passing that as criticism begins at this point so do the peculiar temptations of the critic, of which the first is to dishonesty, the greatest vice possible in criticism. Let it be noted also, even more in passing, that whereas a spontaneous judgment like that about the conditon of the roast is normally sincere, the sequel produced in its revision by the incipient critical faculty often differs from it only by the elimination of sincerity. This is unfortunately especially true of judgments concerning the values called aesthetic, for whatever people believe about the relation of moral and aesthetic value, they seem generally to feel that conscience is involved only in judgments of the former kind.

Criticism, then, is not just evaluation. It is a reflex operation by which we examine a spontaneous evaluation and evaluate this evaluation. How is this operation performed? By bringing to bear upon the first evaluation all the relevant knowledge possible. Knowledge of the processes involved in evaluating itself; knowledge of the thing evaluated--of things of that kind in general and of this specimen in particular; knowledge of the evaluator and his capacities and limitations; knowledge of the situation in which the evaluation occured and the pressures it exerted upon the evaluator; knowledge of everything that might possibly affect the evaluation or enter into its composition.

So there is knowledge, or science, involved in criticism. It is, in fact, this knowledge which distinguishes criticism from lay evaluation. For, apart from this knowledge, or science, or scholarship, by which the primary judgment is judged in relation to the context of its occurence, there is nothing to differentiate the act of final judgment which is critical from the original response which is not. Both perform essentially the same operation, that of estimating worth. We are now in a position, if we wish, to make a more pedantic statement of the critic's function. The function of the critic is to test the relevance of a response to the stimulus which occasions it, in the situation in which it occurs. And the apparatus, the equipment for this testing, which distinguishes the critic from the lay judge, though both perform evalutory acts, is knowledge, or science, or scholarship.

At times we all wish this were not so, but even the little examination we have made is enough to establish that it is so. There is no other account possible of the distinctive equipment of the critic. It is not native cleverness or mother wit, though that is indispensable. It is not sensibility and depth of feeling, though they are precious. It is not imaginative fire or powerful will. The critic should have all these things, yet one may have all these things and not be a critic. Though criticism is not a science, what makes the critic is knowledge. The critic himself may wish it were not so, but it is inexorably so.

It may be said, indeed, that any kind of knowledge will make some kind of critic. But that each kind of criticism requires its own specific knowledge is equally plain. Nothing is of more importance in these matters than that the critic, and his audience, understand precisely what kind of criticism he is practicing at any given moment, and that he possess the particular knowledge required for the practice of that kind. These are three most general kinds of value that may be in question: practical criticism, which is concerned with the goodness of acts, philosophic criticism, which is concerned with the truth of propositions, and aesthetic criticism, which concerns itself with the beauty of things. So far as these three criticisms have different objects to work upon, they are quite distinct things, but so far as the work they perform is critical they are similar. This similarity of general method is no doubt the rea-

son for their constant confusion. But in some objects
of criticism, and poetry is one, the values to which
different criticisms give attention also often coincide, and thus multiply opportunities for confusion.

Whatever be the explanation, it is at any rate
the fact that it is almost impossible to keep any one
critic of poetry to one kind of criticism of poetry.
There would be no harm in this if critics kept their
moral criticism of poetry, which is a perfectly legitimate criticism of poetry, distinct from their philosophic crticiism of poetry, an equally legitimate
criticism; and these both distinct from their aesthetic criticism, which is certainly the most legitimate of all three ways, provided the three be kept
distinct, and, above all, provided the critic is capable of each of the three kinds of evaluation. Actually, critics truly capable of this extended range
are naturally very rare, for what is supposed is
thorough competence over the whole field of action
and of speculation. But nothing is more common than
the criticism which conflates the three kinds and by
confusing vitiates them all. It is true that these
things are related, often very intimately. That is
to say, the danger of confusion is often very great;
this does not diminish the responsibility of avoiding
it.

But I am beginning to prescribe for the critic,
and it is not time for that. This anticipation, however, suggests that I have said what I feel needs
saying about the nature of criticism, about the critical operation and the critic's proper work. Let us
turn, then, directly to the problem for which that
was to prepare us, our stated business, the delineation
of the role of one whose work is of this kind.

It is clear, I think, from this account of the
critic's work what his role must be. It can be sum-
marized in a single word, a word I have not used
much in what I have so far said, but one which expresses a notion implied throughout: discrimination.
The role of the critic is to insure that there be
discrimination in judgment. It is not to provide
judgment; society provides judgment in abundance without calling upon the critic. The critic's function
is to add discrimination to this spontaneous judgment
with which society is always perhaps too ready, to

make discriminations sharper than spontaneous judgment assures, and thus, of course, in time to render spontaneous judgment itself more discriminating. This amounts to saying that the role of the critic is to discipline "taste" by establishing standards, and to improve taste by applying standards, and to preserve taste by maintaining standards.

In our society it is above all this last office that the critic must perform. "What is more insidious than any censorship," T.S. Eliot has said, "is the steady influence which operates silently in any mass society organized for profit, for the depression of standards of art and culture." The steady multitude of influences operating, silently and noisily too, in our society toward the depression of standards is so overwhelming that the critic may well be tempted to give up and retire before its magnitude. He may feel he has all he can do to save himself from the inundation and no energy left for society. Well, in any event he will save society only by saving himself. But perhaps all that society needs in such a crisis is a few people who refuse to succumb, who continue to discriminate, who go on with the process of continual self-examination which is criticism, who keep the standards they have inherited or achieved and will not let them down.

I cannot here discuss the character of those standards or their genesis. I will only say that it is one of the uses of such adversities as those of the intellectual life in our time that they force us, as in periods of more comfort we are not forced, to go directly to the solid foundation at the bottom of all reasoned evaluation for standards which are permanently established in the nature of things. It is hardly necessary today to tell the critic to dig his foundation deep. Unless he digs deep today, he can have no foundation at all.

But there are some less radical admonitions one would like to give the critic, some more general demands I would make upon him for the performance of his role as I envisage it.

I will not say that he must be intelligent, partly because it is so evident that he must be--this above all; partly because if I demand intelligence of

him I shall have forestalled the other demands I want
to make. But he must be informed, aware--instructed,
as the French say; he must not be provincial. He
must be informed concerning his own job, its nature
and its techniques, and he must know something of how
others have practiced it before him and what solutions
they have made of the problems which face him. He
must be informed concerning what he criticizes--he
must have studied the nature of literature and of poetry. He must know as many as possible of the existing
works of literature, and know a few of them as thoroughly as possible. The awareness which comes of
wide acquaintance with literature, and comes only with
wide acquaintance, will save him from provincialism.

Then he must be _disinterested_. I use Matthew
Arnold's word, as consecrated by his use and better
than current alternatives such as _objective_ or _imper-
sonal_. I doubt whether the critic should be or can
be impersonal. But he must not be partisan or sec-
tarian in his criticism. He may belong to a party;
he will not serve it by attempting a partisan criticism. The attempt will fail and his party and his
cause will only be compromised by failure. The attempt must fail, for there never can be any such thing
as partisan criticism--partisanship and criticism are
antithetical notions. It is not my business to prescribe what Catholics should do as Catholics, but I
think the theologians would approve counseling a Catholic critic to remember in dealing with a pagan's
work or a heretic's that these, too, are children of
God to be approached as such reverently and not without adequate preparation. In any case, the Catholic
critic, like the others, must be disinterested and
impartial.

And he should be humble. I will not labor this.
The knowledge on which criticism is founded is always
incomplete, and every particular evaluation is at
best only an approximation. Every critic who takes
his work seriously must find it an endlessly humbling
process.

Finally, the critic should be honest. He can
never be perfectly intelligent, or perfectly informed,
or perfectly disinterested, or perfectly humble, but
it is open to everyone to be perfectly honest, and to
a critic who is perfectly honest his inevitable short-

comings with respect to the rest will easily be for-
given. For honest statement is the soul of criticism;
pretense is incompatible with criticism.

Intelligence, awareness, disinterestedness, hu-
mility, honesty--these are the virtues of the critic,
and together they are the sum of his responsibility.
If in his work of evaluating evaluations, of discriminating, of establishing and maintaining standards
for himself and others, he cultivates these virtues
and represents them, and contributes to their dissemi-
nations, shall we not say that he has performed his
part? Is not this the role of the critic?

---

from Spirit, 13 (1947), 179-186.

D. Craig La Drière, "Scientific Method in Criticism"

The question whether there is or can be a scientific method for criticism is at least as old as Plato's Ion (532C). Explicit discussion of it has naturally increased since the general scientific advances
and conscious refinements of method in recent centuries, but a scientific ideal for the theory and a
generally scientific procedure in the practice of criticism did not, of course, have to await the development of modern science. In later antiquity both were
well established if not universally agreed upon in
detail, and admirable progress was made (most notably
by Aristotle) in scientific investigation of literary
phenomena. The attempt of medieval teachers to re-
tain the ancient knowledge, and their efforts and
those of Renaissance scholars to recover what had been
lost or obscured in it, were largely frustrated by
historical ignorances; and though some significant de-
velopments occurred in the Middle Ages and the Renaissance, it is fair to say that in those periods, and
generally during that of classicism which they prepared and determined, there was less appropriation of
the permanently valid general method of the ancients
than of its temporally conditioned particular results.
So in 1751 Dr. Johnson wrote, "Criticism...has not
yet attained the certainty and stability of a science."
For "certainty and stability" in criticism Johnson
seems to have had a desire perhaps in excess of the

temperate demands of a truly scientific spirit. The
romantics were more moderate in this respect, but the
critical part of their reaction too was a drive, however misdirected, toward surer knowledge and sounder
method; and one of the directions in which the criticism (like the literature itself) of the later 19th
century turned to recover the objectivity it had lost
was that of the developing natural sciences. French
criticism, the most influential of the period, was
indeed then as a whole simply a succession of attempts
to apply to literature formulas supplied by contemporary science, and includes more discussion of the
possibilities and requisites of scientific method in
criticism than we have from any other period or place.
Into our own time such discussion has continued; but
though today one young critic (Bronowski, The Poet's
Defence, 1939) can declare, "I have tried to write
criticism as reasoned as geometry," it is the "considered opinion" of another (Cleanth Brooks) that
literary studies in general "will have to forego the
pleasures of being 'scientific.'" We can hardly say
that the question of Plato's Socrates has been finally answered.

Its answer will depend, of course, upon the definition given its terms. Science may be defined as
systematized conceptual knowledge that is directly or
indirectly verifiable; all questions of its method
are questions of the means proper in a given case to
the attainment and verification and systematization
of conceptual knowledge, or to its communication.
If criticism is conceived as response to a work of
art simply, the adventure of a soul among masterpieces,
it can hardly be scientific, for the operation of
the critic is then wholly or principally affective-
volitional (or "affective-motor"), whereas science
is as such wholly cognitive. It is now generally
agreed that this view of criticism, which fails to
distinguish it from ordinary reading, is wrong; for
such simplification is in practice impossible, and
approximation to it produces results unsatisfactory
precisely because deficient in cognitive value. Criticism is not simply affective response, however sensitive or intense. But neither is it mere cognition
of the object or stimulus, however acute. Arnold's
account of the "endeavor" of criticism, "to see the
object as in itself it really is," though admirably
(if in strict epistemology extravagantly) expressive

137

of one primary aim of both criticism and science
(which it practically identifies), is as incomplete
as the impressionist's; for the critic must not only
"know the best that is known and thought in the world,"
but be able also as far as possible to determine the
meaning and validity of its claim to be best. It is
not, to be sure, judgment or evaluation alone that
criticism adds to the acute cognition of an object
and sensitive response to it which are required of
both critic and lay reader; for the lay reader also
judges or evaluates. Evaluation is truly the ultimate
function of criticism, one which it cannot subordinate
to any other or, in a pseudo-scientific effort toward
the scientific, replace by mere description; to eliminate judgment is to eliminate criticism. But critical judgment is not the direct and spontaneous evaluation in which all reading naturally culminates. It
is a reflex operation by which this evaluation, or
any other proposition about a literary work or process,
is itself evaluated, in the light ideally of everything
than can be known about it and about its occasion.
(In practice the primary and the reflex operations
may be concomitant, the latter controlling the former
as it proceeds; the complete critical process is usually not a separate recapitulation of the normal process of reading but simply an expansion and deepening
of it by addition of concurrent cognitive acts, so
that when the final evaluation emerges its critique
is provided with it. A given criticism, however, may
and usually does involve only a part of this full process, and may evaluate not the final judgment but
only prior incidental evaluations or propositions not
evaluatory at all but simply descriptive or classifying.) The specifically differentiating operation of
criticism is thus not evaluation but discrimination
among evaluations, actual or possible, explicit or
implied; "krinein" meant "to discriminate" before it
meant "to judge." And the principle of this discrimination is cognitive; for the only criterion by which
evaluations can in any sense be tested is that of
relative consistency with all the relevant reality
that is securely known. Criticism thus adds to lay
reading a greater cognitive curiosity and more relevant knowledge and its work is to bring this knowledge methodically to bear upon judgment. But it is
evidently absurd to use for discrimination means selected and applied without discrimination; the knowledge and the method used by the critic must them-

selves be critically evaluated by the criteria appropriate to them. This is to say that they must be scientific. Criticism is not a science, because its concern is with the particular thing or value, whereas science is by definition concerned only with what is general; but it realizes itself and achieves its own ideal only in the degree to which it appropriates and assimilates science and scientific method. Criticism is simply the application to a particular judgment of as much science and as scientific a method as possible.

Scientific method is not attained in criticism by adopting the jargon or the formulas or data that have resulted from its application elsewhere, as those of biology were adopted by French critics in the 19th century or as those of various inchoate systems of psychology or sociology have sometimes been adopted in the 20th. Nor is it the application to literature without modification of the specific method of any of the exact or natural sciences; for every science has its own method, determined by its objects, and the literary datum must determine the peculiar method by which it is to be investigated. Scientific method in criticism means simply bringing to bear upon literary judgment every item of relevant knowledge (conversely excluding from consideration everything that is not relevant knowledge) and restricting judgment to what is warranted or permitted by the sum of this relevant knowledge. The knowledge required for criticism, though all susceptible of scientific scrutiny, is not all science, for much of it is particular (of the particular data immediately concerned, and of other similar or related particulars and their relations, i.e., literary history); but a large part of it is or should be science, for continuous discourse in terms of the particular alone is impossible and the critic's determinations concerning the particular must rest upon some systematic generalized knowledge of the nature and categories of literary phenomena. The ideal of such a science or general literary theory is to provide accurate observation of the literary object and the processes of its production and reception (including evaluation), analysis of these into their elements, and exact description and classification of them in terms of these elements and their combinations.

In the practice of criticism, to be scientific or truly critical is to say nothing that is not somehow grounded in strictly relevant knowledge, and to make this grounding clear. This means in general to avoid merely affective or volitional exclamation, which, though legitimate in itself and for the lay reader often a convenient means of summarily indicating an unanalyzed reaction, is not criticism; in criticism feeling should appear only as a datum for cognition, object of analysis or item of evidence. It means to avoid also multiplication of purely evaluatory propositions on the way to the final judgment; for these, unless only parenthetical, interrupt and embarass the progress of logical argument and create rather than dispose of critical problems. In constructing the descriptive and classifying propositions that should preponderate in critical discourse, to be scientific is to be careful of one's terms, using them as exactly and as univocally as possible and choosing those with plain denotations and without compromising connotations; it is to make all crucial statements as obviously verifiable as possible, presenting or suggesting the means used or the sources relied upon by the critic himself for verification. (For the analytic and comparative observation upon which these statements are based should be as systematic and as controlled as the critic can make it. The findings and the techniques of all the sciences should of course be used wherever they are relevant and applicable; those of physical and physiological phonetics for examination of sound-structures, e.g., those of well certified experimental or clinical psychology or psychiatry for analysis of a meaning or of a creative process or a response. The great controls of modern scientific observation, measurement and experiment, are not often subtle enough for use upon the object of literary criticism. But though strict measurement in literature is possible only with data that is generally not very important to measure, in matters of very specific detail at least the critic can often profitably contrive a kind of measurement by comparing two data with the same third; and simple experiment is not denied him, with the processes of production and reception, by imitating or repeating them under varying conditions, and with the object, by such devices as translation and alteration of structure--insertion, omission, rearrangement. These procedures were all in common, if not always systematic, use in

140

classical antiquity.) But to be scientific is above all to accept the established fact always, whatever its character or one's disposition toward it; and it is sometimes to acknowledge that the fact cannot be established. The critic must not shrink from noting the subjective and the relative as such where they occur, or from confessing that a given object of his attempted scrutiny eludes it, or that in a given case the inadequacy, perhaps the inaccessibility, of reliable knowledge makes evaluation of a judgment impossible. What is unscientific and uncritical is not to observe and report subjectivity, relativity, and ignorance, but to mistake these for or to pretend that they are their opposites.

The ideal suggested by this account of method is not often realized. Most criticism is, perhaps all criticism must be, partial and imperfect. But it is something to recognize the ideal, and to understand that we are truly critical only in so far as we approach its realization.

---

from Dictionary of World Literary Terms, ed. Joseph T. Shipley (Boston: The Writer, Inc., 1970), pp. 364-367.

APPENDIX II: LANGUAGE AND THE STRUCTURE OF SPEECHES

A.   Craig La Drière, "Voice and Address"

     In the analysis of a speech or literary composi-
tion, nothing is more important than to determine precisely the voice or voices presented as speaking and
the precise nature of the address (i.e., specific
direction to a hearer, and addressee); for in every
speech reference to a voice or voices and implication
of address (i.e., reference to a process of speech,
actual or imagined) is a part of the meaning and a
frame for the rest of the meaning, for the interpretation of which it supplies an indispensable control.
It may be added that, though we arrive at the concepts of voice and address from observation of the
fact that speech is now ordinarily the vehicle of a
social process (of communication), the utility of
these concepts once they are arrived at is not compromised, but rather illustrated, by the possibility
or the actual occurence of speech not intended as communicative. To generalize these notions as technical
devices for analysis involves no commitment concerning
the communicative or merely expressive, or other, nature of human speech as such, or concerning the ori-
gins of speech; the concepts are universally applicable to all speech-constructs, normal or eccentric by
whatever standards, whether the indication of specific address in them be obviously explicit (as when,
in a letter or apostrophe, a vocative is used) or only
implied or wholly lacking.

     The significant distinctions as to voice are
those made first by Plato and Aristotle and regularly
applied by critics throughout subsequent antiquity,
according to which a speaker (poet) may (1) speak in
his own person, or (2) assume the voice of another
person or set of persons and speak throughout in a
voice not his own, or (3) produce a mixed speech in
which the basic voice is his own, but other personalities are at times quoted. The first of these forms of
presentation, called by the ancients <u>diegesis</u> or <u>apan-
gellia</u>, produces pure exposition (where the meaning
is reference to ideas of static reality or of process
statically abstracted, i.e., a logical discourse) or

143

pure narration (where the meaning is reference to
events or actions as such, to dynamic reality or reality envisaged as dynamic, i.e., a story). From speech
of this kind direct quotation is excluded; in it quoted matter ("He said, 'I will'") must be cast into
indirect discourse ("He said that he would"), for
the characteristic of this mode is that the speaker
assimilates the speech of all other cited voices into
his own, so that his voice is the only voice heard.
The second mode of presentation was by the ancients
called "imitation" (mimesis); it produces dialogue
(as, where there is a story or action, in drama) or,
if there be only one assumed voice, "dramatic" monologue. (Plato and Aristotle used the same word, "imitation," to designate both this mode of voice in a
composition and the relation to reality of the fictions
of the poetry they chiefly discuss; these two senses
of the word in ancient texts, though related, should
not be confused.) These two modes, with the mixed
third that needs no separate comment, provide in fact
four basic types of structure as to voice, viz. (a)
one in which a single voice is heard throughout, and
this is the voice of the speaker himself (as in the
speech of ordinary conversation or a letter in which
there is no quoted matter), (b) one in which a single
voice is heard throughout, not that of the speaker
but that of a personality assumed by the speaker in
imagination (as in a monologue of Browning, or most
lyric poetry), (c) one in which a single basic voice
(that of the speaker in his own person or of an assumed personality, e.g., that of one of the characters in a story) speaks, but the speech of this voice
is interrupted by direct, verbatim quotation of other
voices as their speech is reported (as in most narrative), and (d) one in which a dialogue of two or
more voices, which in narration would be quoted, is
heard directly without the intrusion of a narrator's
voice (as in drama, where of course action and a setting are added to speech). The progression through
these types of structure is formally a progression
from the extreme of subjective assimilation of objective reality to the extreme of objectivity; and though
of course the things referred to within the framework
supplied by any of these modes will have their own
relative subjectivity or objectivity which may not
seem to correspond to that of the modes employed for
their presentation (so that, e.g., Chekhov or Maeter-
linck may use the drama to present reference to reali-

ty far from "objective," or Joyce the most objective
mode of narrative for presentation of the interior of
a mind, and even the interior of an unconscious mind),
yet obviously either to understand such incongruities
or to penetrate to the insights necessary for their
resolution if that is possible, some such system of
distinctions is required. And the notion of such a
progression, which though its demarcation of types is
definite enough nevertheless presents as a whole a
kind of continuum, provides not the crude and obviously incomplete compartmentalization of narrative, dramatic and lyric that embarrasses much criticism, but
flexible categories that exhaust the possibilities of
both prose and poetry, and modes among which modula-
tion is as easy in theory as it evidently is in practice. For the various types of voice-structure, and
of address, are in literature what the basic colors
of a palette are in painting, or keys in music; the
whole tone and character of a composition is set by
the writer's choice among them, and changed by any
variation from one to another within the work. The
advantage of such a system of conscious distinctions
is that it provides a sure technical foundation for
discussion of all that concerns the "point of view" in
a piece of writing, and a clear view of some of the
major technical relations among works as disparate as,
e.g., the novels of Fielding, Jane Austen, James,
Proust, and Joyce, or Widsith, The Seafarer, Prufrock,
and Yeats' I am of Ireland. Perhaps the most important thing to remember in analyzing the voice of a
composition is that the basic voice need not be the
author's, and may even be that not of a person but of
an abstraction or a thing; the voice may be a wholly
imagined voice, and the process of speech involved
an imagined process in an imagined situation. (Here,
perhaps, is the best handle for a practicable distinction between poetry and prose; it seems possible at
once to reconcile and to illuminate nearly all the
historic characterizations of poetry if we define it
as speech that is not the instrument of any actual
speech-process, or more briefly as "detached speech,"
i.e., actual speech detached, by whatever mechanisms
of meaning, sound, or structure, from any actual
speech-situation.)

The phenomena of address in literature include
all that part of literary meaning which is reference
to specific direction to a hearer and to the relations

145

between speaker and addressee established or presupposed by such direction, or rather by the social situation which occasions and environs it. The mechanisms of address furnish a necessary framework even for poetic form and, since the character of a speech is powerfully affected by the speaker's consciousness of a relation between himself and the addressee, what is usually called the "style" of a composition is in large part a function (in the mathematical sense) of its address. Here the question of first importance for analysis is that of the precise identity and character of the addressee or grammatical second person in a speech (as in the matter of voice it is the identity and operation of the first person). The addressee may be ontologically as well as grammatically a person. In this case, one will naturally distinguish between a singular and a plural addressee, and discriminate further according to what may be roughly called the definitness of the address (address to somebody, address to anybody, address to everybody). With these varieties of address may be classified that in which so little personality is felt in the addressee (and so, correlatively, in the speaker) that the address may be conceived as as impersonal (address to nobody), and thus minimal. But the address may be not to a person, but to a thing or an abstraction; and of address to persons an eccentric variety is that in which the person addressed is the speaker (as in soliloquy). Since, as Aristotle observed, the speaker's end in ordinary speech is in the addressee and the addressee therefore largely determines the character of the speech, each of these varieties of address has its inevitable effect upon the attitude of the speaker, which, reflected in the details of the speech, becomes either explicitly or implicitly a part of its meaning. This part of the meaning, viz. all reference to the attitude of the speaker toward his addressee, is commonly called "tone." The relation between speaker and addressee cannot of course be adequately seized in isolation from the relation of both speaker and addressee to the agencies represented in grammar by the third person, whether conceived as the "subject" reference of the speech or as a true personality present to hear or overhear it. This latter third person, though it be excluded physically in private dialogue, can perhaps never be eliminated psychologically; it is the sum of all the social pressures of the community that provides the

environment in which a speech occurs. The difference
in rhetoric between private speech and public is partly the difference between a singular and a plural addressee (second person), partly a function of the relative consciousness of the presence and pressure of
a third person, definite or vague (the smaller or
larger community or group, linguistic, national, international; society at large; humanity at large, or
in the West, through its whole history). For distinctions such as that by which J.S. Mill differen-
tiated poetry from prose ("Eloquence is heard, poetry is overheard...All poetry is of the nature of soliloquy.") these schemes provide a useful frame of
reference, within which one may pass from such insights
to a plainer view of their implications and difficulties than is possible without such a system. And of
course, it is within such a systematic framework that
the problems concerning the relation of poetry to
communication generally are to be worked out, or at
any rate made practically intelligible.

from Dictionary of World Literary Terms, ed. Joseph
    T. Shipley (Boston: The Writer, Inc., 1970),
    pp. 441-444.

B.   Craig La Drière, "Grammatical and Rhetorical
     Structure"

    In literature, the elements which are organized
together to produce a form are the elements of a language, that is to say, of a conventional system of
significant sounds adapted to the natural human act
of speech. The forms of literary art are produced by
composing together in a given order the phonemes, the
lexemes, the syntagmatic structures provided by a
given language.

    This means that in any speech, and in any product
of literary art, one kind of form that may be discerned will be the simply linguistic form which in
traditonal literary terms we call "grammatical." This
is the form provided for or imposed upon a speech by
virtue of its participation in the systematic structure of a given language (the langue of de Saussure);
the principle of such form, the grammatical principle,

147

is that of the functioning of such a system as an instrument in a social process of communication, specifically as an instrument for the production and practical manipulation of meanings. The ultimate governing principle in linguistic or grammatical construction is the principle of satisfactory communication; but the goal in the grammatical process as such is not the socially acceptable presentation of a meaning (this would shift it from langue to parole, and extend it to the area of the "rhetorical"), but only the production of a construct which shall function effectively in that large social process. The norms of grammar are therefore wholly structural in the strictest sense; the virtue of grammatical speech is constructional "correctness," its value the simplest communicative efficacy, that of the achievement of conventional signification.

Since this is the nature of the grammatical form, it follows that though the whole form of a language is grammatical form, grammatical form can never be the sole or total form of any actual speech. The principle that provides and determines the form of an actual speech is on the one hand always concerned with more than the production of a construct that will present a meaning (correctly), and on the other hand, always involves more than what has been pre-established by conventions, at the very least more than is provided by specifically linguistic convention. Language is something to use in speaking; but speech always involves more than language in this use of it, and its use redisposes the linguistic elements themselves into forms for which the norms of grammatical structure provide no sufficient determining principle.

In the natural process of speech additional formal determination is derived first of all simply from the fact that this process is natural, and its form is "naturally" determined by features of the social situation in which it occurs and by characters in the participants of the process; but it is determined also in the second place by conventional norms for such participation and interaction, since conventional norms of this kind, larger or broader than the purely linguistic, exist in all societies as a necessary part of their constitution as societies.

The art of rhetoric consists in the imposition

upon this natural process of such artistic control as will, without altering the general social and communicative goal of the process, produce a speech (in principle, at least) ideally suited to the achievement of a particular intended effect within the framework of the given social situation and set of circumstances. The virtue of rhetorical speech is "eloquence," its value is that of persuasive, communicative effectiveness. The norms which govern the production of such speech and determine its form are so far from being exclusively linguistic or grammatical that for a required rhetorical effect the norms of grammar may be ignored and its usages transgressed. The operative norms in rhetoric are more general social norms, supplied ad hoc by the particular end in view and the particular social situation and circumstances and of course especially by the character and demands of the addressee or audience. Some of these norms are "natural" or universal; some--doubtless most--are conventional and particular.

In both the natural process of speech and the rhetorical norms other than those supplied by the principle of communicative efficacy may operate to determine form though not as its primary determinant. The most obvious of such attendant or subsidiary norms are those of logic. Logic may of course provide the principle of organization of speech, by fusing, so to speak, with the communicative principle as it does wherever what is to be communicated and the mode of the communication are themselves logical; in philosophical or scientific discourse the logical principle may thus be the primary determinant of form. But this is rarely the case in the normal process of natural speech; and as for rhetoric, what is almost the oldest and still the most profound account of the art, that of Aristotle, notoriously elaborates the distinction between the principle of its organization and that of logical structure. But logical structures are not excluded from either ordinary speech or the productions of rhetorical art, and may have a conspicuous place in the constructions of both; only, in both they will appear in subordination to the principle of socially acceptable communicative efficacy which is the primary determinant of form in such speech.

It is the same with the aesthetic principle.

149

"Elegance" is one of the most ancient adornments of both grammar and rhetoric, and some conceptions of the grand style in the latter--certainly that, for example, of Longinus--include an aesthetic component as did commonly the ancient conception of the "middle" or florid style. But grammar and rhetoric can appear complete without the addition of elegance; and where this or any other aesthetic quality arises in normal speech or in rhetorical art it must be subordinated to the primary principle of communicative efficacy.

But what if the aesthetic impulse should resist such subordination, and itself be strong enough to dominate the principle of sheer communicative efficacy and subordinate it to itself? Then, of course, we have poetry. This is in fact one way of defining poetic speech and the principle determining poetic form: poetry is speech the principle of whose organization is aesthetic rather than practical or utilitarian.

---

from Craig La Drière, "Literary Form and Form in the Other Arts," Stil und Formprobleme in der Literatur, ed. Paul Bochman (Heidelberg: Winter, 1959).

C. Francis Bacon, "Of Studies"

Studies serve for delight, for ornament, and for ability. Their chief use for delight is in privateness and retiring; for ornament, is in discourse; and for ability, is in the judgment and disposition of business. For expert men can execute, and perhaps judge of particulars, one by one; but the general counsels, and the plots and marshalling of affairs come best from those that are learned. To spend too much time in studies is sloth; to use them too much for ornament is affectation; to make judgment wholly by their rules is the humour of a scholar. They perfect nature, and are perfected by experience: for natural abilities are like natural plants that need pruning by study; and studies themselves do give forth directions too much at large, except they be bounded in by experience. Crafty men contemn studies, simple men admire them, and wise men use them; but that is

a wisdom without them and above them, won by observation. Read not to contradict and confute, nor to
believe and take for granted, nor to find talk and
discourse, but to weigh and consider. Some books are
to be tasted, others to be swallowed, and some few
to be chewed and digested; That is, some books are
to be read only in parts; others to be read, but not
curiously; and some few to be read wholly, and with
diligence and attention. Some books also may be read
by deputy, and extracts made of them by others; but
that would be only in the less important arguments
and the meaner sort of books; else distilled books
are, like distilled waters, flashy things. Reading
maketh a full man; conference a ready man; and writing
an exact man. And, therefore, if a man write little,
he had need have a great memory; and if he confer little, he had need have a present wit; and if he read
little, he had need have much cunning, to seem to
know that he doth not. Histories make men wise; poets,
witty; the mathematics, subtle; natural philosophy,
deep, moral, grave; logic and rhetoric, able to con-
tend. Abeunt studia in mores.* Nay, there is no
stone or impediment in the wit but may be wrought out
by fit studies, like as diseases of the body may have
appropriate exercises. Bowling is good for the stone
and reins, shooting for the lungs and breast, gentle
walking for the stomach, riding for the head and the
like. So if a man's wit be wandering, let him study
the mathematics; for in demonstrations, if his wit be
called away never so little, he must begin again. If
his wit be not apt to distinguish or find difference,
let him study the school men; for they are Cymini
sectores.** If he be not apt to beat over matters,
and to call up one thing to prove and illustrate another, let him study the lawyers' cases. So every defect of the mind may have a special receipt.
****

*Abeunt studia in mores: Studies pass into (that is,
     form) manners.

**Cymini sectores: dividers of cuminseed (Matt. 23:
     23), that is, hairsplitters.

151

D.   Daniel Burke, FSC, "Bacon's Essay 'Of Studies'--
     A Rhetorical Analysis"

     Bacon's essay "Of Studies" is one of the oldest
essays in our literature. Its reflections on educational ideals and methods, however, still afford
valuable insights. Hence, the essay can appeal to a
modern reader, even as it appealed, in different ways
perhaps, to an Elizabethan. Our chief concern here
is with the means Bacon uses to achieve effective
communications and the elegance of style for which
his essays are praised.

     Bacon's pioneer effort has most, if not all, of
the characteristics we associate with the essay today.
It has, for instance, a clearly rhetorical purpose:
to explain the broad topic of studies. It instructs
the reader, that is, as to the reasons, the methods,
and the results of studies, and, in the second place,
it persuades him about their utility. As exposition,
the essay is likewise very direct, for the author
loses no time in presenting and developing his subject.
Furthermore the essay is brief; it comprises but one
paragraph containing no digressions, no superfluities.
And yet, there is sufficient elegance of style to
make it unmistakably "literary." Finally, in its approach to the reader, it is markedly objective as it
is too in its approach to its materials. Hence, it is
clearly what we have come to call a "formal" essay.

     As in any rhetorical composition, the basic ele-
ments of the essay are (1) a speaker addressing with
some specific purpose (2) an audience (3) about some
matter. Bacon's stance here as a speaker is rather
magisterial: he is markedly serious and impersonal
as he offers his reflective insights to those who
would hear. He doesn't attempt to ingratiate himself
with his readers either by suggesting pleasant characteristics of his own personality (aside from his wisdom, that is) or by attempting a more emotional involvement of his readers by personal references to
them, humor, and so forth. In fact, with his condensed, difficult style and his shifting positions,
Bacon may intend, as Stanley Fish suggests, to challenge his readers to exercise a more disciplined and
skeptical approach to received opinions on this subject, even to the ideas he is presenting. The audi-

ence, in turn, is assumed to be a rather general and distant one--but one that is interested in self-improvement, in attaining insight--and profiting from its reading.

As to the content, Bacon's main idea is that studies are, or rather, can be beneficial. He commences with a general discussion (comprising the first six sentences) of the uses and possible abuses of study. In the next five sentences, he deals, no less generally, with reading as the chief tool of study. In the third section, sentences twelve to nineteen, the essayist deals with the particular advantages of various types of reading and study.

Bacon begins the first part of the essay with the general statement, "Studies serve for delight, for ornament, and for ability." He then supports this proposition with several instances. In the third sentence, he proceeds to generalize the last instance that he had given, that studies' chief advantage "for ability, is in the judgment and disposition of business." Taking a contrasting line, the essayist adds a word of caution in sentence four against the indiscriminate use of studies, adding in the next that studies, having perfected natural abilities, must themselves be "perfected by experience." Bacon concludes this first section by reiterating that this "experience" can be gained only outside of study.

In the next section the author deals with reading in general, covering briefly several different ideas. First, he considers the proper motive for reading: "Read not to contradict and confute, nor to believe and take for granted, nor to find talk and discourse, but to weigh and consider." Secondly, in the most famous lines of the essay, Bacon counsels that, of books available, "Some are to be tasted, others to be swallowed, and some few to be chewed and digested." Extending the notion of "tasting," he suggests in sentence nine that some books may even be read in the form of "extracts made...by others." Thirdly, in the last two sentences of this part, Bacon considers the most general results of reading and other forms of study."

In the last part of the essay, the author becomes more particular, concentrating on the specific advantages of different studies: "Histories make men wise; poets, witty; the mathematics, subtle..." He supports these assertions with a Latin proverb and with an elaborate comparison of various physical and mental exercises and their advantages: as gentle walking is good for the stomach, so mathematics is good for the mind that cannot concentrate. After other examples of this type, Bacon concludes that "every defect of the mind may have a special receipt."

It can be seen that the over-all design of the essay in the presentation of ideas and in the disposition of major parts has involved a contrast of the general and particular. The essay has moved, that is, from a discussion of the generic advantages of study to a consideration of the specific advantages of individual disciplines. Typically, too, the loose rhetorical "proof" has moved from the general to the particular, for the various assertions have usually been supported inductively by "instances" and "analogies": "Their chief use for delight is in privateness and retiring...," and, again, "natural abilities are like natural plants that need pruning by study."

Bacon has presented these basic ideas and supporting notions in a distinctive style. His diction, for instance, aside from the archaism the modern reader first notes, is remarkable for its drift toward general terms--delight, ornament, ability, privateness, retiring, and so forth. But it is the sentence structure and the figuration that it involves that is, perhaps, most peculiar. Bacon seems to depend very heavily on the compound sentence of three clauses (or elliptical clauses), frequently joined without benefit of conjunctions ("asynedton"). In sentences two and six, as well as many others throughout the essay, Bacon shows clearly how important an adjunct of his style he considers this particular combination of sentence structure and figure. Furthermore, this combination usually involves what is perhaps Bacon's fundamental figure of words, that is, "balance." Such balance is often accompanied by repetition of identical words at the beginning or ending of the parallel members and by an equal, or nearly equal, measuring of the members ("isocolon"). The most notable appearance of this larger complex of figures is in the "Some books..." passage, but it appears also, more or less completely, in sentences two, four,

six (first part), ten, and eleven. There are other
varieties of balance, of course, and it should be
noted that in most cases the balance is less than
exact:

> Their chief use
>> for delight is in privateness and retiring;
>> for ornament, is in discourse;
> and for ability, is in the judgment and disposi-
> tion of business.

In some ways, Bacon's most important figure is
"sententia," the maxim. While he actually uses only
one traditional proverb (<u>Abeunt studia in mores</u>), he
presents his own insights so compactly and precisely
(the asyndeton is important here) and in such a serious and "pedagogical" tone that all the assertions
seem like aphorisms: "Studies serve for delight, for
ornament, and for ability," "To spend too much time
in studies is sloth...," and so forth. Other passages
of the essay have been quoted so frequently that they
have indeed become traditional maxims; this is especially true of the "Some books..." phrase. And the
aphoristic style is difficult to bring off successfully. As Catherine Drinker Bown has remarked, it
requires "almost unbounded imagination, cruelly disciplined by precision of utterance." But it is in
this way, especially, that Bacon makes his own essay
something "to be chewed and digested" thoughtfully
and appreciatively.

E.   Robert M. Browne, "The Shropshire Lad as Funeral
         Orator"

I have elsewhere argued that rhetorical analysis
of the proper kind is a necessary part of the work of
the analyst of poetry, and I wish in this paper to
illustrate the utility of such analysis through a consideration of Housman's "To An Athlete Dying Young."

The proper kind of rhetorical analysis, to my
mind, respects the integrity of the poetic construct
and does not attempt to reduce the poem to its author's
extrapoetic persuasive intentions. These intentions
may, perhaps must, be there behind the poem, and it
is legitimate to analyze a poem from this point of

view, assisted by what we know of the poet's biography and the rest of the historical context. But such analysis deals with the external rhetoric of the poem, its functioning in a persuasive process involving poets and readers in extrapoetic relations. It may not be necessary for a poem to be a good poem to function well in a process of external rhetoric. Thus a bad love poem may have its intended effect on a girl because she responds to the man who wrote it for her, even though his poem is null aesthetically. In principle, the analysis of external rhetoric does not have to concern itself with poetic merit.

But the analyst who wishes to deal with poetry as poetry must ask about the relation of rhetorical structure to the aesthetic structure of the poem. The kind of rhetoric that will interest him is the internal rhetoric of the poem, the persuasive or other communicative processes involving the speakers and addressees of the poem. Not all poetry has a highly articulated rhetorical structure, but nevertheless it will always have some address, minimal though it may be, and hence some kind of rhetorical purpose. In such cases rhetorical analysis may be brief and may merely be used to point out the inconsequentiality of the rhetorical structure before the analyst goes on to more pertinent matters.

Yet some poems exhibit marked rhetorical structure. This is not surprising in view of the importance of rhetoric in Hellenistic and Roman education and in the European school curriculum after the Renaissance. Product of such an education and professor of Latin, Housman frequently presents the Shropshire Lad as engaged in argument, not simply reflecting or meditating. "To An Athlete Dying Young" is an excellent example of a poem with a fully developed rhetorical structure. The poem is best understood when it is considered as a funeral oration, delivered by a townsman of the dead athlete, apparently at the graveside ceremony, in the presence of the mourners. It has a specific addressee, the dead man, and a specific purpose, to persuade him that he's better off dead.

Yet the mere statement of these facts is enough to show that this rhetorical situation is a bizarre one. Rhetoric is not normally employed to speak to dead men, nor for such a purpose. It is true that

"normal" rhetoric might occasionally address the dead
man, as a literary device or to demonstrate faith in
immortality, but its normal addressee would be the
appropriate deity or the assembled mourners. Here
the address to the dead man is not occasional but consistent throughout.

And if we suppose that, even so, the address remains a literary device and the real audience is an
assembly of mourners, we have still not returned the
poem to the world of ordinary rhetoric. For it is
hard to conceive a real audience to whom this rhetoric
would be appropriate. Is it to be conceived as a
group of Shropshire villagers? The sturdy English
colloquiality of the opening stanzas and the use the
poem makes of the well-known English enthusiasm for
sports suggests as much. But such an audience would
be scandalized by the pagan sentiments of the last
five stanzas. Furthermore, the poem is full of classical references, which at first seem only part of
the stock in trade of the well-read village poet, but
which become dominant at the end of the poem. It is
slightly ambiguous whether the dead athlete is to
take these references to the pagan underworld literal-
ly or figuratively. The same for the mourners. The
result is to create a certain ambiguity about the literal time and place: nineteenth century rural England
or the pagan countryside of classical times?

As there are difficulties in conceiving either
of these in literal terms, it is perhaps best to take
the scene as an imaginary and idealized pagan countryside, having features both ancient and modern. Only
in such a context can the orator sound so English yet
express such un-Christian sentiments in public. From
the rhetorical point of view the important thing is
that this conjunction, together with the other depar-
tures from normal rhetoric which I have mentioned,
serves to make the rhetoric of the poem an ideal rhetoric, detached from a real occasion and therefore
more readily foregrounded as a conspicuous part of
the aesthetic structure. This way of using rhetorical
structure is common in classically influenced poetry.
One sets up a situation where the speaker, or the addressee, or the subject, or the purpose so deviates
from normal rhetoric that it becomes a figurative
rhetoric.

In such poetry the speaker involved in the fictive rhetorical process is likely to appear oblivious
of the fact that the process is fictive. The speaker
of Housman's poem does not appear to be aware of any
oddity in the situation. He takes his role as funeral orator with due seriousness and is completely
faithful to his task from beginning to end, as a brief
analysis will show.

The two opening stanzas are narrative in form,
but the narrative details are carefully selected to
suit a forthcoming argument. The first stanza recalls
a past victory of the athlete, the triumphal procession through the market place of the town. This is
epideictic rhetoric, and such an opening recalling
past glories is very appropriate for the purpose of
praising the young man. Then the speaker shifts to
the present occasion, also a normal part of epideictic
rhetoric. But he describes the funeral procession
in terms closely paralleling those used to describe
the victory procession. In both cases the runner is
borne shoulder-high, in both cases he is surrounded
by his townsmen. The phrase "the road all runners
come" insists on the similarities between racing (and
its accompanying celebration) and dying (and its accompanying celebration). This is not free-flowing
narrative, motivated by the need of a story-teller
to recount his story properly, but a carefully controlled juxtaposition of related scenes for other purposes, the most immediate being an argumentative one.

However, the juxtaposition could well serve different kinds of argument. For instance, racing could
have been used to stand for spiritual combat, as in
Saint Paul. Instead, the youth is congratulated in
stanza three for his cleverness in dying early and
avoiding the disadvantages of living too long. Such
a paradoxical thesis is of course a clear departure
from conventional funeral rhetoric. Perhaps to mark
it more clearly, there is a breach of social decorum
in the language. "Smart lad," says the speaker, fa-
miliarly and almost jocularly. Then for three stanzas (three to five), he presents arguments to persuade the young man that he has done the right thing.
Each rhymed couplet seems a separate argument, and
each is a justification for calling the young man a
smart lad. Epideictic rhetoric has at least momen-
tarily changed to forensic rhetoric, the defense of

the young man's wisdom in having chosen to die young.

These three stanzas of forensic argument are of course deeply involved in absurdities that would be fatal to normal arguments. The speaker has to make the following claims: (1) that the young man has chosen death freely (though there is no hint of suicide); (2) that the young man did so on rational grounds; and (3) that he in fact made the right choice; that an early and glorious death is preferable to a late and inglorious one.

To defend these positions he uses a variety of arguments, but they are always arguments addressed to the young man. They use elements that appeal directly to his experience as a small-town athlete. Lines 9-10 involve the pathetic argument: they compliment the young man on the intelligence he has illustrated in having chosen death; Aristotle says that in rhetoric "all things are (to be considered) good which men deliberately choose to do." But the lines also imply a logical argument involving enthymeme:

The athlete should die while his glory is still
    with him (implied principle).
The glory of an athlete is with him only in early
    life (1. 10).
Therefore the athlete should die in early life. (1.9)

The "and" beginning the next couplet shows that it is a continuation of the argument. "Laurel" and "rose" are signs which by metonymy stand for athletic glory and the beauty of young girls, respectively. The argument is an a fortiori one, based on the assumption that what is true of the signs is true of the things signified. The rose is known to be short-lived, and so, it is argued, is the thing it signifies, the beauty of girls. If the laurel, another sign, has an even shorter life, so must the athletic glory it signifies. This couplet supports the minor premise of the enthymeme of the preceding couplet: it "proves" the brevity of athletic glory.

In the next stanza the speaker daringly takes on the biggest obstacle to his case: the dark, silent isolation that can be imagined for existence in the grave. He drops the pretense that death is chosen; it is "shady night" and "earth" that act. But apart

from these personifications, he says only what is li-
terally true: dead men's eyes "cannot see the record
cut," and dead men's ears are as indifferent to silence as to cheers. Still, these literal facts are
cunningly chosen: these things that cannot be seen
and heard are only things that would be painful to
perceive anyhow. The hearer is offered a choice between two things. No other possibility is conceded:
the implication is that the life of an aging athlete
consists largely of painful happenings.

The first couplet of stanza five is also literal-
ly true and also compares nothingness with painful
existence. The second couplet argues more metaphori-
cally, treating the retired runners first as losers
in a race, then as possessors of dead names. The
dead young athlete has avoided this fate. Once again
the concentration has been on the disadvantages of
living as compared with extinction; no positive advantages to dying have yet been mentioned.

The end of stanza five completes the forensic
part of the argument, the defense of the young man's
past action. But the opening of six ("so" followed
by an imperative) seems to imply that the following
command is a logical consequence of the preceding argument. It shifts the type of rhetoric once more,
this time to deliberative rhetoric, the rhetoric that
deals with future choices. The young man is already
dead, but once again there is the flattering pretense
that he has a choice. Since stanza three has already
stated that he has made the choice, the argument is
logically superfluous. But the point insisted on
more forcefully here is the urgency with which the
choice must be made. In a striking hyperbole he is
urged to get from the finish-line of the race to the
threshold of the grave so quickly that the sound of
his running will still be echoing back at the finish-
line when he arrives. In one sense this is simply a
way of urging him to be quick about it, like the bu-
reaucratic command "this order must be complied with
yesterday." But metaphor as well as hyperbole is
involved: the fading of echoes stands for the fading
of glory. The argument is basically the same as that
of "Smart lad, to slip betimes away / From fields
where glory does not stay"; but now presented in a
deliberate framework, it is more dramatic. The deliberative framework qualifies the rest of the stanza;

160

the stress is on the fact that the challenge cup will
be "still-defended" and can be displayed on the low
lintel.

The seventh and last stanza of the poem also
seems at first to have a deliberative function. It
offers an incentive to encourage the young man to step
over the threshold. He will be surrounded by admirers
as he was in the first scene; and his laurels, already
shown to be briefer than a girl's garland of roses if
he lives, will be forever unwithered. These are more
positive advantages to dying than those offered in
the middle section of the poem. Yet even conceived
in pagan terms the argument seems less weighty than
the hardboiled literal arguments of stanza four. For
pagans did not really conceive the underworld as a
happy place. The argument is ingenious, but is becoming more purely literary, a graceful way of providing a satisfactory ending, an ending that tends to
return the poem to its epideictic beginnings.

This analysis has attempted to show that the
speaker of this poem has composed a speech that is a
skillfully controlled piece of rhetoric. But normal
rhetorical functioning is blocked by the fact that
the hearer is dead and by the fact that even if he
could hear it is doubtful he would be reconciled to
his own death by such arguments. Yet the reader of
the poem, who is outside its rhetorical circle, can
respond to the arguments on an aesthetic basis. He
can admire them because first of all they are consistently ingenious and appropriate to a fantastic situation. Very rich rhetorical structure is to be found
there, richer than that found in normal, "real" rhetoric. In addition he can see the ingenious rhetorical
structure as not a pure exercise in meaningless argument, but as itself a kind of vehicle for an extended
trope. It would be foolhardy to try to give too precise and propositional form to the tenor of this vehicle, but I think it would have something to do with
Housman's well-known pessimism. The implication is
that life is so dreadful that if we were logical about
it we'd argue somewhat as this speaker has argued and
prefer a short happy life to a long miserable one.
The speaker's dubious rhetorical arguments have their
truth or at least their emotional validity. The reader need not be a pessimist to admire the way this
understandable human attitude is made part of a rich

verbal structure. As in other instances of good poetic metaphor, we do not go through the vehicle only to seek the tenor. The structure is valued for its wholeness, for the relations that bind together vehicle and tenor.

The points I have just made indicate ways in which the rhetorical structure of this poem can be itself considered as aesthetically interesting. But the rhetorical structure is implicated in aesthetic structure in another, less direct way, because the structure of argument carries with it an implied narrative. The first two stanzas present two moments in the career of an athlete, two moments carefully established as parallel with each other. The admirers of the athlete bring him "home" in the first stanza, to his "threshold" in the second. The admirers (pallbearers) have brought him to the edge of the grave.

This narrative element, slight as it is, is suspended during the three stanzas of argument. But stanza six, although it is cast in argumentative form, also implies an action. The invitation to set "the fleet foot on the sill of shade" is a natural accompaniment to the next step of the funeral ceremony, the lowering of the body into the grave. Once there, the athlete will make himself at home by putting his challenge-cup over the lintel. Then in stanza seven, he will meet his new "townsmen." Stanzas six and seven complete the slight narrative action begun in one and two, and carry it beyond the grave. The pattern is very neat. We have seen that stanzas one and two are parallel to each other, though there are slightly different emphases: stanza one stresses the reception by the townspeople, stanza two the procession to the hero's door. The last stanzas reverse this pattern: first the ceremony around the door is picked up and completed, then the reception by the townspeople takes place.

The poem involves the interplay of a number of aesthetic patterns. Within the structure of argument there is the ingeniously developed fictive rhetoric, manipulating the forms of rhetorical argument for ends that are more aesthetic than persuasive. There is also the progression of types of argument from epideictic to deliberative, returning at last to the epideictic beginning. There is a pattern of relations between the structure of argument and the structure of narrative. Narrative dominates the first two stanzas, disappears in the next three, and returns, though indirectly, in the last two. And this structure of narrative involves the recurrence of similar elements in chiasmic order: a victory parade is reflected, in reversed images, by a funeral procession extended in imagination beyond the grave.

The same elements participate in the structure of argument, the narrative structure, and the aesthetic structures that make use of these others and bind them together. I hope I have shown the importance of the rhetorical structure, but also its interrelations with other structures, particularly the aesthetic or poetic structure. Rhetorical analysis is a basic tool, but rhetorical structure has no priority over other structures in a poem; on the contrary, unless it is somehow secondary to an aesthetic pattern the poem is only nominally a poem.

As a postscript I might add that there are many ways in which rhetorical structure functions in poems. The poem I have chosen to analyze exhibits some of these ways, and because it is a traditional poem, it exhibits some traditional ways of employing rhetorical structure. With modernist poetry the task is more difficult. We cannot make many generalizations about it without many studies, but it is certainly not characterized by the kind of neat, self-contained but fictive rhetorical structure seen here. To determine what the rhetorical situation is in a modern poem is often the major task of the analyst, the end rather than the beginning of his labors. The rhetorical situations of a "Prufrock" or a "Peter Quince at the Clavier" do not yield themselves at first glance. Yet if we ask questions about the rhetoric of these or of any poems we are asking questions that are meaningful and that will lead us to a better grasp of what we are studying.

from The Quarterly Journal of Speech, 57 (1971), 134-139.

APPENDIX III: THE SMALL POETIC STRUCTURE

A.   Jan Mukařovský, "Standard Language and Poetic
      Language"

     The problem of the relationship between the stan-
dard language and poetic language can be considered
from two standpoints.   The theorist of poetic language
poses it about as follows: is the poet bound by the
norms of the standard?   Or perhaps: how does this
norm assert itself in poetry?   The theorist of the
standard language, on the other hand, wants to know
above all to what extent a work of poetry can be used
as data for ascertaining the norm of the standard.
In other words: the theorist of the standard language
is mainly interested in the similarities between them.
It is clear that with a good procedure no conflict
can arise between the two directions of research;
there is only a difference in the point of view and
in the illumination of the problem.   Our study approaches the problem of the relationship between poetic
language and the standard from the vantage point of
poetic language.   Our procedure will be to subdivide
the general problem into a number of special problems.

     The first problem, by way of introduction, con-
cerns the following: what is the relationship between
the extension of poetic language and that of the
standard, between the places of each in the total system of the whole of language?   Is poetic language a
special brand of the standard, or is it an independent
formation?--Poetic language cannot be called a brand
of the standard, if for no other reason, then because
poetic language has at its disposal, from the standpoint of lexicon, syntax, etc., all the forms of the
given language, often of different developmental phases thereof.   There are such works in which the lexical material is taken over completely from another
form of language than the standard (thus, Villon's or
Rictus' slang poetry in French literature).   Different
forms of the language may exist side by side in a
work of poetry (for instance, in the dialogues of a
novel dialect or slang, in the narrative passages the
standard).   Poetic language, finally, also has some
of its own lexicon and phraseology, as well some grammatical forms, the so-called poetisms, such as zor

(gaze), oř (steed), pláti (be aflame), third person
singular muž (can; cf. English -th, plg.) (a rich
selection of examples can be found in the irǫnic description of "moon language" in (Svatopluk) Čech's
(1846-1908, a realist) Vulet pana Broučka do měsíce
(Mr. Brouček's Trip to the Moon). Only some schools
of poetry, of course, have a positive attitude toward
poetisms (among them the Lumír Group including Sv.
Čech), others reject them.

Poetic language is thus not a brand of the standard. This is not to deny the close connection between the two, which consists in the fact that the
standard language is for poetry the background against
which is reflected the aesthetically intentional distortion of the linguistic components of the work, in
other words, the intentional violation of the norm of
the standard. Let us, for instance, visualize a work
in which this distortion is carried out by the inter-
penetration of dialect speech with the standard; it
is clear then that it is not the standard which is
perceived as a distortion of the dialect, but the dialect as a distortion of the standard, even then, if
the dialect is quantitatively preponderant. The violation of the norm of the standard, its systematic
violation, is what makes possible the poetic utiliza-
tion of language; without this possibility there would
be no poetry. The more the norm of the standard is
stabilized in a given language, the more varied can
be its violation, and therefore, the more possibilities for poetry in that language. And on the other
hand, the weaker the awareness of this norm, the fewer
possibilities for poetry. Thus, in the beginnings of
Modern Czech poetry, when the awareness of the norm
of the standard was weak, poetic neologisms, with the
purpose of violating the norm of the standard, were
little different from neologisms designed to gain
general acceptance and become a part of the norm of
the standard, so that they could be confused with
them...

This relationship between poetic language and
the standard, one which we could call negative, also
has its positive side which is, however, more important for the theory of the standard language than for
poetic language and its theory. Many of the linguistic components of a work of poetry do not deviate from
the norm of the standard because they constitute the

background against which the distortion of the other components is reflected. The theoretician of the standard language can therefore include works of poetry in his data, with the reservation, that he will differentiate the distorted componenets from those that are not distorted. An assumption that all components have to agree with the norm of the standard would of course be erroneous.

The second special question which we shall attempt to answer concerns the different <u>function</u> of the two norms of language. This is the core of the problem. The function of poetic language consists in the maximum of foregrouding of the utterance. Foregrounding is the opposite of automatization, that is the deautomatization of an act; the more an act is automatized, the less it is consciously executed; the more it is foregrounded, the more completely conscious does it become. Objectively speaking: automatization schematizes an event, foregrounding means the violation of the scheme. The standard language in its purest form, as the language of science with formulation as its objective, avoids foregrounding (aktualisace): thus, a new expression, foregrounded because of its newness, is immediately automatized in a scientific treatise by an exact definition of its meaning. Foregrounding is, of course, in the standard language, for instance, in journalistic style, even more in essays. But it is here always subordinate to communication: its purpose is to attract the reader's (listener's) attention more closely to the <u>subject matter</u> expressed by the foregrounded means of expression. All that has here been said about foregrounding and automatization in the standard language, has been treated in detail in Havranek's paper in this cycle; we are here concerned with poetic language. In poetic language foregrounding achieves maximun intensity to the extent of pushing communication into the background as the objective of expression and of being used for its own sake; it is not used in the services of communication, but in order to place in the foreground the act of expression, the act of speech itself. The question is then one of how this maximum of foregrounding is achieved in poetic language. The idea might arise that this is a quantitative effect, a matter of the foregrounding of the largest number of components, perhaps of all of them together. This would be a mistake, although only a

theoretical one, since in practice such a complete
foregrounding of all the components is impossible.
The foregrounding of any one of the components is necessarily accompanied by the automatization of one or
more of the other components; thus, for instance, the
foreground intonation in (Jaroslav) Vrchlikỳ (1853-
1912, a poet of the Lumír Group, see above) and (Svatopluk) Čech has necessarily pushed to the lowest level of automatization the meaning of the word as a
unit, because the foregrounding of its meaning would
give the word phonetic independence as well and lead
to a disturbance of the uninterrupted flow of the
intonational (melodic) line; an example of the degree
to which the semantic independence of the word in
context manifests itself also as intonational independence can be found in (Karel) Toman's (1877-1946,
a modern poet) verse. The foregrounding of intonation as uninterrupted melodic line is thus linked to
the semantic emptiness for which the Lumír Group
has been criticized by the younger generation as being
"verbalistic."--In addition to the practical impossi-
bility of the foregrounding of all components, it can
also be pointed out that the simultaneous foregrounding of all the components of a work of poetry is un-
thinkable. This is because the foregrounding of a
component implies precisely its being placed in the
foreground; the unit in the foreground, however, occupies this position by comparison with another unit
or units that remain in the background. A simultaneous general foregrounding would thus bring all the
components into the same plane and thus become a new
automatization.

The devices by which poetic language achieves
its maximum of foregrounding must therefore be sought
somewhere else than in the quantity of foregrounded
components. They consist in the consistency and systematic character of foregrounding.

---

from A Prague School Reader on Esthetics, Literary
Structure and Style, tr. and ed. Paul L. Garvin
(Washington: Georgetown University Press, 1964),
pp. 17-20.

B.   Roman Jakobson, "Linguistics and Poetics"

   Language must be investigated in all the variety
of its functions. Before discussing the poetic function we must define its place among the other functions of language. An outline of these functions demands a concise survey of the constitutive factors
in any speech event, in any act of verbal communication. The addresser sends a message to the addressee.
To be operative the message requires a <u>context</u> refe-
renced to ("referent" in another, somewhat ambiguous,
nomenclature), seizable by the addressee, and either
verbal or capable of being verbalized; a <u>code</u> fully,
or at least partially, common to the addresser and
addressee (or in other words, to the encoder and de-
coder of the message); and, finally, a <u>contact</u>, a
physical channel and psychological connection between
the addresser and the addressee, enabling both of
them to enter and stay in communication. All these
factors inalienably involved in verbal communication
may be schematized as follows:

CONTEXT

ADDRESSER _____ MESSAGE _____ ADDRESSEE

CONTACT

CODE

   Each of these six factors determines a different
function of language. Although we distinguish six
basic aspects of language, we could, however, hardly
find verbal messages that would fulfill only one function. The diversity lies not in a monopoly of some
one of these several functions but in a different
hierarchical order of functions. The verbal structure
of a message depends primarily on the predominant
function. But even though a set (<u>Einstellung</u>) toward
the referent, an orientation toward the <u>context</u>--
briefly the so-called <u>referential</u>, "denotative," "cognitive" function--is the leading task of numerous
messages, the accessory participation of the other
functions in such messages must be taken into account
by the observant linguist.

   The so-called <u>emotive</u> or "expressive" function,

169

focused on the addresser, aims a direct expression
of the speaker's attitude toward what he is speaking
about. It tends to produce an impression of a certain emotion whether true or feigned; therefore, the
term "emotive," launched and advocated by Marty has
proved to be preferable to "emotional." The purely
emotive stratum in language is presented by the interjections. They differ from the means of referential language both by their sound pattern (peculiar
sound sequences or even sounds elsewhere unusual) and
by by their syntactic role (they are not components
but equivalents of sentences). "Tut! Tut! said
McGinty": the complete utterance of Conan Doyle's
character consists of two suction clicks. The emotive
function, laid bare in the interjections, flavors to
some extent all our utterances, on their phonic, grammatical, and lexical level. If we analyze language
from the standpoint of the information it carries,
we cannot restrict the notion of information to the
cognitive aspect of language. A man, using expressive
features to indicate his angry or ironic attitude,
conveys ostensible information, and evidently this
verbal behavior cannot be likened to such nonsemotic,
nutritive activities as "eating grapefruit" (despite
Chatman's bold simile). The difference between (big)
and the emphatic prolongation of the vowel (bi:g) is
a conventional, coded linguistic feature like the difference between the short and long vowel in such
Czech pairs as (vi) "you" and (vi:) "knows," but in
the latter pair the differential information is phonemic and in the former emotive. As long as we are
interested in phonemic invariants, the English /i/
and /i:/ appear to be mere variants of one and the
same phoneme, but if we are concerned with emotive
units, the relation between the invariant and variants
is reversed: length and shortness are invariants im-
plemented by variable phonemes. Saporta's surmise
that emotive difference is a nonlinguistic feature,
"attributable to the delivery of the message and not
to the message," arbitrarily reduces the informatio-
nal capacity of messages.

  A former actor of Stanislavskij's Moscow Theater
told me how at his audition he was asked by the famous
director to make forty different messages from the
phrase Segodnja vecerom "this evening," by diversi-
fying its expressive tint. He made a list of some
forty emotional situations, then emitted the given

phrase in accordance with each of these situations, which his audience had to recognize only from the changes in the sound shape of the same two words. For our research work in the description and analysis of contemporary Standard Russian (under the auspices of the Rockefeller Foundation) this actor was asked to repeat Stanislavskij's test. He wrote down some fifty situations framing the same elliptic sentence and made of it fifty corresponding messages for a tape record. Most of the messages were correctly and circumstantially decoded by Moscovite listeners. May I add that all such emotive cues easily undergo linguistic analysis.

Orientation toward the addressee, the conative function, finds its purest grammatical expression in the vocative and imperative, which syntactically, morphologically, and often even phonemically deviate from other nominal and verbal categories. The imperative sentences cardinally differ from declarative sentences: the latter are and the former are not liable to a truth test. When in O'Neill's play The Fountain, Nano, "(in a fierce tone of command)," says "Drink!"--the imperative cannot be challenged by the question "is it true or not?" which may be, however, perfectly well asked after such sentences as "one drank," "one will drink," "one would drink." In contradistinction to the imperative sentences, the declarative sentences are convertible into interrogative sentences: "did one drink?" "will one drink?" "would one drink?"

The traditional model of language as elucidated particularly by Buhler was confined to these three functions--emotive, conative, and referential--and the three apexes of this model--the first person of the addresser, the second person of the addressee, and the "third person," properly--someone or something spoken of. Certain additional verbal functions can be easily inferred from this triadic model. Thus the magic, incantatory function is chiefly some kind of conversion of an absent or inanimate "third person" into an addressee of a conative message. "May this sty dry up, tfu, tfu, tfu, tfu" (Lithuanian spell). "Water, queen river, daybreak! Send grief beyond the blue sea, to the sea-bottom, like a grey stone never to rise from the sea-bottom, may grief never come to burden the light heart of God's servant, may grief

be removed and sink away" (north Russian incantation).
"Sun, stand thou still upon Gibeon; and thou, Moon,
in the valley of Aj-a-lon. And the sun stood still,
and the moon stayed..." (Josh. 10.12). We observe,
however, three further constitutive factors of verbal
communication and three corresponding functions of
language.

There are messages primarily serving to establish,
to prolong, or to discontinue communication, to check
whether the channel works ("Hello, do you hear me?"),
to attract the attention of the interlocutor or to
confirm his continued attention ("Are you listening?"
or in Shakespearean diction, "Lend me your ears!"--
and on the other end of the wire "Um-hum!"). This
set for <u>contact</u>, or in Malinowski's terms <u>phatic</u> function may be displayed by a profuse exchange of ritua-
lized formulas, by entire dialogues with the mere
purport of prolonging communication. Dorothy Parker
caught eloquent examples: "'Well!' the young man
said. 'Well!' she said. 'Well, here we are,' he
said. 'Here we are,' she said. 'Aren't we?' 'I
should say we were,' he said, 'Eeyop! Here we are.'
'Well! she said. 'Well!' he said, 'well.'" The endeavor to start and sustain communication is typical
of talking birds; thus the phatic function of language
is the only one they share with human beings. It is
also the first verbal function acquired by infants;
they are prone to communicate before being able to
send or receive informative communication.

A distinction has been made in modern logic between two levels of language, "object language" speaking of objects and "meta-language" speaking of language. But metalanguage is not only a necessary scientific tool utilized by logicians and linguists; it
plays also an important role in our everyday language.
Like Moliere's Jourdain who used prose without knowing
it, we practice metalanguage without realizing the
metalingual character of our operations. Whenever the
addresser and/or the addressee need to check up whether they use the same code, speech is focused on the
<u>code</u>: it performs a <u>metalingual</u> (i.e., glossing)
function. "I don't follow you--what do you mean?"
asks the addressee, or in Shakespearean diction, "What
is't thou say'st?" And the addresser in anticipation
of such recapturing questions inquires: "Do you know
what I mean?" Imagine such an exasperating dialogue:

"The sophomore was plucked." "But what is plucked?"
"Plucked means the same as flunked." "And flunked?"
"To be flunked is to fail in an exam." "And what is
sophomore?" persists the interrogator innocent of
school vocabulary. "A sophomore is (or means) a second year student." All these equational sentences
convey information merely about the lexical code of
English; their function is strictly metalingual. Any
process of language learning, in particular child ac-
quistion of the mother tongue, makes wide use of
such metalingual operations; and aphasia may often be
defined as a loss of ability for metalingual operations.

We have brought up all the six factors involved
in verbal communication except the message itself.
The set (Einstellung) toward the message as such, focus on the message for its own sake, is the poetic
function of language. This function cannot be pro-
ductively studied out of touch with the general problems of language, and on the other hand, the scrutiny
of language requires a thorough consideration of its
poetic function. Any attempt to reduce the sphere of
poetic function to poetry or to confine poetry to
poetic function would be a delusive oversimplification.
Poetic function is not the sole function of verbal
art but only its dominant, determining function, whereas in all other verbal activities, it acts as a subsidiary, accessory constituent. This function, by
promoting the palpability of signs, deepens the fundamental dichotomy of signs and objects. Hence, when
dealing with poetic function, linguistics cannot limit itself to the field of poetry.

"Why do you always say Joan and Margery, yet never Margery and Joan? Do you prefer Joan to her twin
sister?" "Not at all, it just sounds smoother." In
a sequence of two coordinate names, as far as no rank
problems interfere, the precedence of the shorter
name suits the speaker, unaccountably for him, as a
well-ordered shape of the message.

A girl used to talk about "the horrible Harry."
"Why horrible?" "Because I hate him." "But why not
dreadful, terrible, frightful, disgusting?" "I don't
know why, but horrible fits him better." Without
realizing it, she clung to the poetic device of paronomasia.

173

The political slogan "I like Ike" /ay layk ayk/,
succinctly structured, consists of three monosyllables
and counts three dipthongs /ay/, each of them symmetrically followed by one consonantal phoneme, /..l..
k..k/. The make-up of the three words presents a
variation: no consonantal phonemes in the first word,
two around the dipthong in the second, and one final
consonant in the third. A similar dominant nucleus
/ay/ was noticed by Hymes in some of the sonnets of
Keats. Both cola of the trisyllabic formula "I like/
Ike" rhyme with each other, and the second of the
two rhyming words is fully included in the first one
(echo rhyme), /layk/--/ayk/, a paronomastic image of
a feeling which totally envelops its object. Both
cola alliterate with each other, and the first of
the two alliterating words is included in the second:
/ay/--/ayk/, a paronomastic image of the loving subject enveloped by the beloved object. The secondary,
poetic function of this electional catch phrase reinforces its impressiveness and efficacy.

As we said, the linguistic study of the poetic
function must overstep the limits of poetry, and, on
the other hand, the linguistic scrutiny of poetry
cannot limit itself to the poetic function. The particularities of diverse poetic genres imply a differently ranked participation of the other verbal
functions along with the dominant poetic function.
Epic poetry, focused on the third person, strongly
involves the referential function of language; the
lyric, oriented toward the first person, is intimately linked with the emotive function; poetry of the
second person is imbued with the conative function
and is either supplicatory or exhortative, depending
on whether the first person is subordinated to the
second one or the second to the first.

---

from Style in Language, ed. Thomas A. Sebeok (New
     York: MIT Press and John Wiley, 1960), pp. 353-
     357.

C. Daniel Burke, FSC, "A Sampler of Figures and
     Tropes"

"There is no small difficulty in talking about

the figures of discourse," observed the rhetorician Alexander (2nd century A.D.), "for the figures themselves are difficult to delimit, since some authors say they are infinite in number, and others, while they assert the figures are not infinite, yet say they are so many as to be inexhaustible; furthermore it is not easy to distinguish figure from trope" (see the translation by Benedict Einarson in Longinus on the Sublime and Joshua Reynolds Discourses on Art (Chicago, 1945), p. 81). Nevertheless, Alexander proceeds to distinguish between figures and tropes--and several other types of small poetic structures. "The figure," he says, "differs from trope in that a trope is an excellence...concerned with a single word, whereas a figure is a good arrangement...concerned with several words." And again, "a figure differs furthermore from a trope in that the trope contains an extraneous word in the place of the word peculiar to the thing expressed, for it takes its deviation from the proper word, as in 'head of the fountain' and 'the lowest foot of Ide,' whereas the figure keeps the word peculiar to the thing, but the word is placed in a certain way...as in 'Against yourself you summon him, / Against the laws you summon him.'"

These distinctions do not take one very far in the whole range of poetic devices, but they are a good point of departure and they remain serviceable today. The following examples of tropes and figures are drawn from the Rhetorica ad Herennium that at one time was attributed to Cicero (see the Loeb Library edition by Harry Caplan, 1954), with many of the illustrations suggested by Sr. Miriam Joseph, Shakespeare's Use of the Arts of Language (New York, 1947). For further discussion of individual figures see Quintilian, Institutio Oratoria, VIII-IX; George Puttenham, The Arte of English Poesie; Charles S. Baldwin, Ancient Rhetoric and Poetics (New York, 1924); Warren Taylor, Tudor Figures of Rhetoric (Chicago, 1937); Joseph R. Shipley, Dictionary of World Literature (New York, 1953); Alex Preminger et al., eds., Encyclopedia of Poetry and Poetics (Princeton, 1965); Richard A. Lantham, A Handlist of Rhetorical Terms (Berkeley, 1968).

Figures of Words

A. Repetition of individual words:

175

1. Anaphora - repetition of the same word at
            the beginning of successive
            phrases, clauses, sentences.

    Some glory in their birth, some in their
      skill,
    Some in their wealth, some in their body's
      force,
    Some in their garments...(Sonnets, XCI)

2. Antistrophe - repetition of a word at the
            end of succeeding phrases,
            clauses, sentences.

                    anon with great disdain,
    She shuns my love, and after by a train
    She seeks my love...(Henry Peacham)

3. Symploce - combination of anaphora and an-
            tistrophe.

    Son. How will my mother for a father's death
    Take on with me, and ne'er be satisfied!
    Father. How will my wife for slaughter of
            my son
    Shed seas of tears, and ne'er be satisfied!
            (3 Henry VI, II.v.106)

4. Homoioteleuton - like ending in words; rime.

    How churlishly I chid Lucetta hence
    When willingly I would have had her here!
    How angerly I taught my brow to frown...
            (Two Gentlemen of Verona, V.i.210)

5. Antimetabole - words repeated in the same
            sentence but in an opposite
            connection.

    The fool doth think he is wise, but the wise
    man knows himself to be a fool...
            (As You Like It, V.i.35)

B. Play on meaning in one or more words:

6. Traductio - repetition of a word in different
            senses, and/or different forms.

Society is no comfort to one not sociable.
        (Cymbeline, IV.ii.12)
But day doth daily draw my sorrows longer
And night doth nightly make grief's strength
   seem stronger...(Sonnets, XXVIII)

7. Antanaclasis - pun in which repeated word
                 shifts from one of its mea-
                 nings to another.

To England will I steal, and there I'll
   steal...(Henry V, V.i.92)

8. Paronomasia - same as (7) except that re-
                peated words are nearly but
                not precisely alike in sound.

Were it not here apparent that thou art
   heir apparent...(I Henry IV, I.ii.64)

9. Antimetabole - see (5) above.

C. Larger arrangements:

10. Antithesis - clauses or sentences contrasted
              with each other in the position
              of their words and/or meaning.

Drown desperate sorrow in dead Edward's
   grave
And plant you joys in living Edward's
   throne...(Richard III, II.ii.99)

Through tatter'd clothes small vices to
   appear
Robes and furr'd gowns hide all.
         (Lear, IV.vi.166)

11. Balance - clauses or sentences paralleling
             each other in the position of their
             words and/or meaning.

Never have you tasted our reward
Or been reguerdon'd with so much as thanks...
       (I Henry VI, III.iv.24)

12. Asyndeton - omission of conjunctions be-
              tween phrases, clauses

All hail great master! Grave sir, hail!
I come to answer thy best pleasure; be't
    to fly,
To swim, to dive into the fire, to ride
On the curl'd clouds...(<u>Tempest</u>, I.ii.189)

13. <u>Polysyndeton</u> - use of conjunctions between
                      phrases, clauses.

    'Tis as I should entreat you wear your
        gloves
    Or feed on nourishing dishes, or keep you
        warm
    Or sue to you to do a peculiar profit
    To your person...(<u>Othello</u>, III.iii.77)

14. <u>Isocolon</u> - construction of different parts
                  of the same sentence with a like
                  (not necessarily equal) number
                  of syllables.

    Your reasons at dinner have been sharp and
    sententious; pleasant without scurrility,
    witty without affectation, audacious without
    impudency, learned without opinion, and
    strange without heresy.
                    (<u>Love's Labour's Lost</u>, V.i.2)

15. <u>Exclamatio</u> - exclamation, usually of indig-
                    nation or sorrow

                            O sun,
    Burn the great sphere thou mov'st in!
      Darkling stand
    The varying shore o' th' world! O Antony!
    Antony! Antony!
                    (<u>Antony & Cleopatra</u>, IV.xv.9)

16. <u>Interrogatio</u> - question, usually rhetorical

    O heavens! is't possible a young maid's wits
    Should be as mortal as an old man's life?
                    (<u>Hamlet</u>, IV.v.159)

17. <u>Sententia</u> - expression of a truth in a short
                    pointed way; maxim

    Who steals my purse steals trash...

But he that filches from me my good name
Robs me of that which not enriches him
And makes me poor indeed.
                (Othello, III.iii.161)
There's a divinity that shapes our ends,
Rough-hew them how we will.
                (Hamlet, V.ii.11)

18. Definitio - definition; a brief explanation

                        Love is not love
Which alters when its alteration finds
Or bends with the remover to remove.
O, no! it is an ever-fixed mark
That looks on tempests and is never shaken.
                (Sonnets, CXVI)

19. Gradatio - climax; a graded succession of
                words, phrases, clauses.

And let the kettle to the trumpet speak,
The trumpet to the cannoneer without,
The cannons to the heavens, the heavens to
    earth...(Hamlet, V.ii.896)

20. Praeteritio - the pretense of omitting what
                is mentioned in the omission.

Let but the commons hear this testament,
Which (pardon me) I do not mean to read,
And they would go and kiss dead Caesar's
    wounds
'Tis good you know not that you are his
    heirs...(Julius Caesar, III.ii.151)

21. Occupatio - the rebuttal of anticipated
                objections

22. Dubitatio - pretense of not knowing where
                to begin or stop or of being
                able to express oneself; doubting
                of and deliberating with oneself.

I cannot tell if to depart in silence,
Or bitterly to speak in your reproof,
Best fitteth my degree of your conviction.
                (Richard III, III.iii.141)

179

Tropes

1. <u>Antonomasia</u> - substitution of another word
   for a proper name; denoting
   the possession of a quality by
   a proper name readily associated
   with it.

   A Daniel come to judgement! yea a Daniel!
   O wise young judge, how do I honour thee!
                    (<u>Merchant of Venice</u>, IV.i.222)

2. <u>Metonymy</u> - designation of a thing not by its
   proper name by by an adjunct, at-
   tribute,. relation.

       a. substitution of quality for sub-
          ject

          Conferring them on younger
          strengths...(<u>Lear</u>, I.i.41)

       b. cause for effect

          (of music being played) is it
          not strange that sheep's guts
          should hale souls out of men's
          bodies? (<u>Much Ado About Nothing</u>,
             II.iii.61)

       c. effect for cause

          All torment, trouble, wonder
          and amazement inhabits here.
          (<u>Tempest</u>, V.i.105)

3. <u>Synecdoche</u> - substitution of genus for species,
   species for genus, part for whole,
   whole for part.

   Pour down thy weather! (<u>King John</u>, IV.ii.109)

   Like to a pair of lions smear'd with prey.
                    (<u>Two Noble Kinsmen</u>, I.iv.18)

4. <u>Metaphor</u> - transfer of a word from its proper
   significance to one which it does
   not commonly denote at all.

180

What plume of feathers is he that indited
   this letter?
What vane?   What weathercock?
                    (<u>Love's Labour's Lost</u>, IV.i.95)

5. <u>Catechresis</u> - transfer similar to metaphor,
                    but usually a verb or an adjec-
                    tive which implies a metaphor.

Supple knees Feed arrogance.   (<u>Troilus</u>, III.
   iii.48)

Your ears...so fortified against our story.
                    (<u>Hamlet</u>, I.i.31)

I will speak daggers to her, but use none.
                    (Hamlet, III.ii.414)

6. <u>Permutatio</u> - saying one thing in words and
                    another in meaning.

   a. <u>per similitudinen</u>:   simile, parable, com-
                               parison

       Our bodies are our gardens, to the which
       our wills are gardeners, so that if we
       will plant nettles or sow lettuce, set
       hyssop and weed up thyme, supply it with
       one gender of herbs or distract it with
       many--either to have it sterile with
       idleness or manured with industry--why,
       the power and corrigible authority of
       this lies in our wills.
                    (<u>Othello</u>, I.iii.322)

   b. <u>per contrarium</u>:   use of words in a sense
                            opposite their meaning;
                            irony

       For Brutus is an honorable man,
       So are they all, all honorable men.
                    (<u>Julius Caesar</u>, III.ii.88)

7. <u>Periphrasis</u> - circumlocution, e.g., use of
                    a descriptive phrase for a com-
                    mon name.

Most sacrilegious murther hath broke ope

181

The Lord's anointed temple...
                    (<u>Macbeth</u>, II.iii.7)

8. <u>Hyperbole</u> - exaggeration

This horseback-breaker, this huge bill
of flesh... (<u>1 Henry IV</u>, II.iv.268)

APPENDIX IV: THE INTERMEDIATE POETIC STRUCTURE

A.   Robert M. Browne, "The Nature of Convention"

     What are the aspects or qualities of existent
poems from which our idea of convention arises?   The
section on "Convention" in the glossary to Brooks
and Warren's Understanding Poetry will provide a convenient starting point:

>   Though the poet must finally work
>   out a form for each particular poem,
>   this does not mean that he may not
>   make use of elements of form handed
>   down from other poets--elements such
>   as metrical patterns, symbols, and
>   ways of relating images to a theme,
>   etc. Such elements, when their use
>   has become fixed and recognized, are
>   called conventions.

     The elements generally called "conventions" ac-
tually include many more things than Brooks and Warren
felt the need of listing for their undergraduate
audience, as well as elements which are not always
thought of as formal. Convention can govern the characteristic voice or voices heard in the poem, the
addressee, the references made by the voice or voices,
and the relations among all these. It can govern the
kind of meanings structured (e.g., "love," "war") as
well as the structuring of these meanings (e.g., literal or figurative language). In can affect both
the quantity and quality of sounds. In short, every
aspect of sound and meaning in a poem can be conven-
tionalized.

     Furthermore, unlike many arts, poetry works with
a material which is itself radically conventional--
language. Any two poems in a given language share
at least one convention--the language itself. It is
evident that Brooks and Warren are not thinking of
this type of convention in the passage quoted, but of
a more properly literary kind. Such is generally the
case when literary men discuss "convention" without
further specification: they mean poetic rather than
linguistic convention. Nevertheless, the fact that

linguistic convention affects every poem must never
be forgotten.

The employment of convention by poets gives rise
to poems some of whose aspects are evidently similar
to aspects of other poems. It is these aspects which
we are to consider first. The mere fact that they
are similar to aspects of other poems does not necessarily make them conventional aspects: to be conventional, they must be "handed down from other poets."
More exactly, they must have been accepted by a group
of poets, either poets of the present, or of the
past, or both. This acceptance, whether conscious
or unconscious, is an act of choice on the part of
the group, which selects certain ways and means of
constructing poems and makes these standard. The
standard ways and means are what Brooks and Warren
call "elements of form" or "conventions": they are
not present in actual poems, but they give rise to
standardized, conventional aspects of actual poems.

All similarities among aspects of different poems
are not traceable to convention, however. In comparing two poems from two completely separated cul-
tures, for example, English and Tibetan, one might
find many similarities derived from the fact that both
are poems rather than some other kind of speech. One
might also find points of similarity in the way in
which they employ one or more of the three great forms,
expository, narrative, and dramatic. In the absence
of cultural exchange, we would not explain the existence of these similarities by convention; the English
and the Tibetans lack that sense of a common past and
a common present which is needed to make convention
possible.

Nevertheless a satisfactory explanation of certain basic similarities between a given English and
a given Tibetan poem could be based on the nature of
poetry, on the fact that all poems are both speeches
and productions of fine art. Because poems are
speeches, they must conform to the nature of speech:
they will as a consequence imply a speaker and a
hearer, they will be cast in one or more of the three
major forms, they will conform to the nature of the
language in which they are written, and so on. Because they are productions of fine art, poems must
also conform to the nature of fine art: they will in

consequence be designed to serve the ends of contemplation rather than practicality, to be beautiful rather than ugly, and so on.

There are thus two sources from which common aspects of poems may derive, convention and nature; and we may in general classify all aspects of poems as conventional or natural aspects. Conventional aspects find their immediate source in some kind of group acceptance; natural aspects are based directly on the requirements of poetry.

This does not mean that convention and nature are of equal significance as sources of poetry; for while natural aspects need no further explanation for their existence than the fact that they are natural, conventional aspects need ultimately to be based on nature and to be, in some way, natural. Let us take as an example an extremely conventional form, the sonnet. There is no reason in nature why the orthodox Petrarchan sonnet should have fourteen lines and a break in sound and meaning after the eighth line. The existence of such a pattern is most directly explained by convention, by the fact that, as Brooks and Warren say, its "use has become fixed and recognized."

Nevertheless there must be something natural about this pattern, too. The first man who wrote a sonnet obviously did not find it so conventional a form as we do; it must have seemed a good and relatively natural way of setting up a poem with a closely knit two-part pattern. For this kind of poem the nature of poetry in general offers few specific principles; no specific number of lines or rhyme scheme or placing of the division of parts. Faced by the bewildering multiplicity of natural possibilities, the poet often, and quite understandably, has recourse to some specific embodiment of natural principle which has previously demonstrated its utility, such as the sonnet form. He, and others with him, set up a convention; but as we have seen, the thing which they conventionalize, the sonnet form, is made the basis of convention precisely because it is an adequate embodiment of natural principle. Convention, says J.C. La Drière, "is ideally a conscious or unconscious adjustment to and interpretation of nature."

Convention, then, presupposes nature: and conventional aspects of poems are in some way natural. The reverse is generally true also: the natural generally receives some sort of conventionalization. Now that it is solidly established in English verse, it is easy for us to think of iambic meter as an extremely natural prosodic pattern, one which is peculiarly suited to the nature of the language. Nevertheless, iambic meter was not so obviously natural to poets in the Old English period, and its merits only slowly came to be recognized after the Norman conquest. Its adoption and perfection would not have taken so long a time if it had been self-evidently a usable and natural principle of versification. In the hypothetical case that every English poet had to start his work in complete ignorance of his predecessors, it is not likely that a great many poets would have discovered the iambic principle. Nevertheless, once given the example, English poets made great strides in perfecting the iambic instrument in the short space of time between Wyatt and Shakespeare.

They did so because the natural principle of iambic verse had become a convention; its natural efficacy had been greatly reinforced by general acceptance. Depending on which aspect we may wish to emphasize, then, we may think of iambic meter as a natural or as a conventional aspect of a given poem.

From the foregoing discussion it should be clear that "natural" and "conventional" are often only relative terms. Thus language, the material of the poem, is in itself conventional as we have seen earlier; but we have also seen that in a given poem the language belongs on the side of nature: the poem being a speech, the poem is to a greater or lesser extent limited by the laws of the language in which it is written. But if poems must conform to the nature of language, it is natural for language to change; hence to conform to the nature of the language poets must constantly be adjusting their language to fit contemporary linguistic convention. Paradoxically, poets who do so successfully are thought of as employing very natural speech, while those who do not are said to make use of conventional speech. Actually, if one were striving for the utmost precision one could not contrast natural speech with conventional speech, since a given language is essentially conventional. One could only contrast language which reflects live conventions, and which therefore is more "natural" speech, and language which reflects dead or dying conventions, and which is therefore less natural speech. The distinction of natural and conventional here is only one of degree.

The same kind of relativity is apparent when we turn from the material of poetry to its structure. A device which is natural with the originator of a form will be conventional with the imitators of that form. However, if one of these imitators adopts the conventional form so that it fits the requirements of the poem he is writing, the device could be said to be a natural part of that poem, despite the conventionality of its origin. It is natural because it is a necessary part of that poem's structure. When the very same device is inappropriately present in another poem, its conventionality will of course be more conspicuous.

The fact that aspects of poems may be either natural or conventional, depending on the principle of classification employed, is not evidence that the distinction is useless. Employed with discrimination, the distinction can be very enlightening. On the other hand, failure to distinguish between absolute and relative senses of "convention" and "nature" has often confused the issues in literary controversies of the past.

Conventional aspects of poems, then, can be divided into those which derive from linguistic and those which derive from poetic convention, and they can be distinguished from relatively natural aspects. The existence of such aspects is the source of our thinking about convention, but nevertheless we do not strictly apply the term "convention" to them. To these aspects we apply the adjective "conventional"; we reserve the noun "convention" for something external to individual poems.

This "something external" to the poem is something internal to poet and readers; it is primarily a state of mind, but a state shared in varying degrees and manners by many different minds. This is the second facet of convention that we are going to examine: convention as historically existing in and

determining minds; not the actual conventional aspect,
e.g., Milton's invocation to the Muses in <u>Paradise</u>
<u>Lost</u>, but whatever it is in our minds that makes us
recognize this passage as conventional, and whatever
it was in Milton's mind that led to the writing of
the passage.

"Convention" thus restricted to the mind can be
divided in two categories, for both of which the
single term "convention" may be currently employed.
One of these is often otherwise designated by such
terms as "agreement," "acceptance," "consent," "con-
currence," "assumption," "custom," "usage." The
other may be referred to as " a rule," "a practice,"
"a device," "a method," "a custom," "a usage." What
is being referred to in the first is the assent of
the will or wills to something; in the second it is
the something assented to. In speaking of a contract,
we may use the term "agreement" to refer to the state
of mind of the participants or to the actual provi-
sions of the contract. The term "convention" likewise has this double meaning.

---

from Robert M. Browne, <u>Theories of Convention in Con-</u>
<u>temporary American Criticism</u> (Washington: Catho-
lic University Press, 1956), pp.2-6.

B.   Aristotle, "The Parts of Tragedy"

Our discussions of imitative poetry in hexameters,
and of comedy, will come later; at present let us
deal with tragedy, recovering from what has been said
so far the definition of its essential nature, as it
was in development. Tragedy, then, is a process of
imitating an action which has serious implications,
is complete, and possesses magnitude; by means of
language which has been made sensuously attractive,
with each of its varieties found separately in the
parts; enacted by the persons themselves and not presented through narrative; through a course of pity
and fear completing the purification of tragic acts
which have those emotional characteristics. By "language made sensuously attractive" I mean language that
has rhythm and melody, and by "its varieties found
separately" I mean the fact that certain parts of the

play are carried on through spoken verses alone and others the other way around, through song.

Now first of all, since they perform the imitation through action (by acting it), the adornment of their visual appearance will perforce constitute some part of the making of tragedy; and song-composition and verbal expression also, for those are the media in which they perform the imitation. By "verbal expression" I mean the actual composition of the verses, and by "song-composition" something whose meaning is entirely clear.

Next, since it is an imitation of an action and is enacted by certain people who are performing the action, and since those people must necessarily have certain traits both of character and thought (for it is thanks to these two factors that we speak of people's actions also as having a defined character, and it is in accordance with their actions that all either succeed or fail); and since the imitation of the action is the plot, for by "plot" I mean here the structuring of the events, and by the "characters" that in accordance with which we say that the persons who are acting have a defined moral character, and by "thought" all the passages in which they attempt to prove some thesis or set forth an opinion--it follows of necessity, then, that tragedy as a whole has just six constituent elements, in relation to the essence that makes it a distinct species; and they are plot, characters, verbal expression, thought, visual adornment, and song-composition. For the elements by which they imitate are two (i.e., verbal expression and song-composition), the manner in which they imitate is one (visual adornment), the things they imitate are three (plot, characters, thought), and there is nothing more beyond these. These then are the constituent forms they use.

---

from Aristotle, Poetics, trans. Gerald F. Else
    (Ann Arbor: University of Michigan Press, 1967),
    pp. 25-27.

C.   Daniel Burke, FSC, "Some Questions for Narrative
     Analysis"

     In narrative, a speaker or writer uses words
basically to refer to actions and, necessarily, to
the "people" performing the actions. Some of the
smaller and scattered meanings (e.g., references to
a gesture, a change of facial expression, or some
activity like running) are built into episodes. The
episodes, in turn, are built into the larger action
which is the whole plot.

     Other meanings (e.g., references to physical ap-
pearance, to thoughts, or ways of feeling) are built
into fictional "personalities" who perform actions,
cause them to be performed, or are affected by them.
Such characters may be developed at great length and
may enter into many changing relations with other
characters so that a larger pattern of characterization is built up. Like episodes, therefore, the
characters of a story are units of meaning. They are
patterns of meaning, composed of smaller units of
meaning and, like "settings" and "themes" similarly
developed, they become units in the larger and more
complex patterns which make up the whole story.

     As individual words refer to things so do "epi-
sodes" and "characters." But they refer to something
which exists only in the story, not of course in real
life. In a certain sense, therefore, these units do
not so much refer to something as they "present" some-
thing--what has been created in the units and by the
units themselves. We can see and appreciate the characters and actions of a story, then, only by seeing
how the words enter these patterned units, how they
interact with one another, qualifying earlier denotations and connotations, modifying one another in
contrasts, emphasizing themselves in repetitions, until the final and total meaning emerges.

     In analysis of narrative, therefore, it is under-
stood that we are not dealing with real people and
real actions, but with constructions of meaning. This
emphasis does not exclude, of course, what is our frequent and clear experience of characters and plots--
that they really engage our interest when their traits,
qualities, and interactions convincingly resemble

those of real life, or real life heightened or changed in some way, or life as we might like it to be. Fiction gives us the pleasure, that is, of recognizing what we know in other contexts while at the same time signalling to us that this is somehow different, that this is fiction.

The present note raises questions about many aspects of narratives; only some of these aspects will be operative in particular stories. The note will be useful, therefore, only if it is used to locate what is important or striking--and to analyze that feature more thoroughly. It should be added, too, that the distinction between elements and patterns of meaning here has not been rigorously drawn.

I. ELEMENTS OF MEANING

    A. First Person Meaning: The Narrator

        Some writers appear to tell a story in their own voice: some introduce modifications of their usual way of speaking, their opinions, attitudes, etc.; some create a wholly new character to tell the story. Despite the first possibility, it is usually safe to assume that the narrator is as much a fictitious creation as any character in the story he tells. In any event, it is necessary to have some idea of the narrator since he exerts the primary control over the story.

        1. Who is the narrator? Does he identify himself directly? Indirectly? Does he, at least, refer to himself, that is, use the pronoun "I"? Or is he an "impersonal" speaker? Is it one person? Or several, speaking at different times?

        2. Does the narrator reveal any "character" or "personality" of his own? (See the questions on character traits in third person meaning.)

        3. What specifically are the attitudes of the narrator? Toward the story in general? Toward the characters and what they do? Toward his presumed reader?

4. Does the narrator state or imply any purpose in his story?

B. Second Person Meaning: Addressee

Meanings in a story that refer to an addressee
or audience are typically very tenuous and
slight. But it is important to advert to
these meanings, for in choosing or assuming
a particular audience or addressee to be reflected in his story, the writer sets the basic tone and character of his narrator's
speech. Many of the questions raised about
the narrator can be raised about the addressee
as well but some others are worth raising.

1. Is the addressee a person, a thing or abstraction (apostrophe), the speaker himself (soliloquy)?

2. Is the audience an individual or a group?
How definite--anybody, somebody, everybody?

3. How personalized is the audience (see the
questions on traits, attitudes of narrator,
and characters).

C. Third Person Meaning

1. Characters

A character is a set of "traits," meanings
that present or suggest persistent, differentiating features--mental, volitional,
emotional, even physical--for an agent in
a story. Characters, however, can often
be the most fascinating part of a story,
not simply puppets used to forward a plot,
but "personalities" in their own right.
Characters like Hamlet, Frankenstein, Sher-
lock Holmes (or Superman) seem even to out-
live their original stories and take on a
life of their own as later writers build
stories around them. There has also been
a tendency in modern fiction to focus attention on characters, no longer considered
primary as agents in a series of actions

but simply as fictional creations interesting in themselves. When this tendency
is pursued the "story" becomes a character
sketch or a group of character sketches
related in various ways perhaps by one character (or more) getting an insight into
his situation. Analysis of such work will
naturally be concerned with characterization. However, even in the more traditional story where action is primary, the characters and their relations to the action
may be important problems for analysis.

a) Aside from the narrator, if he is a
character in the story, who are the
major characters? Who are the minor
characters?

b) What traits are important in an individual character? Are there traits
of mind, will, sensibility (passions
and emotions)? Are these traits connected with a particular way of
thinking, choosing, reacting or with
a particular thing the character is
preoccupied with in these areas of
inner activity?

c) Which traits suggest the age group,
the profession, the class, the nationality, etc. the character may be
assigned to? Are there any traits
inappropriate to the class, nationality, etc. which have been assigned?
Which traits seem to be universally
human?

d) Is there a dominant trait in the cha-
racteriztion? Does one trait dominate so completely or is it so exaggerated that the character is a type
or caricature? Or is the characterization more complex? What balances
or contrasts make it complex?

e) Is the character "realistic"? That
is, does he (1) bear resemblance to
an actual historical personage or

have many traits which seem universally human and (2) do traits which
are more essentially fictitious,
which are peculiar, exaggerated,
idealized harmonize with the first
kind of qualities? Is the harmony
such that the character is convincingly what he is supposed to be?
Are peculiar, exaggerated, or idealized traits so emphasized that the
character must be described as eccentric, romantic, fantastic?

2. Events

Action considered here is exterior action
like speaking and fighting as opposed to
interior action like thinking and willing.
As we have already seen the two types of
activity are closely connected; in narrative analysis, however, we tend to look at
interior activity from the viewpoint of
characterization, at exterior activity from
the viewpoint of plot. Considered in itself, actual physical activity has little
significance. It becomes significant in
relation to the person performing it (e.g.,
king, clown) and this person's motives and
purposes (e.g., charitable, malicious); in
relation to the person or thing affected
by the action (e.g., other men, nature);
in relation to external norms and laws
(e.g., etiquette, the natural law). In
fiction as well, physical actions as such
rarely have much significance. They are
given significance by references to the
elements just mentioned. Such relations
play an important role as the actions are
being combined into elementary patterns
throughout the story (e.g., the recurrence
of a particular kind of action) or into
separate units of action which we call episodes.

a) What is the nature of the actions in the
   story? Do they explicitly or implicitly involve any conflict? With other
   characters, a social institution, en-

vironment, fate--or with a weakness in
the character himself?

b) What is the quality of (all, most, a
significant group) actions in the story?
Does the fact that (all, most, a significant group) actions are of the same
kind create a peculiar texture or quality of action, e.g., a series of social
actions (courtships, tea-parties) as
opposed to a series of anti-social actions (crimes, wars).

c) Are the actions generally performed in
any special way? Is their nature or
importance affected by this manner (e.g.,
heroic, awkward) or by the situation
(time and place) in which they are performed?

3. Time and Place

Time and place, temporal and social ambi-
ence, environment are usually minor elements in narrative, especially in short
stories. But they can be important in
creating the atmosphere of the story and
in influencing characters, events, developing ideas, especially in naturalistic
writing where the impact of the environment
is major.

a) What are the places (exterior, interior,
city, country) and times of the story?
What qualities of these times and places
are emphasized explicitly (as in set descriptions) or implicitly?

b) Are time and place presented with realistic or with other conventions?

c) Do time and place or the social setting
have implied meanings that create symbolic functions for them?

d) What atmosphere, general emotional
feeling, are created by the elements of
time and place?

4. Ideas

   General and abstract concepts, attitudes
   toward life, moral norms may be presented
   at length or only incidentally in the comments of a narrator or the conversation of
   characters. But, indirectly, any event,
   character, or setting may imply such ideas
   or attitudes.

   a) What explicit or implicit ideas and
   value judgments are presented in the
   story?

   b) How simple or complex are these ideas?
   To what more general world views or philosophies do they relate? How are
   they emphasized?

IV. PATTERNS OF MEANING

A. The Narrator

The narrator stands in certain relations to
the story he is telling. These relations
suggest the "angle" from which he tells the
story. The first questions here are concerned
with this "point of view."

1. Is the narrator a character in the story?
   Is he exterior to the story, simply reporting what he had no part in? Or does he
   tell the story from the angle of one of
   the characters (James's Centre of vision)?

2. If he is a character in the story, is he
   the major character telling his own story
   in the fashion of autobiography? Or is
   he a minor character telling the story of
   a major character? Or do several characters tell the story (as in The Ring and
   the Book)? Or does the point of view otherwise shift (War and Peace)?

3. In any of these cases, is the narrator om-
   niscient, describing the characters, their
   thoughts, feelings, etc. as if he knew
   everything about them? Or is he an objec-

tive narrator describing only what he can
see and hear--and deduce? Or is he limited
somewhere between these extremes?

4. What vividness, intimacy, sense of cold
   objectivity, etc., is created by the point
   of view?

5. Does the character of the narrator show
   any pattern of development? Do his attitudes to the action or characters change?
   Where? Are these changes consistent with
   what we know of the narrator, of the action
   or characters?

6. What are the functional relations of the
   narrator to his story? Does he tell long
   stretches of the action in detail or does
   he summarize often? Does he comment little and allow the characters to tell and
   to present the story? Beside narrating,
   does he explain and comment on the action
   at length? Does he introduce speculations
   of his own? Are these digressive? What
   is the extent and quality of the speculation?

B. Addressee

1. What is the relationship of the narrator
   to his assumed audience? What are his attitudes toward that audience? Does he
   share any assumptions with them--about life,
   morals, society?

2. Are there any discernible effects of the
   addressee on the way the narrator presents
   his story, or his style, etc.?

3. Does the narrator betray any purpose in
   telling his story to this addressee?

C. Third Person Meaning

1. Characters

   A pattern may be discerned in the "development" of a character considered in itself,

that is, in the various stages of its development. Patterns exist also in the re-
ciprocal and changing relations of a character to other characters and to the action.

a) Is the characterization created fully
   at the beginning of the story to remain
   practically unchanged until the end?
   Or, at the other extreme, is their a
   gradual growth and maturing in the characterization? Or are there sudden and
   radical changes in the pattern of development? Do all changes follow logically and probably from what has pre-
   ceded them and can the characterization,
   therefore, be said to be consistent?

b) What are the relations among the characters, e.g., social relations? Are
   certain characters related in such a
   way that they may be said to constitute
   a group, e.g., the schemers?

c) What changes do relations among characters undergo? What effects these changes? In what manner do they occur?
   When? Are they indicated explicitly
   or implied in some way? Are these changes consistent with earlier stages in
   the development of characterization?
   Are they appropriate to other elements
   in the story?

d) In terms of which character is the story
   told, whom does it revolve about? Is
   there any shift in this "focus of character" to another?

e) How do the opinions and attitudes (and
   emotions) of a character influence his
   decisions and consequent actions? Which
   actions throw new or important light
   on his motives and decisions.

2. Plot

The pattern or "combination of incidents,

198

or things done in the story" is the plot.
Questions of special importance concerning
plots are the position of an incident in
relation to other incidents, the nature
of the connections between incidents, and
the combination of incidents into a pattern of action "rising" to a climax.

a) What are the episodes of the story?
   What is their complexity (number of actions combined in the episodes; number
   of characters involved), duration (see
   questions on "tempo" in the next section), and scale (the amount of space
   they occupy in the whole story; the
   amount of detail in their description
   or presentation)? Which are the minor
   incidents?

b) Is there a pattern of action rising to
   a climax within the individual episode?

c) Are the incidents of the plot connected
   in a close causal sequence, that is,
   does one episode lead to or cause another? Or is there a loose connection
   between episodes, and hence, does the
   story have an "episodic" structure?

d) Are the causes for actions grounded in
   the characterization, in the moods, reactions, decisions of the characters? Or
   are episodes motivated by accident,
   chance, or "fate"?

e) Is the relation of earlier incidents
   to the final outcome of the story clearly indicated; is it hinted at, "fore-
   shadowed"? Or is this relation obscure
   and uncertain? Does the uncertainty
   result in any suspense?

f) What is the tempo of the story, that is,
   what is (1) the relation of the episodes
   to the time scheme indicated in the
   story itself (e.g., many episodes in a
   short time) and (2) the relation of the
   episodes to the extent of their develop-

ment (e.g., few episodes described
in great detail)? Is the tempo the
same throughout? Are there changes of
tempo (in sense 2, shifts among sum-
marizing, fuller description of action,
even more leisurely presentation of
scenes with complete dialogue implying
and referring to action)?

g) Which incidents constitute the beginning, middle, and end of the story? Do
the incidents occur in their "natural"
(the chronological order of the fiction)
order or are there "flashbacks"?

h) Which incidents are involved in these
parts as functions in the typical narrative:

   (1) exposition - reporting previous ac-
       tion while establishing the ba-
       sic situation of the story (cha-
       racters, setting)

   (2) trigger event - the episode which
       actually begins the main action
       of the story, sets the story
       going in a determinate direction

   (3) conflict - the event or series of
       events leading to the climax

   (4) climax - the moment of highest in-
       terest and meaning, focusing and
       integrating all previous inci-
       dents

   (5) denouement - the final situation in
       the story, the statement of out-
       comes and effects?

i) Are the incidents leading to the climax
alike in any way? Do they illustrate
in slightly different ways the nature
of the conflict (e.g., of character with
character, of character with forces of
environment)? What, then, is the pattern of incidents leading to the climax?

j) Is anything revealed in the climax
which casts unexpected light on earlier
episodes of the story, any "discovery"?
Does this discovery effect any radical
change in, any "reversal" of, the direction the story has been moving in
(e.g., the underdog suddenly triumphs)?

k) What is the relation of one part of the
plot to another in terms of size? Indicate these relations in a graph of
the plot line with the climax as the
highest point. Is there any dispropor-
tion among the parts? Does the length,
the scale of the whole story seem justified?

3. Setting

a) Is the setting single and unified--or
are there different times and places
involved? If there are a series of settings, are there repetitions, contrasts
(e.g., summer/winter) or balances developed?

b) How is the setting developed, e.g., accumulated by brief and incidental references to time and place or presented
in paragraphs or detailed "scenery" at
the beginning of the story?

c) What aspects or qualities (e.g., wild-
ness, tameness) of the setting dominate
and possibly relate to meanings of other
major parts of the narrative?

4. Ideas

a) In what stages or parts are the propositional ideas or value judgments of
the narrative developed? Are there repetitions, contrasts, or balances of
these meanings?

b) Are there standard logical (e.g., cause
and effect) or rhetorical patterns in
the development of the ideas?

c) How can the resulting thematic structure
of all explicit and implicit ideas be
described? Is it dominated by one notion, complicated by subtle contrasts
of several ideas, etc.?

It should be emphasized again that the checklist
of questions here is focussed on individual parts of
a story, one or other of which may strike one as
needing more particular analysis. Any part, however,
has its ultimate function and value in the total structure of the story, the total set of appropriate relations. While it is helpful, therefore, to reduce an
individual part to its basic elements and relations,
this process may finally be important only as an
opening to the total structure.

The questions raised here are numerous, but each
is open to further refinement. For more detailed analysis, the following modern theorists and critics
can be consulted:

Booth, Wayne. The Rhetoric of Fiction. Chicago:
University of Chicago Press, 1961.

Brooks, Cleanth and Robert Penn Warren. Understanding Fiction. New York: Crofts, 1943.

Chatman, Seymour. Story and Discourse. Ithaca:
Cornell University Press, 1978.

Crane, R.S. "The Concept of Plot and the Plot
of Tom Jones" in Critics and Criticism:
Ancient and Modern, ed. R.S. Crane. Chicago: University of Chicago Press, 1952,
pp. 616-648.

Forster, E.M. Aspects of the Novel. London:
Edward Arnold, 1927.

Genette, Gerard. Narrative Discourse, trans.
Jane Lewin. Ithaca: Cornell University
Press, 1980.

Halperin, John. The Theory of the Novel. New
York: Oxford University Press, 1974.

Holloway, John. Narrative Structure: Explana-

tory Essays. Cambridge: Cambridge Univer-
Press, 1979.

Lodge, David. Language of Fiction. New York:
Columbia University Press, 1966.

Lubbock, Percy. The Craft of Fiction. New
York: Viking, 1957.

Van Ghent, Dorothy. The English Novel: Form
and Function. New York: Rinehart, 1953.

D. Daniel Burke, FSC, "Versification"

Versification is the act, art, or practice of
making poetic lines or verses. In particular, versification is concerned with the patterns of sound
which characterize verse. Such patterns are studied
for the practical purpose of explaining some of the
elementary conventions for writing verse and, as in
the scansion taught in schools, for reading it properly. More detailed study may seek to understand
how verse was written by one poet or by a group of
poets in one or more historical periods. Descriptions
of this type may further provide the basis for judgments about the aesthetic value of poems or for theorizing about the nature and function of sound patterns
in verse and about poetry itself.

Patterns of sound in verse are of two general
types--qualitative and quantitative. First are those
patterns which involve the repetition and variation
of the kinds or qualities of speech sounds. By this
is meant those elements which differentiate one sound
or letter from another, as "a" from "o" or "b" from
"k" without reference to the intensity, duration, or
musical pitch with which either sound is pronounced.
These latter are the quantitative elements and are
the basis for another large design of sound in verse.
In the study of a poem's versification, both of these
designs of sound, the qualitative and the quantitative,
are considred in abstraction from the various patterns
of meaning with which they occur simultaneously. But
it is in the harmonious interplay of all such patterns
that the poem exists and is enjoyed.

Design for Qualities of Sound

Rhyme, alliteration, assonance, and other figures usually associated with the "melody" of verse are basically repetitions of the qualities of sounds, of their inherent characters. The most important of these figures are repetitions of whole syllables or of parts of syllables. Thus rhyme may repeat a whole syllable (supplied...replied) or an essential part of a syllable (braid...jade)--normally, that is, the vowel and any consonant which may follow it. Complete repetition of syllables (braid...braid) has not been considered normal rhyme. As in other figurations and designs, a play of sameness and difference is expected. Hence, in normal rhyme, initial consonants contrast with syllabic elements otherwise repeated (raid...made).

Two major varieties of rhyme are traditionally distinguished: masculine, which repeats the final stressed syllables of words (arcade...brocade) and feminine, which begins the repetition on a syllable other than the last (tending...mending). Repetition of more than one syllable in masculine rhyme is unusual (recline...decline), but is normal, of course, in feminine (thundering...sundering). Such richness of repetition may extend to lines and whole stanzas of refrain. However, in modern verse, especially, even full single rhymes are sometimes avoided for more subtle figurations called imperfect or slant rhymes (blade...bled, cat...cad) which only approximate one of the elements of repetition. Between the extremes of complete sameness (braid...braid) and complete differnece (braid...so), slant rhyme moves beyond normal rhyme in the direction of difference.

Taking the same direction are some of the simpler traditional figures, such as alliteration, consonance, and assonance, and the less formal patterns of repeated sounds which occur in verse. While there is not complete agreement about terminology, alliteration is the name usually given to the repetition of a consonant or vowel at the beginning of words: "Apt alliteration's artful aid." Consonance repeats the same consonantal sound after different accented vowels, as in pressed...past, while assonance repeats the same vowel with different consonants following, as in man ...hat. What also differentiates these simpler fi-

204

gures from the whole family of rhymes is the fact
that the character of the syllable is not repeated.
Even the repetition of p...t in a slant rhyme like
pit...pat creates the effect that part of a syllable
is being repeated. When only a single sound is repeated in contrasting syllabic contexts, as p in tip
...pool or in pit...pool, the effect is quite different.

Beyond these figures, there are an indeterminate
number of more random and casual phonetic echoes, as,
for instance, the patterns of r, s, and n which support the alliteration of rains...ruins in Swinburne's
line: "For winter's rains and ruins are over." While
all these figurations are basically repetitions of
qualitative or so-called "segmental" elements of
sound, it is clear that "suprasegmental" figures like
stress affect the formulization and, in large measure,
the conspicuousness of sound patterns. Thus, a
stressed syllable is not ordinarily rhymed with an un-
stressed, and end rhyme (that is, rhyme at the end
of metrical lines) is normally more conspicuous than
internal rhyme (rhyme at the middle and end of the
same line). Modern descriptive linguistics has provided the researcher with rather precise tools for
weighing the effect of these factors.

In most cases, patterns of the qualities of sound
present themselves as distinct but sporadic concen-
trations of similarity in a sequence of dissimilar
syllables. The total design of sound qualities em-
braces, of course, the distinct patterns as well as
their less organized background. Many of the finer
effects of verse depend upon the poet's "ear" for the
proper adjustment of pattern and background as much
as on the conscious creation of the figures themselves.

Qualitative figures of sound play a role in the
verse of all languages. End rhyme, for example, frequently contributes to the elaboration of larger metrical systems like stanzas. Rhyme was, however,
practically unknown in classical Greek or Latin verse,
though it became a familiar feature in medieval Latin
and thence in the Romance languages. It is basic
to Chinese verse, but generally avoided in Japanese.
Arabic is peculiar in using a single rhyme throughout
a poem. Assonance is also frequent in Romance verse
of all periods, while alliteration is a prominent

feature of early Germanic verse. The older forms of
Celtic verse, especially Welsh, employ all the forms
of qualitative figuration of sound in the greatest
elaboration. The taste for richness in such figuration varies considerably; especially identified with
this taste in English poetry since the early Renaissance are John Skelton, Edmund Spenser, William Shakespeare, John Milton, John Keats, Edgar Allan Poe, Al-
gernon Swinburne, Gerard Manley Hopkins, and Dylan
Thomas.

Design for Quantities of Sound

The study of the sound patterns usually called
rhythm and meter has generally been more systematic
and detailed than the corresponding analysis of rhyme
and other design of the qualities of sound. The term
prosody is often applied to the former study, as is
metrics and, less frequently, rhythmics. Prosodic
study began quite early in the West. Aristotle, for
example, already invokes a tradition of such study
as he discusses in the Poetics the appropriateness of
certain meters to satire, tragedy, and epic, and in
the Rhetoric, the use of less obtrusive rhythms by
the orator. The philosopher is important, too, for
drawing a clear distinction (Poetics, 1447a, 11.18ff.)
between the art of poetry, with its own patterning
of sound, and the arts of music and dance with which
it had been and would continue to be closely associated. Aristotle's pupil Aristoxenus of Tarentum wrote
a treatise on rhythm; part of the second book survives.
The earliest complete treatise on metrics extant is
by Hephaestion (130-169 A.D.). Like most of his predecessors, Hephaestion offers more information on
types of metrical feet than on the precise basis of
Greek meter.

From the beginning, however, there has been general agreement about the large object of prosodic study: it is the quantitative aspects of sound (length
or duration, relative pitch, and intensity or force)
and, in particular, the harmonious patterning of these
elements in the flow of speech. For a poet creates
a rhythm or meter by arranging the elements of conspicuousness or emphasis operating in his ordinary
language. Rather than the haphazard prose arrangement
of emphases, though, in a sentence like "The plowman
is plodding his weary way homeward" (o ó o o ó o o ó

o ó ó o), a poet like Thomas Grey may create a more
formal and stylized pattern with "The plowman homeward plods his weary way" (o ó o ó o ó o ó o ó).

Types of Basic Rhythm

     The conventions which govern the creation of
such patterns and, indeed, the particular quantifia-
ble elements which may be patterned, vary from language to language and even, at times, from period to
period of the same language. In Indo-European, a
basic type of meter seems to have utilized the lengths
of speech sound and this mode developed into the "durational" or so-called "quantitative" meters of San-
skrit and Greek. A basic principle affecting these
meters in Greek was the distinction between short and
long syllables, the latter considered twice the
length of the former. Various combinations of long
and short syllables were possible; the resulting elementary units (feet) could then be repeated to form
a longer rhythmic series. In Greek epic verse, for
example, the dactylic foot (one long syllable followed
by two shorts: - ᵕ ᵕ) was repeated with only occasional
variations by other feet of equal duration, like the
spondee (two long syllables: --). The regular patterned effect of alternating long and short durations
was further formalized by the division of the whole
metrical series into lines which, though they might
vary from twelve to seventeen syllables, had an equal
durational value (namely, twenty-four short syllables).
Other common feet besides the dactyl and spondee were
the iamb (ᵕ-), anapaest (ᵛ ᵛ -), trochee (- ᵛ), pyrrhic
(ᵛ ᵛ), cretic (-ᵛ-), paeon (- ᵛᵛ ᵛ), and choriamb (-ᵛᵛ-).
More complicated than the regularly repeated dactylic
verses of epic or the iambic lines of dramatic dialogue were the meters of Greek lyric. In these, different feet were combined in large rhythmic phrases
(cola) and then arranged in stanzas.

     Early Latin meters, in particular the Saturnian
verse of Lucius Livius Andronicus and Gnaeus Naevius,
appear to have been constructed on the basis of syllabic intensities rather than durations. But under
the prevailing influence of Greek culture the "quantitative" system was adopted some time before the end
of the second century B.C. Thereafter, one finds
Virgil imitating the dactylic verse of Homer, and
Horace and other lyric poets the stanzas of Sappho

and Alcaeus.

In the first centuries of Christianity, however,
the linguistic distinction of long and short syllables fell into decay. At the same time, poets like
St. Augustine and St. Ambrose introduced hymn meters
in which lines had an equal number of syllables and
concluded with simple rhymes. In addition, rhythmic
figures similar to the end patterns of classical
prose (<u>clausulae</u> or <u>cursus</u>) occurred in the middle
and end of these lines. It was, perhaps, the extension of these patterns, based now on the intensities
of regular word accents rather than on the duration
of syllables, that led to a fully accentual meter.
The transition, observable in hymns like the <u>Pange</u>
<u>Lingua</u> <u>Gloriosi</u> and <u>Vexilla</u> <u>Regis</u> <u>Prodeunt</u> of Venan-
tius Fortunatus (c. 530-c.600), was completed by the
tenth century; the earlier quantitative system, however, continued an artificial existence into the Renaissance. The versifications of the various Romance
languages inherited from medieval Latin the principle
of stable line length maintained by count of syllables. Their fundamental rhythmic effects, though,
depend more on the manipulation of pauses and of stronger and weaker syllables in the phrases created by
pauses, than on the regular recurrence of an accentual
foot. In its long history, therefore, Latin verse
utilized different aspects of sound as the basis of
its verse rhythms. Originally this basis was intensity, in the classical period it became duration, and
later it returned to intensity. (The other quantifia-
ble element of sound, pitch, is never used as the basis of rhythm and meter; but in some languages, notably Chinese, it is used as an important adjunct to a
rhythm the basis of which is count of syllables.)

Total Rhythmic Design

The total design for the quantities of sound is,
however, more complicated than the steady pulse of
a meter or the looser harmony of a rhythm. Even in
a very regular accentual meter, the simple alternation
of light and heavy stresses has its variations. To
begin with, there is some inequality in the stresses
being patterned. For example, phrases like "and thus
invoke" (o ó o ó), "another's hermitage" (o ó o ó o ò),
and "half-acre tombs" (ò ó o ó) all have iambic cadences, though various degrees of light and heavy

stress occur. The iambic cadence requires simply that a less conspicuous sound precede a more conspicuous one. The measure of more or less is a relative one provided by the immediate context of syllables; it tolerates a certain range of difference. Another element of complexity is metrical variation, or the use of feet different from the one normally repeated. In English iambic meter, for instance, a trochee is frequently used to begin a line. This is the case in the first line of Shakespeare's Sonnet 30, which also has a pyrrhic and a spondee: "When to the sessions of sweet silent thought" (ó o o ó o o ó ó o ó).

More subtle variations are provided by the natural groups into which syllables fall as they cluster around strong stresses. Such groups are then separated by slight hesitations and pauses. For example, "tomorrow and tomorrow and tomorrow" (o ó o, ò o ó o, ò o ó o). Grouping occurs in all speech, but, with the greater deliberateness used to enunciate verse, groups in verse tend to be smaller and more frequent. The boundaries of groups may coincide with or overlap the boundaries of feet and thus provide a play between the conspicuousness of the two kinds of units. One can contrast, for example, the two textures in these passages of iambic meter from John Donne's "Canonization":

> And if unfit for tombes and hearse
> Our legend bee, it will be fit for verse
>
> o ó, o o ó, o o ó, o ó,
> o ó o, ó, o o ó, o o ó, o o ó
>
> As well a well wrought urne becomes
> The greatest ashes, as halfe-acre tombs
>
> o ó, o o ò ó, ó, o ó,
> o ó o, o o, o ò ó o, ó

Given the basic rhythmic effect with its consistent or varying textures, the total design for the quantities of sound is further developed by larger systems and balances. For instance, in metrical verse like Alfred E. Housman's "To an Athlete Dying Young," the basic but varied pattern is iambic. This serial recurrence is sectioned into lines of four feet. (The lines in eight instances are varied by omission of a

syllable and once by the suggestion of a run-on-line,
that is, a line in which a phrase is carried on to
the next line.) The lines are then combined in couplets and the couplets repeated in seven four-line
stanzas or quatrains:

> The time you won your town the race
> We chaired you through the market place;
> Man and boy stood cheering by,
> And home we brought you shoulder-high.

Thus, a total rhythmic design is usually a complex
hierarchy of line and stanza patterns developed from
the basic rhythm of the poem and elaborated within
individualized norms of repetition and variation.

Line and Stanza Patterns

The names of metrical lines have traditionally
indicated the basic foot and the number of times it
is repeated or varied in the line: iambic dimeter,
anapaestic trimeter, trochaic pentameter, and so
forth. Stanzas combine lines of similar or different
lengths and emphasize their unity by a pattern of end
rhymes. The history of versification traces the rise
and fluctuating popularity of a great variety of line
and stanza patterns. In the verse of different languages, these patterns frequently become associated
with special forms and genres of literature. The dactylic hexameter, for example, was associated chiefly
with classical epic. It was combined with a dactylic
pentameter in the elegiac distich, a couplet that was
a staple of Latin love poetry. Among Romance poets,
the troubadours of Provence were especially inventive
in stanzaic patterns, sometimes with intricate rhyme
schemes, like the ballade, rondeau, triolet, and ses-
tina. Their followers in Italy produced the inter-
twining tercets called terza rima and the sonnet, a
14-line stanza with a slightly variable rhyme scheme.
The latter was to have a distinguished history in
most European literatures, and especially in English
with Wyatt, Spenser, Sidney, Shakespeare, Donne, Milton, Wordsworth, Keats, and others. Comparable to
the popularity of the sonnet in Western literature
is the hokku in Japanese poetry; this is a short "stanza" of 17 syllables divided into three lines of five,
seven, and five syllables respectively. Among important lineal forms in the modern period have been the

iambic pentameter in English (rhymed in couplets or "blank"), the 12-syllable iambic Alexandrine in French, and the hendecasyllabic in Italian. Major stanza forms utilizing the iambic pentameter in English are rhyme royal (rhyming ababbcc), the Spenserian stanza (ababbcbcc), which ends with an Alexandrine, and ottava rima (abababcc), borrowed from Italian narrative poetry, as, for instance, by Lord Byron for his Don Juan. These and numerous other types continue to flourish despite the 19th and 20th century experiments in free verse, which sought original effects outside the conventions of metrical, lineal, and stanzaic patterns.

The variety of contemporary English verse reflects a rich and complex history. Unfortunately, the details of this history and even the fundamental nature of the rhythms involved are still matters of debate by prosodists. Existing differences of opinion can be surveyed in Thomas S. Omond's English Metrists (Oxford and New York, 1921) and Pallister Barkas' A Critique of Modern English Prosody (Halle, Germany, 1934).

The nature of accentual meter is especially debated. Some maintain that its rhythm depends on recurring cadences of syllables more and less conspicuously stressed, others that it is a matter of recurring isochronous durations (that is, of feet or of intervals between stresses). It is generally agreed that in addition to metrical verse, there are at least two other varieties of English verse that demand a different kind of analysis. Old English stress verse or alliterative verse, practiced into the Renaissance and revived in the 19th century by S.T. Coleridge and G.M. Hopkins, had basically a loose rhythm of natural groups. In the repeated line unit, however, a sense of isochronous balance was created by the use of a determinate number of heavily stressed (often alliterated) syllables and by a strong medial pause. Free verse of the 19th and 20th centuries relies for its rhythmic effects on a simple combination of different but harmonious cadences of natural groups. In the poetry of T.S. Eliot, Ezra Pound, and their followers, it is influenced to some extent by the separate traditions of metrical verse and stress verse.

from The Encyclopedia Americana (1962).

APPENDIX V: THE TOTAL POETIC STRUCTURE

A.   Craig La Drière, "Form"

Form is the character of an object as experienced, or the structure into which the elements of
an experience or a thing are organized. The concept
of form, or obvious analogues, is older than the
earliest documents of critical theory, and occurs in
the East as generally as in the West, especially in
speculation about the process of creation (par excellence, creation of the world by God or gods), in which
the mental notion or image of a thing-to-be-produced
is regarded as the form or formal principle of that
thing. (W.F. Albright, From Stone Age to Christianity, 1940, p.130: "a precursor of the Indo-Iranian
arta and even of the Platonic idea is found in the
Sumerian gish-ghar, the outline, plan or pattern of
things-which-are-to-be, designed by the gods at the
creation of the world and fixed in heaven in order
to determine the immutability of their creation.")
Plato so conceived the forms or ideas of all things,
even trivial human artefacts, to have an eternal and
absolute pre-existence apart from the accident of
their mundane production, which was thus an imitation,
more or less feeble, of their being (Rep.X). For
Aristotle (Met.1032b1) the human mind is the immediate
source of forms or characters which we perceive in
the works of human art; but since the mind derives
forms from the external reality it experiences, the
form of a work of art may "imitate" that of some objective reality. Modern use of the word form in analysis or description of works of art is in part a survival of long established Platonic and especially
Aristotelian terminology, in part an instance of a
natural tendency, illustrated by that terminology,
to refer to the character or structure of a thing or
an experience as its shape or form.

In the Aristotelian system, the form is one of
the four causes which account in full for the mode
of being of any thing. Two of these causes (the efficient cause, or producer; the final cause, the purpose or end) are extrinsic to the thing. The other
two, the formal and the material, are intrinsic; the
matter is that of which a thing is made, the form

that which makes it what it is. For Aristotle therefore form is not simply shape but that which shapes,
not structure or character simply but the principle
of structure, which gives character. So for the Aristotelian form in a work of art is not structure (in
a narrow sense) alone, but all that determines specific character; meaning or expressiveness, as well as
structure, is a formal element. (But meaning, besides
possessing structure and conferring it, since it involves relation is itself a kind of structure.) Actually, the Aristotelian will find in a work of art
not one form but many, a complexity of formal elements
or formalities (structures and meanings), the totality of which is the form (the structure, the meaning,
the character) of the work as a whole. This total
form will extend ideally throughout the work; the work
will be all meaning, all structure. But it will
equally be all that which is given meaning, that which
has structure; matter, as well as form, will be every-
where in the work, though ideally the mind in behol-
ding the object will know it not as matter, but only
as what is formed, as what has structure and meaning.
Where there is form there will be matter, informed;
where there is matter there will be form, informing.
To separate the matter and the form of the work will
require a mental abstraction; in the actual thing
the two will be a unity, since it is only by their
union that the thing exists.

    Such are the proper sense and implication of the
Aristotelian terms form and matter. So understood,
they are in full harmony with the results of modern
analysis, and remain, if used with precision, valuable
technical terms. The difficulties notoriously attendant upon their use in modern criticism are due to
their not being always used with precision, to the
use of other terms for reference to these concepts
and to the use of these terms for reference to other
concepts, especially to elements in other dichotomies
with which this one may be confused. Thus the matter of a literary work is commonly identified with
its "subject," or with the thought or feeling about a
subject to which the meaning of the work is a reference, or with this meaning itself; and form can then
only be what is left of character in a work when its
meaning has been subtracted, viz., its bare physical
structure, and especially, structure of sound. The
word content often replaces matter in this opposition,

and then form may be conceived as the accidental
vehicle, trivial container, or frivolous wrapping,
of a "content" regarded as alone significant and sub-
stantial; indeed, the word substance is then often
used in turn to replace content, or in conjunction
with it. These dichotomies are of course constantly
identified with that of thought and expression; and
the word style is freely used to replace either expression or form. So the alternative terms for reference to what purports to be a single distinction
become so numerous, and the distinction so patently
shifts with the terms, that what results may fairly
be called chaos. What is needed to dispel or reduce
the confusion is simply recognition of the fact that
more than one distinction is implied in this collection of terms.

Form and Matter

The first of these, the traditional Aristotelian
distinction, is a formula intended for analysis of
objects as objects. To apply it with precision, as
has rarely been done, it is necessary to keep this
fact constantly in mind; and with it the fact that
such a formula is useful only if we approach the object to be analyzed with a simplicity that some may
feel amounts to crudeness. The questions posed by
this formula are: What, in this thing, is material
of which something is made, and what is that which
is made of this material? To the first of these questions the general answer of objective analysis must
be that in a literary work the matter out of which
the thing is made is language; as Mallarmé is reported
to have told Degas, "Ce n'est pas avec des idées qu'on
fait des vers, c'est avec des mots." The matter out
of which a poet makes his poem is a language as it
exists in his time and place. But this language is
by no means a wholly formless matter when the poet
begins to work with it; it is itself the product of
more or less art, of ages of human imposition of form
upon matter. In language the basic matter, a matter
so solidly material as to fall within the province
of the physicist, is sound. This is given form by
selection, differentiation (e.g., of consonant from
vowel), and construction (syllable, phrase), by having
significations, natural or conventional, attached to
it (the word), and by conventional systematization
of all these things (grammatical and syntactic "con-

tructions"). When the writer begins to work, therefore, his material is already full of formal elements.
But these, though they remain always formal elements
and as such appear still in his finished work, are
for him part of the matter which he is to inform;
the form of his work is a form he imposes upon his
mass of forms and purer matters by shaping it as a
whole to a structure and a meaning determined by himself. The form he imposes is the peculiar total character of the speech he makes. Until the work is
finished, this new form which he imposes upon his language is an idea, more or less dimly apprehended, in
his mind; the idea of a thing (a speech) to be made.
Such formal ideas are rather ghosts than ideas; they
are not notions which can be signified or expressed.
For them there is no sign, no translation possible.
They are not concepts but conceptions, conceptions
of a thing to be made; and they can be externalized
only by the making of a thing. The impulse they ge-
nerate in the mind is therefore not to expression,
but simply to production, to making a thing. The
difference, which is very important, is made clear by
P. Valéry: "Si donc l'on m'interroge; si l'on s'in-
quiète (comme il arrive, parfois assez vivement),
de ce que j'ai 'voulu dire' dans tel poeme, je reponds
que je n'ai pas <u>voulu</u> <u>dire</u> mais <u>voulu</u> <u>faire</u>, et que
ce fut l'intention de <u>faire</u> qui a <u>voulu</u> ce que j'ai
<u>dit</u>." So far is the poet from preoccupation with
saying or expressing something that in fact what is
said or expressed may originate within, and as a mere
accident of, the process of composing a speech. Yet
of course in a poem something is expressed. Therefore it has been easy for an incomplete analysis to
suppose that in what is expressed the matter of the
poem is to be found; that the matter out of which a
poem, or any speech, is made is whatever is expressed
in it, <u>viz</u>., some thought or feeling about some reality or experience itself. Actually we have here a
confusion of related but by no means identical processes and things. Reality exists in the world round
the poet, and he experiences it; this is one process
(not peculiar to the poet). This reality comes to
him as a more or less confused chaos, and his mind
organizes, imposes order, form, upon this chaotic matter; this is a second process. Then, he may express
in language, i.e., use language to refer to, this order or form, his thought; this is a third process.
But all these processes are distinct from that of ma-

216

king a poem, though in the process of making a poem
the last (which occurs whenever anybody speaks) may
incidentally be involved, and so the others be implied as preliminaries to it. In the poem, the expression of thought exists only as a structure of
meanings. The meanings are there in the poem; the
thought is not, nor is the reality about which the
thinking is done. The poet makes his poem not of
reality or his experience of reality, not of his
thought or ideas, but in part of the meanings he finds
in words and words have meanings. (If words did not
have meanings, perhaps he would not want to make
poems of them; but as things are, words have meanings,
and it is of words that poems are made.)

Form and Expression

     To express anything it is necessary to impose
a form upon a matter and conversely the imposition
of a form upon a matter inevitably renders that matter expressive of something. Hence arises the confusion from which result most of the difficulties
connected with the use of the word form; for, as expressiveness is a formal element in an object and so
may be identified with form, the process of informing
a matter may be identified with the process of expressing something by means of informed matter. From
suggestions afforded by this identification modern
aesthetic has learned much that it must not forget,
and it is not the function of the present article to
judge, but only if possible to clarify by providing
a framework for, such theories of poetry and fine art
as (in opposition to Valery and to most of the prac-
titioners of the arts who have expressed an opinion)
make expression the only operation of the artist and
find in the whole constitution of a work of art nothing but expressiveness. But for such clarification
it is essential at least in abstraction to distinguish
the process of expressing a thought or other exprimend from that of giving a matter a form. The crucial
difference between the processes lies in the fact
that when matter and form are united their sum, as
Hardy puts it, is unity; whereas no matter how perfectly any thing is expressed, what is expressed and
what expresses it must always be distinct. Identity
of the expressed with what expresses it is an impos-
sibility, since it involves contradiction; if an expression were identical with what it expresses it

217

would be not the expression of that thing, but the
thing itself. This necessary discontinuity of exprimend and expriment implies no inferiority in expression to the process of informing, by which a fusion is achieved; for, though romantic expressionism
has perversely made an impossible fusion the goal of
expression, there is nothing in fusion as such that
requires admiration. In the simplest object, as long
as it remains that object, matter and form are united;
what we value in more complex things is not simply
the union of matter and form in them, but the experience provided by the form. And in this expressiveness may be the most precious element. The true goal
in the construction of a work of art is not some impossible identity of an exprimend with an expriment,
but the consistent adjustment of individual formal
elements into a perfectly harmonious whole. And it
is the work of achieving this that constitutes the
artist's informing. We admire in a perfect work not
the fact that matter and form are united in it, but
the admirable form that has been united with a matter.
At whatever stage the artist leaves his work, it will
have a matter and a form, and they will be united;
the question is whether the form is that of a sketch
or botch or of a finished and exquisite thing.

Form and Style

Style is a given way, or manner, or fashion, of
doing any thing, of going through any process; the
concept of style cannot in practice be dissociated
from that of some process. This is sufficient to distinguish it from the concept of form, since as we
have seen form is a concept relevant only to objects
as such, to things and not to processes. But what
is a formal element in an object from the point of
view of analysis of the constitution of that object
may be an element of style from the point of view of
analysis of a process in which the object is involved.
Some formal elements in things are indeed simply suggestions of process. These may be, like the brushwork in a painting, themselves vestiges of the process that produced the thing; or they may, like the
eccentricities of a pianist, be incidents in a process concomitant with and necessary to our apprehension of the thing. A Gothic arch has a form, and a
Romanesque arch has a different form. If we think of
both as performing the common function of arching a

space, the difference between them, without ceasing
to be a formal difference in the things, becomes the
difference between two ways or styles of executing
a process. So in all consideration of style there
is something constant or common, the process, the
thing that is done, and something variable and individual, the way of doing the thing, the style. To
find a style in a literary work is impossible unless
we conceive that something is being done in the work
or with it, that is not just an object but an element
in or embodiment of a process; and is impossible unless we conceive that the thing done might be done
or have been done otherwise, in some other way or
style. But once we do conceive a process, and set
the work within it, then formal elements become "stylistic" elements. In short, what is form in the object conceived as such is style in the process in
which the object is conceived as being involved. Since
it is harder to set poetry within process than prose,
and less relevant to consider (even only theoretically) alternative executions of any process we associate
with a poem, on the whole we use the word <u>style</u> rather
of prose than of poetry.

<u>"Organic" Form</u>

No survey, however vrief, of the idea of form
can omit reference to the distinction, common in English criticism since Coleridge, between <u>organic</u> and
<u>mechanic</u> (or abstract) form. "The form is mechanic,"
says Coleridge, "when on any given material we impress
a pre-determined form, not necessarily arising out
of the properites of the material; as when to a mass
of wet clay we give whatever shape we wish it to re-
tain when hardened. The organic form, on the other
hand, is innate; it shapes, as it develops, itself
from within, and the fullness of its development is
one and the same with the perfection of its outward
form. Such as the life is, such is the form." (<u>Lec-
tures on Shakespeare</u>, i.) The intent of this passage
is excellent, and the result of Coleridge's insistence
upon this principle has been wholly good for criticism.
But the terms of his statement involve a conflation
of the distinction between form and matter with that
between an expression and what it expresses, the ra-
mifications of which it would take long to untangle.
Fortunately the principle has been more accurately
stated by T.S. Eliot in his recent Ker Memorial Lec-

ture: "Some (structural) forms are more appropriate
to some languages than to others, and all are more
appropriate to some periods than to others. At one
stage the stanza is a right and natural formalization
of speech into a pattern. But the stanza--and the
more elaborate it is, the more rules to be observed
in its proper execution, the more surely this happens
--tends to become fixed to the idiom of the moment
of its perfection. It quickly loses contact with the
changing colloquial speech, being possessed by the
mental outlook of a past generation; it becomes dis-
credited when employed solely by those writers who,
having no impulse to form within them, have recourse
to pouring their liquid sentiment into a ready-made
mould in which they vainly hope that it will set. In
a perfect sonnet, what you admire is not so much the
author's skill in adapting himself to the pattern as
the skill and power with which he makes the pattern
comply with what he has to say. Without this fitness,
which is contingent upon period as well as individual
genius, the rest is at best virtuosity." Mr. Eliot
does well to invoke the principle by its name: fitness. It is not a question of the form's "arising
out of the properties of the material," which is impossible; it is not a question of the "innate" except
as genius for perceiving relations and establishing
them is innate. The problem is that of such perfect
fitting together of structural elements and meanings
as will produce for a mind that contemplates the
completed structure a sense of perfect harmony and
consistency: that is, of perfect order.

----

from Dictionary of World Literary Terms, ed. Joseph
     T. Shipley (Boston: The Writer, Inc., 1970),
     pp.167-171.

B.   Craig La Drière, "Literary Form and Form in the
     Other Arts"

     Poetry is speech whose form is determined, not
by the linguistic-social norms of grammar with its
ideal of correctness, and not by the more general social norms of rhetoric with its ideal of eloquence
and its goal of effective communication--though these
may operate within it in subordination to the aesthe-

tic--but by norms derived from a principle which, though it may operate in linguistic materials, is not itself linguistic, and, though it may operate within a framework of social communication, is not itself social.

It is easier to experience the effect of the operation of this principle than to define its nature. Of all the principles I have mentioned as capable of providing norms for the organization of a speech, it is the most difficult to seize in abstraction. This may be because it is in fact the most abstract of all. All structure is based upon, indeed is constituted by, relations; and for each of the other kinds of structure I have mentioned there is a particular kind of relation which we can identify as the basis of that structure and as relevant to that kind of organization of elements. Logical structure is based upon logical relations among its elements; we know, or can be informed, what logical relations among such elements are. Grammatical relations we can similarly identify as relations of a particular kind, which we can understand once we know something of the nature of language and its use; and, though rhetorical relations are more subtle than these, we can identify and in a measure isolate them likewise once we have an adequate grasp of social reality and the process of communication or persuasion. Each of these relations is a relation of a distinct, particular kind. But there does not seem to be any particular kind of relation which is distinctly aesthetic. Indeed, each of these other kinds of relations may on occasion have the character of an aesthetic relation. We are forced to conclude that whereas a grammatical structure is an organization of elements in terms of grammatical relations, and logical structure an organization of elements in terms of logical relations, and rhetorical structure in terms of rhetorical relations, a structure whose principle of organization is aesthetic is a structure simply of relations, a structure in terms of relation simply as such.

If this makes the aesthetic or poetic principle, as I have said, the most abstract and generalized of the possible principles of organization for a speech, what this means in fact is not that a structure organized by this principle is at any point less evi-

221

dently based upon a specific kind of relation, but
only that the kind of relation upon which it is based
is not specified a priori as in the other types of
structure. The aesthetic impulse may choose any kind
of relation as the ground of its construction; it
may elect a plurality of relations and work with
several at once or in succession. But it must make
a choice of some kind, for if there is to be construction at all it must be in terms of some kind, or
kinds, of relation. We may indeed specify or limit
the aesthetic principle somewhat by observing that,
since this principle brings to its construction no
pre-established extrinsic norms like those provided
by the practical ends of grammar and rhetoric, or the
speculative ends of logic, the relations with which
it works must be those of the intrinsic characters
or properties of the elements which it relates together. But to say this is not to specify very much
the operation, or to limit very much the freedom, of
the aesthetic principle, for such intrinsic characters
and properties in any kind of material or element are
so numerous and so various that for the constitution
of each individual structure a choice must be made
among them. And there is no a priori prediction of
this choice where the aesthetic principle is in control. It is for this reason that each individual
work of fine art provides the only relevant norms both
for apprehension of its form and for judgment of its
value. We know beforehand what it is to be grammatically correct, or logically coherent or rhetorically
effective; and we judge the individual grammatical,
or logical, or--within limits--rhetorical construct
in terms of such antecedent awareness and expectation.
But of the beautiful, the aesthetically satisfying,
all we know beforehand is that it will have coherence,
or unity, or some such abstraction. What it is that
will cohere, what the mode of its coherence will be,
we cannot know before the event. We can be sure only
that this coherence will not be simply grammatical coherence, or logical, or rhetorical: the coherence of
a poetic speech will not be that of any other kind
of speech, since clearly if it were then the speech
would be a structure of one of those other kinds and
not a poem.

     I have said that all literary art uses for its
constructions the materials provided by a language;
so poetic construction uses as its elements those

which are furnished by the phonemes, the lexemes, and the syntagmatic structures of a given language. But poetic construction works with these elements not as such--for as such they are grammatical units--but as having intrinsic properties of which structures can be made. Poetry dissolves the units of the language it employs into their natural components, and uses these components as the elements of its own constructions. The elements of poetic structure are sounds as such and meanings as such; and of the natural aspects of sounds as such and of meanings as such, their intrinsic properties, poetry builds structures by relating them together in terms of similarly intrinsic relations. It must be noted here only in passing that for such construction too, like that of grammar or logic, there arise conventional procedures, so that we can speak of conventions of poetic form as of those of others, and in a given culture the conventions of poetic form may be as numerous and as complicated as those of grammatical form; but the conventions of poetic form are always conventional procedures for the attainment of form that at least in principle is itself not conventional but natural.

The relation, or class of relations, which is fundamental to poetic structure is the simplest and most basic of all kinds of relation, the relation of identity and diversity or of sameness and difference. All poetic structure is a structure of sameness and difference in sounds and in meanings: poetic structure is structure of sounds simply as sounds, and meanings simply as meanings, in terms of the relations of sameness simply as sameness and difference simply as difference. It is easier perhaps to see this in structures of sound than in those of meaning, but the two kinds of structure, though always distinct, are fundamentally alike. It is not difficult, for example, to see that rhythmic structure of sounds is based upon likeness and unlikeness of stress and unstress; it is less immediately obvious, but upon examination equally apparent, that all poetic structure of meaning too is based upon likeness and difference among individual meanings--and this not only in such conspicuous, though representative, instances as "Shall I compare thee to a summer's day? Thou art more lovely and more temperate..." or the likeness and difference of Creon and Antigone, Hamlet and Claudius. Whether in sound or in meaning, it is the relation of

sameness and difference that provides all the repetitions, recurrences, balances, symmetries, and all contrasts, tensions, and conflicts, that constitute artistic form.

The two principles, of sameness and of difference,
operate together and by interaction in the constitution of all such form; neither can work without the
other. But in terms of their mutual interaction, and
of emphasis now upon one and now upon the other, we
can distinguish two great types of organization, that
of the series and that of the system. Serial organization is the order of recurrence of some identity;
such organization operates to diffuse an established
identity: it is exemplified typically by metrical
rhythm. Systematic organization, on the other hand,
operates to establish new identities by concentration,
or cumulation, of elements into relatively discrete
unitary entities. To take an example again from
rhythmic structure, the foot is a small system; the
strophe a larger system. The normal interaction of
the two types of organization is illustrated in these
examples. You must have some systematic unit, which
may be repeated, before you can have a series: you
must have a foot if you are to have a meter. But you
can constitute a larger system serially, simply by
"marking off" a certain number of repetitions of the
smaller system: so lines and stanzas may be constructed, by serial organization of small units (feet) into cumulative systems of a larger order; and then these
larger systems in turn may be repeated serially again,
or ordered into yet larger systems. The interaction,
or interinvolvement, of the two types of order occurs
at all levels and tends always to be complementary.
I have said that to have a meter you must have a foot;
but one cannot say you must first have a foot, for
until it is repeated the thing is not a foot, and so
one might with equal propriety say that to have a foot
you must have a meter. If the thing which repetition
makes a foot appears only once in a flow of speech
and is not repeated, we may not observe in it any such
unitary systematic character as it appears to have in
a repetitive series. Serial repetition can thus in
a sense create systems; but the systems it creates
may require for their maintenance as systems that they
be held within the series which created them, and
without the support of which they would dissolve into
mere potentialities. What made them discrete and re-

latively discontinuous units was paradoxically their
assimilation into a continuous series.

This interdependence of elements and types of
order, and the generation of one type, so to speak,
out of another, with all that it implies of complexity and intricacy, is universal in all artistic form.
In poetry, systems and series appear in both structures of sound and structures of meaning. But it
seems that some elements or aspects have a natural
affinity for the one type of organization, and some
for the other. Rhythmic structure is typically
serial, and in it we see system constantly absorbed
and re-absorbed into series. The structures of alliteration and assonance are, on the one hand, not
susceptible of strict, continuous serial regularity;
their patterns appear not as series but as occasional
systematic congestions in a flow of sound characterized more by differences than by samenesses, and
serial recurrence in them produces the effect of discrete systematic cumulation or concentration. The
smallest units in any kind of structure are necessarily systematic; and perhaps one may say that the largest unit, the figure of the whole, is in all structures also a system, if only by virtue of the closure
provided externally by its beginning and its end.
But, once we have recognized the interaction and interdependence of series and system throughout all
structure, we may distinguish some total forms as emphasizing the serial in their internal structures,
and others as emphasizing the systematic. Dylan Thomas, for example, was thinking in terms of such difference in character of total forms, and of his own
preferred or predestined poetic form as serial rather
than systematic, when in a letter to Henry Treece
he wrote, "...it consciously is not my method to move
concentrically round a central image...making a full
circle...I do not want a poem of mine to be, nor can
it be, a circular piece of experience placed nearly
outside the living stream of time from which it came;
a poem of mine is, or should be, a watertight section
of the stream that is flowing all ways..." The whole
is a system ("watertight"); but some such systems are
constituted internally rather by a cumulation which
is like serial structure than by the concentration
which is typically systematic.

Series and systems are types of organization, as

we say, of <u>units</u> of some distinguishable kind. In
poetry, as in the other types of speech, our awareness of a given structural design, and hence our analysis of it, is in terms of units; but here again
the poetic structure is different from the others in
that units of poetic structure are not <u>a priori</u> distinguishable. Each of the other types of speech
seems to have its characteristic type also of basic
unit: in grammar the word and then the sentence, in
rhetoric the the word or word-group and the "period"
(if we follow the ancient rhetoricians; and there are
almost no others to follow). But in poetry there
appears to be no such fixed basic unit. Some poems
are constructed of units of the size or order of
the sentence or period, some of units of the size or
order of the phrase or of the word; but poems are
also constructed of units which do not correspond to
any of these. Each poem must be approached as in
this respect, like one of the angels, a genus in itself, and allowed to establish for our perception its
own divisions and combinations. We know there will
be units of some kind; of what kind we do not know
until they are presented to us in the poem.

---

from Paul Bockman, ed. <u>Stil und Formprobleme in der
    Literatur</u> (Hiedelberg: Winter, 1959), pp. 31-
    35.

C. Seymour Chatman, "On Defining 'Form'"

"Form" and "Content"

        I should argue, from a rather straightforward
Aristotelian position, that there really is no alternative to form, that no discourse, indeed no communication, can avoid having a form, as it cannot avoid
having a content. I know that it is popular to argue
monistically, that form and content are one, a position ultimately Plato's, but which gained great support in the Romantic period. In the twentieth century, it has had powerful defenders like Croce and
W.K. Wimsatt. A recent, sophisticated version is
that of French Structuralism--deriving from Russian
Formalism and Saussurean-Hjelmslevian linguistics.
For example, Roland Barthes, in an essay entitled

"Style and Its Image," has argued that "one can trans-
form a given text into a more schematic version, provide a metalanguage which is no longer the language
of the original text, without changing the narrative
character of the text" (for example, replace Balzac's
description of an old man who "conservait sur ses
levres bleuatres un rire fixe et arrete, un rire im-
placable et goguenard comme celui d'une tete de mort"
by any statement which simply "tells that the old man
had something fantastic and funereal about him"), but
it is erroneous to assume that one has thereby
"stripped off" the form and got down to the content.
"What this stripping-off reveals is not a content, a
signifie, but another form, another signifiant, or
if one prefers a more neutral term, another level,
which is never the last, because the text is always
articulated in terms of codes which themselves will
never be exhausted." According to this view, what
is essential to discourse is the quality of "layerd-
ness" (feuillete): "If up until now we have looked
at the text as a species of fruit with a kernel (an
apricot, for example), the flesh being the form and
the pit the content, it would be better to see it
as an onion, a construction of layers (or levels, or
systems) whose body contains, finally, no heart, no
kernel, no secret, no irreducible principle, nothing
except the infinity of its own envelopes--which en-
velop nothing other than the unity of its own sur-
faces." As an example he cites another sentence from
Balzac's "Sarrasine":

> ...the sculptor Sarrasine is the
> lover of a prima donna who, unknown
> to him, is a eunuch; he abducts
> her, but the pretended songstress
> defends herself: "L'Italienne était
> armée d'un poignard. Si tu approches,
> dit-elle, je serai forcée de te
> plonger cette arme dans le coeur.

Barthes asks, "Is there behind the expression a signifie?" And answers, "No, the sentence is an inter-
weaving of several codes: a linguistic code (the
French language), a rhetorical code (antonomasia, in-
terpolation of an inquit, apostrophe), an actional
code (the armed defense of the victim is a unit in
the sequence Abduction), a hermeneutic code (the
eunuch conceals his real sex by pretending to defend

his virtue as a woman), and a symbolic code (the
knife is a symbol of castration).

But granted the existence of these codes and the
legitimacy of this kind of analysis, granted the
reality of the complex and mixed character of literary and other kinds of discourse, it is difficult to
understand why one should deny that there are, ultimately, contents or signifiés referred to. The very
use of the term "code" necessarily entails a concomitant, namely "message"; and though there may be no
single message in a literary statement, no single
signifié, surely one can say that there is some reasonably specifiable number of messages. (Indeed,
Barthes himself has spoken of the message as something separate from the sign: "la littérature n'est
rien qu'un langage, c'est-à-dire un système de signes:
son être n'est pas dans son message, mais dans ce
système.") The linguistic code is indeed the French
language, and then at least something of the message
would remain. (If it is not message, what is it?)
So too with the other codes: alterations could be
made, and yet something like a reference or content
would persist. True, the message will be altered
by the change in form; but to say that form and content co-vary is not at all the same thing as saying
that they are indistinguishable, or that the latter
does not exist. There must finally be a signifié;
otherwise there can be no signifiant.

"Style"

The reverse point must be made about the term
"style" in at least one of its senses, namely "texture," that is, local or "small-scale" form (the
fourteenth sense listed in the Oxford English Dic-
tionary--"Those features of literary composition
which belong to form and expression rather than to
the substance of the thought or matter expressed").
Thus, Monroe Beardsley defines "style" (tentatively)
as "the recurrent features of its texture of meaning."
As an example he offers the difference between "I
am here" and "Here I am," the latter implying, for
example, "I have been long awaited or searched for."
But is this stylistic or only stylistic? More impor-
tantly, what sense does it make to say that the
style feature, the stylisticum, is "detail of meaning"
and nothing else? Surely any bit of meaning or mea-

ning distinction can only come into existence if it is signalled. Even if we were to agree that there is only a stylistic difference between "I am here" and "Here I am" we would still have to distinguish its form--namely the inverted word order--from its content ("I have been long awaited or searched for" or whatever). To say--as Beardsley does elsewhere--that style is "nothing but meaning" seems to deny the fundamental semiotic principle that there can be no reference, hence no meaning, without a feature-element, that is, a sign. We can say that signs have (or signal or evoke or whatever) meanings; we cannot say that they are meanings. We can say that a stylistic choice entails differences in meaning, but not that it simply amounts to those meaning-differences and to nothing else. It has a shape as well as a substance. There can be no signifié without a signifiant.

What then is the distinction between "form" and "style"? The trouble with "style" as a critical term, as I have argued on several occasions, is the confusion of senses that has arisen, and the way those senses collect prescriptive overtones. The OED lists twenty-eight senses of the word, but there are four in particular which tend to overlap distressingly. The "small-scale form" definition has already been mentioned above: this appears as the first part of the fourteenth entry in the OED. But to the end of that definition is added the observation "Often used for: Good or fine style," a phrase which seems to suggest that prescriptive confusions are unavoidable. But "style" as "excellent writing" is obviously a separate definition. (Other entries tack on the same amendment: 13b for example: "Used for: A good, choice, or fine style." And similarly the other arts and walks of life: to 23, for example, "Manner of executing a task or performing an action or operation. Often with references to athletics, racing, games: The manner of action of a particular performer, race-horse, etc." is added 23b "Used absol. for: Good or fine style.") A third sense (and the only one I should like to see used in serious literary discussion) is 13a, "The manner of expression characteristic of a particular writer (hence of an orator), or of a literary group or period." It, too, has a prescriptive amendment: "writer's mode of expression considered in regard to clearness, effectiveness, beauty, and the like." Here, again, the dictionary introduces

229

normative implications, needlessly, since one can
think of famous styles which do not necessarily evoke
characterizations like "clear," "effective," or "beautiful" in usual senses of those words. It is evident
that stylistics, like linguistics before it, must
rid itself of normative preoccupations if it is ever
to get around to the task of describing its object.
"Manner" and "characteristic" seem clear enough, although "expression" is the kind of word that needs
to be watched closely. This, of course, is the definition of Buffon--"The style is the man"--although
his definition, like Beardsley's, is too reductive.
Individuals <u>have</u> a variety of styles; a poet's style
of writing a sonnet may have very few features in common with his way of writing a letter, or even a novel,
let alone his way of playing tennis. In its favor
it should be noted that this sense has been the most
productive of new extensions in English (see articles
twenty-three through twenty-six in the <u>OED</u>). The
fourth definition is that of the fifteenth article in
the <u>OED</u>: "A manner of discourse, or tone of speaking,
adopted in addressing others or in ordinary conversation." This is the meaning referred to in expressions
like "colloquial style," "formal style," and so forth,
and, indeed, in the classical theory of style "levels."
It is used today even in sophisticated linguistic
circles, like that of the British school. Its basis
is the class-structure of society; stylistic choice
in this sense means the selection of vocabulary and
forms to match the element of society that one is de-
picting or wishing to emulate or communicate with.
But "social dialect" seems a better term for expressing this meaning.

I think it is particularly important to avoid
using "style" as a term for "small-scale form." "Texture" is infinitely preferable. "Form" then is a
general class term (as opposed to "content") comprised
of two sub-classes--"texture" or small-scale form vs.
"structure" or large-scale form.

Furthermore, I should argue that it is as meaningful to apply "style" to matters of content as to matters of form. It is clearly useful to be able to say
that Hemingway's <u>style</u> includes the choice of characters that are he-men, boxers, toreadors, deep-sea
fishermen, big-game hunters, and so on, while James'
style sees the world in terms of quite different

"types"; or that Shakespeare's sonnet style runs to
love, the immortality of art, the urge to procreation,
and so on, while Wordsworth's is more often concerned
with the visible beauties of nature or political up-
heaval. These are stylistic statements, that is,
they have to do with those particular choices, among
all the alternatives in the world, that these writers
elected to make. A clear statement of this principle
has been made by Richard Ohmann:

> The very many decisions that add
> up to style are decisions about what
> to say, as well as how to say it.
> They reflect the writer's organi-
> zation of experience, his sense of
> life, so that the most general of
> his attitudes and ideas find ex-
> pression just as characteristically
> in his style as in his matter, though
> less overtly. Style, in this view,
> far from being intellectually peri-
> pheral ornament, is what I have called
> "epistemic choice," and the study of
> style can lead to an insight into
> the writer's most confirmed epistemic
> stances.

I should only add that choices in "matter" have a
stylistic dimension as choices in language.

Now "choice" is ambiguous--it may mean the act
of choosing or the product. Ohmann's use of the word
"decision" obviously refers to the former, and the
clearest explanation of this point is made in Craig
La Drière's classic article, "Form":

> Style is a given way, or manner, or
> fashion, of doing any thing, of going
> through any process; the concept of
> style cannot in practice be disso-
> ciated from that of some process.
> This is sufficient to distinguish it
> from the concept of form, since as
> we have seen form is a concept rele-
> vant only to objects as such, to
> things and not to processes.

What often confuses people is that a given feature

may be at once an element in the form, that is, part
of the object, and a stylisticum, that is, part of
the process. Thus the brushwork in a painting is a
formal (more exactly a textural) element but at the
same time stylistic insofar as it is a _vestige_ of
the process of painting it. Furthermore, what is signalled by that particular brushwork (or use of the
past participle, or whatever the feature) is the artist himself; from the stylistic point of view, he
is the referent, whatever the internal, that is, formal reference or function may be, the role that the
feature plays in the economy of the whole work of
art. What we are doing when we say "Ah, that must
be Rembrandt" or "That must be Milton" is recognizing
certain recurrences among style features (vestiges
of the process of composition) on the basis of previous experiences with that artist's work.

If "style" is best taken as manner, then stylistics is a discipline which is inescapably comparatist:
one of the stylistician's tasks is to measure the
style he is interested in against other styles, that
is, other manners of doing the same or highly similar
things. Like the psychologist, he needs a "control,"
though he is under no pressure to pick some "zero
degree" or "norm" of behavior. It makes more sense
to measure Keats's style against Shelley's than
against an "average speaker's" or a contemporary jour-
nalist's or even against Jane Austen's. To facili-
tate comparison one may seek out texts with minimally
different contents, looking for what Craig La Drière
calls the most "common function":

> A Gothic arch has a form, and a
> Romanesque arch has a different
> form. If we think of both as per-
> forming the common function of
> arching a space, the difference
> between them, without ceasing to be
> a formal difference in the things,
> becomes the difference between
> two ways or styles of executing a
> process. So in all consideration
> of style there is something con-
> stant or common, the process, the
> thing that is done, and something
> variable and individual, the way of
> doing the thing, the style. To find

232

> a style in a literary work is im-
> possible unless we conceive that
> something is being done in the work
> or with it that is not just an ob-
> ject but an element in or embodiment
> of a process; and is impossible
> unless we conceive that the thing
> done might be done or have been done
> otherwise, in some other way or
> style.

That is to say, even if one were to write an account
of Keats's style without referring to any other poet's
style, there would still be tacitly presupposed the
possibility of other ways of expressing the matter
that Keats conveys.

Craig La Drière's example suggests further distinctions. "Gothic" and "Romanesque" are not the
styles of individuals but of whole epochs or periods.
What precisely is a "period style"? Is it, as Lau-
rence Lerner's discussion seems to suggest, something
qualitatively different from individual style? If
we follow the praiseworthy rigor of Craig La Drière's
account we must disagree. Gothic and Romanesque
arches have distinct forms, technically "Gothic and
Romanesque arch forms." The processes by which the
architects did their work are the Gothic and Romanesque
arch styles. Many individual architects followed
these two processes, so it makes sense to call each
a group style. Not every Gothic arch, however, is
like every other Gothic arch, and to the secondary
formal differences (in shape, texture or whatever)
there correspond individual stylistic, that is, process differences. Thus, differences exist between
the individual style of Gothic-arch architect A and
that of Gothic-arch architect B. Their stylistic similarities, that is, the similar aspects of the processes which they followed, as deduced from vestigial
evidence in the objects, the arches themselves, aspects which were also followed by all those whom ex-
perts choose to call Gothic-arch stylists, amount to
the group style called the "Gothic-arch style." Thus,
a group style may be defined as the sub-set or common core of shared processes associated with features
of the total set of formal features authoritatively
assigned to a group. A diagram will make this statement clearer:

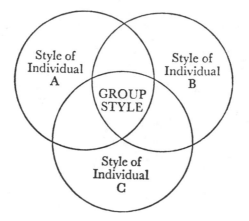

Period style is simply that kind of group style in which the principle of grouping is historical. Thus, the period style called "English Romantic" may be represented as follows:

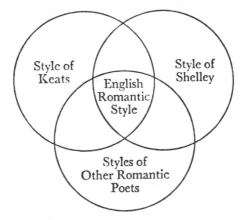

"Genre" style is that kind of group style in which the principle is not historical, but definitional or "divisional," that is, based on distinctions between forms, taking the term "genre" as a qualitatively distinct set of formal elements, or more simply, a distinctive form. Thus, the genre-style corresponding to the form "English sonnet" may be represented as follows:

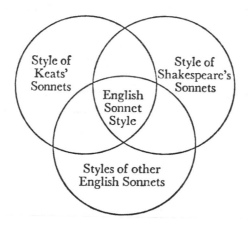

If this formulation is accepted, then the distinction between individual and group style is merely quantitative, rather than qualitative; that is, the two differ only in respect to the number of features comprehended.

The structure-texture dichotomy is rich in implications for stylistic analysis. The textural side of form has been more often worked over and is better understood from the stylistic point of view than the structural. Meter, the figures of speech and so on are more often invoked as part of the description of styles than are the "topics of invention" and other large organizational principles. Our best formal and stylistic descriptions of individual authors--like Wimsatt's study of Johnson and Bates's of Keats--are predominately based on units smaller than the sentence.

Though there are many analyses of larger literary structures, some notable, like R.S. Crane's work on plot, very few treat structure as simply one more stylistic option. There is normally no recognition that a characterization of a writer's large-scale structural propensities is a stylistic observation: an account of Samuel Johnson's "style" is more likely to tell us about his penchant for antithesis than for short essays or "philosophical" tales (as opposed to other possible structures). Crane's discussion, of course, was concerned rather to illustrate a concept of plot in general than to contribute to our knowledge of Fielding's style.

What is needed in stylistics is analysis that leads to terms for characterizing large-scale structures on their own, terms like that of "merry-go-round" for Arthur Schnitzler's Reigen, or "hour-glass" for France's Thais and James's The Ambassadors; and, further, an integration of these with the more molecular aspects of an author's style.

Form: Syntax and Discourse

But to get back to the question of form, and particularly the form-content dichotomy: What is the nature of literary content? Craig La Drière argues that the "matter out of which the thing (the literary work) is made is language." But here "matter" signifies materia, material or substance, in the sense that stone is the matter of a sculpture, or oil pigment and canvas the matter of a painting. Content is surely not that. In the figurative arts, content is ordinarily taken to be the object represented in the matter as it has been shaped by the form--"David" in Michaelangelo's sculpture or "the Mona Lisa" in Leonardo's painting. So the content of a literary work is not the language but what the language stands for, its reference. Further, as Craig La Drière points out, the language itself, though it is a matter or materia in relation to the overriding literary form, is itself a form or set of forms in relation to content, the set of referents which it expresses. Thus the literary form of an author's work is best seen as

> a form he imposes upon his mass of
> forms and purer matters (language)
> by shaping it as a whole to a struc-
> ture and a meaning determined by
> himself. The form he imposes is the
> peculiar total character of the
> speech he makes.

And the language is a mediating form between the literary form (structure-texture) and the ultimate

236

content.

Linguistics has shown that Craig La Drière's "mass of forms" is really an elaborate set of systems --phonological, morphological, syntactic, semantic, discursive, etc. Little work has been done in linguistics at the level of discourse, but it is clear that the development of such analysis would provide a powerful tool for literary studies. What seems particularly interesting and as yet infrequently considered is the relation between syntactic and discursive structures. This is an important way, for example, of accounting for such rhetorical notions as emphasis, as Ohmann has suggested in his analysis of the last sentence of Conrad's "The Secret Sharer."

My own present concern is, rather, esthetic, namely, how to account for the impression of diversity, where form varies around a more-or-less constant content. A classic instance is provided by the first seventeen sonnets of Shakespeare. These are in a way counterparts at higher levels of what preoccupied Beardsley in "I am here" and "Here I am." That is, they share a relatively common message--the "motive to procreation." The addressee is urged to marry so that his excellencies may be preserved in his offspring. What is remarkable is how the combination of relatively few elements of syntactic and discursive form creates such a variety of expression.

The basic English sentence types are declarative, imperative, and interrogative, and there are some additional minor types like exclamation and call. Of course, no necessary connection exists between syntactic feature and discursive function, since a given feature may have several functions--or, in another terminology, participate in one or several different kinds of "illocutionary speech act." An interrogative may not function as a real but rather as a rhetorical question, in which case it asserts rather than solicits an answer. Shakespeare's sonnets play richly on these possibilities. For example, the speech act of exhorting, the most essential in the group, does not inevitably take the syntactic form of imperative. Not only are obvious alternatives, auxiliaries like "should" and "must," used--"Against this coming end you should prepare" (XIII,3) and "And you must live, drawn by your own sweet skill" (XVI,14)--but other

237

locutions, like "be for someone to"; "That's for thyself to breed another thee" (VI,7). An exclamation may also serve a hortatory function, as in "For shame ..." (X,1). Conversely, what is syntactically imperative sometimes does not function as a direct exhortation: in "Pity the world, or else this glutton be, / To eat the world's due, by the grave and thee" (I,13-14) only "Pity" is hortatory; the imperative "Be" is only syntactically, not discursively, parallel, since the poet is not urging the young man to be a glutton (as he is urging him to pity the world), but rather imagining the consequences of his not performing an action. That is, the imperative is used to make the speech act of predicting. (Some linguists might argue, however, that "be" is not an imperative at all but simply an elliptical form of "will be.") Similarly, "grant" in "Grant, if thou will, thou art beloved of many, / But that thou none lov'st is most evident" (X,3-4) is not an exhortation but rather a concession--it could as easily have been phrased "Let us grant that..." or "It may be granted that..." or in a number of other ways. Further, the sonnets use non-imperative structures like declaratives (posing observations or predictions) or interrogatives to provide a supportive context for the implied or expressed exhortation. All of these means, of course, are adjusted to the exacting requirements of the stanzaic pattern of the genre. Therefore, it is not the number of elements employed in each system (which is necessarily small) but rather the considerable number of combinations they can make that gives the cycle sonneteer the freedom to achieve exquisite variations on a common theme. These elements may be listed as follows:

Syntax	Discourse
Imperatives	Exhortation
Interrogatives	Rhetorical or Real Questions
Declaratives	Observations
Exclamations	Predictions

In addition, most of the discursive elements may be either specific or general; thus there occur many general observations which sound much like adages.

Since the common theme is "urging" or exhortation, one might expect a heavy use of the imperative mood.

238

There are some, but the art of the sequence is that relatively few are needed. Only five poems rely on imperative constructions for explicit exhortation. If the traditional order is accepted, it is significant that these are distributed evenly: they are numbers 1, 3, 6, 10, and 13. And even if this order is not what Shakespeare intended, indeed even if the whole matter of order is irrelevant, the fact that there are only five suggests at least that he might have been careful not to overuse the directest linguistic means of injunction. They provide a framework, a context in terms of which less overt structures can be meaningful.

Further, considerable variety is achieved within the marked imperative group by placing them in different positions in the sonnet: at the beginning (number three), at the end (numbers six and thirteen), in the middle (number one), and in all three positions (number ten). The imperative is most insistent in only the two middle poems, six and ten: Number six has four and number ten has six imperatives (although not all are hortatory). If one accepts the ordinary grouping, this increase may be seen as a formal reflection of the increased, climactic urgency suggested by these two sonnets. But my thesis would not be totally invalidated by the acceptance of another sequence, since all I really wish to argue is that some part of the richness of structure that readers sense inheres in the interplay of several different systems --the syntax of English, the functional or illocutionary speech act system, and the relative position within the metrical framework of the poem--and that it is in part this interplay that keeps the repetition of the message from seeming tedious. Though the number of elements within any one of these systems is comparatively small, their combinatory possibilities are considerable. And it is as aspects of literary form, I think, that such phenomena are best considered.

from New Literary History, 2 (1971), pp. 218-225.

D.   Daniel Burke, FSC, "Classifying Forms and Genres:
        the Novel"   .

        The nature of forms and genres is a rather com-
plicated theoretical question; there is not even
agreement among theorists about what the most general
classes or kinds of literature are or how more specific kinds are related to them.   The theory of classification offered here emphases certain basic parts
of the natural structure of speeches--the number of
speakers; the general kind of object reference; the
specific attitude of the speaker(s); the specific
object reference.   It suggests that certain combinations of these elements are the basis of the forms
and genres, that the combinations themselves constitute the conventional patterning of speech elements
that influence and limit writers in the ways we have
been describing.

        We can begin analyzing and classifying forms and
genres by reviewing the basic speech elements mentioned and adding a few.   One distinction that we will
expand later and will have to assume here is the simple one between verse (speech with regular patterns
of sound) and prose (speech with irregular patterns
of sound).   We can then proceed by noting in speeches
whether they are in monologue alone, dialogue alone,
or both monologue and dialogue mingled.   Thus an
essay is in prose monologue; a lyric, in verse monologue.   A play is completely in dialogue, either in
verse or prose.   A story is in a mixture of monologue
with dialogue, either in verse (as an epic or ballad)
or prose (as a novel or short story).   Another aspect
of the speech to consider here is whether or not it
is presenting action (as a play or story) or only
states of mind or ideas (as in a lyric).   If it presents action, we can call it dynamic speech; if it
does not, we can call it static speech--though these
are not standard terms.

        All of these aspects just mentioned can be pre-
sent in any of the three modes of discourse or language which we discussed earlier.   For example, a history book can be presenting an action and can be
using a mixture of monologue and dialogue in doing it.
Philosophy can be presented, as that of Plato was, by
dialogue.   Therefore, we may outline the possible combinations of these factors in this way:

                            240

Modes of Language	General Pattern Of Sound	Type of Speaker	General Object Reference
Poetry	Verse	Monologue	Dynamic -- e.g., Dramatic monologue
			Static -- e.g., Lyric
		Dialogue	Dynamic -- e.g., Play
			Static -- e.g., Debate
		Monologue & Dialogue	Dynamic -- e.g., Ballad
			Static -- e.g., Sketch
	Prose	Monologue	Dynamic -- e.g., Dramatic monologue
			Static -- e.g., Sketch
		Dialogue	Dynamic -- e.g., Play
			Static -- e.g., Dialogue
		Monologue & Dialogue	Dynamic -- e.g., Novel
			Static -- e.g., Sketch

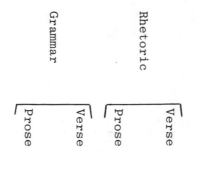

$$
\text{Rhetoric}
\begin{cases}
\text{Verse} \\
\text{Prose}
\end{cases}
\qquad
\text{Grammar}
\begin{cases}
\text{Verse} \\
\text{Prose}
\end{cases}
$$

(Similar combinations of these factors occur in Rhetoric and Grammar, though many of the resulting forms are rare.)

It is clear, however, that more specific characteristics are combined in the various kinds of literature. As we move on to discuss these, we should note
that these various combinations of conventional traits
are involved in our definitions of types of literature. When we give a logical definition of the novel
(which we shall take as our example here), we include
the basic similarities among those works we usually
call "novels." In such definitions we make a rough
division between important general and important specific characterizations of these works. The general
characteristics of the novel are those which relate
it to other types of literary works in a still larger
class, story. In our definition of the novel, we simply name this large class to imply these general characteristics (cf. "animal" in the definition of man).
The specific characteristics of the novel, then, are
those which define its own place within the larger
class (cf. "rational" in the definition of man). We
say, then, that a novel is a story which...

Now the largest classes of literary works are
the forms. Forms are a classification of literary
works based on two characteristics: the number of
speakers in the work and the general type of reality
referred to. Thus, to repeat, literary works may have

    a. a single speaker (monologue)

    b. two or more speakers (dialogue)

    c. a single basic speaker quoting other
       speakers (monologue and dialogue)

Ballads, short stories, and novels are usually a mixture of monologue and dialogue; they all belong to the
form characterized by this mixture.

The second characteristic of the forms is that
they refer to either of two very general types of
reality--to static reality like states of mind or
things, or to dynamic reality like events or actions.
The first and second characteristics described here
combine in different ways so that theoretically
speaking six forms are possible:

    Static --   Exposition

243

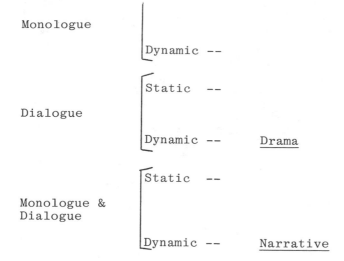

Monologue

⌐ Dynamic --

Dialogue

⌐ Static --

Dynamic -- <u>Drama</u>

Monologue &
Dialogue

⌐ Static --

Dynamic -- <u>Narrative</u>

However, we usually think of three <u>major</u> forms among
these, those indicated as exposition, drama, and
narrative. (And these three terms are related to typical enumerations of the major literary types as
"lyric," "tragedy," and "epic" or "lyric," "drama,"
and the "novel.") More technically, the novel belongs to the <u>form</u> narrative. In it a basic narrator
(monologue) and other quoted characters (dialogue)
refer to dynamic reality, a series of actions.

At the other end of the scale, the most specific
classes of literary works are the <u>genres</u>. Genres
are a classification of literary works based on the
specific object referred to (e.g., love, adventure,
doctors, detectives) and/or the specific attitude taken toward this subject (e.g, comic, satiric). Thus
science fiction, epics, romances are genres; comedy,
tragedy, and satire are genres. There are hundreds
of literary genres.

Obviously, the novel as a class is larger in
scope than the genres, for the novel itself breaks
down into many genres--novels of love, adventure,
comic fantasy, and so forth. On the other hand, the
novel as a class is smaller in scope than the form
narrative. Therefore, it must exist and be defined

somewhere between these extremes, between the general forms and the very specific genres.

We can anticipate some of our findings about the level or scope of the novel as a class by considering some of the many definitions that have been given to it historically and which attempt to pinpoint its peculiar qualities. Actually most of these definitions stress the same elements. If we were to construct from these definitions two that were typical they would be the following:

    a. the novel is a long prose narrative;

    b. the novel is a realistic study of human relationships, of men in conflict or in vital relation and action with themselves, with nature, with society at large.

Now the first definition suggests characteristics of length or quantity and of the way sounds are patterned in the speech. These elements draw the class "novel" to the level of classes like the short story (a short prose narrative), the verse tale (a short verse narrative), the sonnet (a lyric with fourteen lines of iambic pentameter and a particular rime scheme), the ballad, and so forth. These classes are determined at least partially by characteristics of length and of sound pattern. Usually, these classes are rather wide in scope; they include a number of genres. Therefore, we might think of them on a level of generality below the forms.

The second definition of the novel given above draws it as a class toward the level of genre classes which, as we have seen, are defined by specific matters and attitudes. The term "realistic" in the definition suggests an attitude, but an attitude that is not so specific as "bitterly satiric" or "comic," for example. The phrases "human relationships" or "men in conflict, in vital relation" suggest a subject matter, but, once again, not a very specific subject matter, not the matter of a genre in the sense that shepherds are the subject of the pastoral.

The class "novel," therefore, may be thought of as having an intermediate scope in literary classification. It belongs to a larger class, the form "narrative," and it controls many smaller classes or genres. Its specific and individual qualities are at once those of a "sub-form" based on conventional elements of length and pattern of sound and those of a "super-genre" based on a very wide subject matter and a very general attitude. Our definition, therefore, might be that:

> the novel is a long prose narrative
> which treats realistically of human
> relationships and actions.

So it is clear that we classify works of literature at different levels:

1. Forms -- based on number of speakers and general type of object reference

2. Intervening classes --

    (a) based on length and patterning of sound, e.g., sonnet

    (b) based on general subject matter and general attitude, e.g., Elegy

3. Genres -- based on specific subject matter and specific attitude, e.g., satirical novel

What is most important to note again in our discussion of form and genre is that what exists as an abstract, traditional set of characteristics, a model influencing a writer (e.g., the "novel" or the "sonnet") emerges in his work as definite parts of the structure--as the "stream-of-consciousness" narration of Mrs. Dalloway or the stanzaic structure of "Altarwise by owl-light." Here in the interplay of convention and originality may be important sources of a work's success or failure.

APPENDIX VI: LITERARY AND OTHER VALUES OF LITERATURE

A. Craig La Drière, "Fitness"

Fitness may be defined as the conformity of related things to each other, the conformity in a relation to some recognized ideal for such relations, the
coincidence, in matters of relatedness, of what is
with what ought to be. Since everything in the universe stands in some relation to other things, the
idea of fitness, under this name or another (propriety,
congruity, aptness, harmony) is involved in all normative or evaluatory speculation; but it is especially
important in normative theory of art and of aesthetic
experience, which is concerned with judgment of relations in general and simply as such. The idea of fitness is so simple and abstract that attempts to reduce it to any concrete formula are likely to produce
either mere tautology or a description of some other
idea. Upon empirical grounds we can certainly relate
it to the idea of unity (q.v.). But fitness seems
to be prior to unity; it is rather because its internal relations are fit that a structure presents itself as unified than because it is unified that its
relations seem fit. And fitness is an idea of more
extension than is unity, for it applies equally to
relations within an object and to relations between
the object and other things, e.g., the end or purpose
of a process in which the object serves as instrument
or means (functional fitness). Puttenham, following
ancient masters, well summarizes the complexity of
fitness in speech: "by reason of the sundry circumstances that means affaires are, as it were, wrapt in,
this decencie comes to be very much alterable and subject to varietie, insomuch as our speech asketh one
manner of decencie in respect to the person who
speakes, another of his to whom it is spoken, another
of whom we speake, another of what we speake, and in
what place and time and to what purpose." The search
for general norms of fitness is naturally much complicated by these problems of the relative and the
particular. "Vt enim in uita," says Cicero, "sic in
oratione nihil est difficilius quam quid deceat ui-
dere." Of possible objective norms of fitness the
only sources are evidently (1) nature and (2) convention or custom, the latter presumably founded upon the

former and only so far valid as adequate correspondence is felt to exist between the two. Norms supplied by convention are objective enough, and indis-
putable as long as the convention continues in effect;
indeed, even where a discrepancy has been felt between nature and convention, a conventional norm may
for a time persist as an acceptable alternative for
a natural one. So Bacon says, "What is setled by
Custome, though it be not good, yet at least it is
fit." Natural norms of fitness are harder to establish. More or less definite norms of fitness in relation to a single and definite end are sometimes
plainly supplied by the end itself; but ends may be
variously complicated, and in judgment of aesthetic
objects as such considerations of external finality
are in any case at most only incidental. In the internal structure of such objects we may certainly
require that there be manifest relevance or consistency among all related elements, that there be no
unresolved conflict or contradiction; but it is hard
to say whether this is really more concrete specification or tautological repetition of the requirement
of fitness. (Perhaps its repugnance to specification
is evidence that the idea of fitness is specific
enough without reduction to any more concrete formula,
and directly applicable to experience without being
made less abstract. Perhaps its very obdurate ab-
stractness, its resistence to assimilation by any particular context and its consequent elasticity in application to all contexts, explain its hardy persis-
tence, and its permanent value, as an ultimate principle for aesthetic judgment.) In any case there remains always the problem of determining whether in a
specific relation there is actual conformity to such
general prescriptions; for in aesthetic as in moral
evaluation judgment is always ultimately the special
case and the special case is always unique. To make
this ultimate judgment is not to apply a formula
(though to express it may be to find a formula for it);
one is here at the bare experiential ground of all
knowledge and judgment, and for the critic or the
reader as for the artist, or indeed for the scientist
when he enters this region, the only recourse is to
direct intuition, and the only ultimate test of one
intuition is corroboration by others (spontaneous or
induced by discriminating examination and discussion).
The intuition ideally required here is of course that
of the Greek pepaideumenos or phronimos, Arnold's

"judicious" man; if it be referred to "taste," Dante
reminds us that this involves not only a sensitive
palate, but also sound teeth and a competent tongue.

   In aesthetic and artistic, especially in literary, theory, speculation concerning fitness or involving it is continuous throughout history in both
Orient and Occident. Among the Greeks, it seems to
have originated in musical theory, from which it passed
to rhetoric, where the idea of fitness (to prepon)
first appears as a practical principle in the work of
Aristotle, whose influential disciple Theophrastus
included it among the required "virtues" of style.
The Stoics especially emphasized the idea in their
ethical teaching, and their great influence further
entrenched it in literary theory. It furnished the
cardinal principle for all rhetoric and poetic in the
first century before and after Christ, i.e., for the
matured theory of classical antiquity, in which, e.g.,
the theory of style and its kinds is as a whole simply
a theory of the fitness of specific means to specific
ends in a poetic situation. Any part of a writing
that lacks fitness, says Dionysius of Halicarnassus,
"fails, if not entirely, certainly in what is most important." Cicero, translating the Greek prepon by
the Latin decorum, recurs to the idea again and again.
In the theory of Horace fitness or decorum is the fundamental principle. For Quintilian too the idea of
the fit is at once the source of all true rules for
art and the only recourse of the artist when rules
fail him. In the middle ages (when, for example,
S. Thomas so described the beautiful that a modern interpreter can summarize his statements by defining
beauty as "purely objective fitness"; these ideas per-
sisted, e.g., in Dante; but their survival has not
been adequately studied. At the Renaissance and
through the classical period they were of course re-
emphasized, especially in France; in England first by
Puttenham, Sidney, and Jonson. Though the idea of
decorum (q.v.), especially in drama, was for the average theorist of that time mainly one of merely conventional propriety, the norms of which (supplied by
over-rigid and historically naive interpretation of
such ancient statements as those of Horace) were not
critically enough examined, the more general concept
which the ancients had in mind was never abandoned.
Dryden defines wit in writing generally as "a propriety of thoughts and words." "Propriety of thought,"

he explains again, "is that fancy which arises naturally from the subject, or which the poet adapts
to it. Propriety of words is the clothing of those
thoughts with such expressions as are naturally proper to them; and from both these, if they are judi-
ciously performed, the delight of poetry results."
In the eighteenth century, notably in Johnson, the
concept appears with renewed clarity. The romantic
movement in criticism may indeed be conceived as simply a reinterpretation of its implications, in which
the overemphasis of classical critics upon convention
was replaced by overemphasis upon nature as the source
of norms.

---

from Dictionary of World Literary Terms, ed. Joseph
    T. Shipley (Boston: The Writer, Inc., 1970),
    pp. 172-174.

B.   Monroe C. Beardsley, "The Classification of Cri-
     tical Reasons"

     When a critic makes a value-judgment about a
work of art, he is generally expected to give reasons
for it--not necessarily a conclusive argument, but at
least an indication of the main grounds on which his
judgment rests. Without the reasons, the judgment is
dogmatic, and also uninformative: it is hard to tell
how much is being asserted in "This painting is quite
good," unless we understand why it is being asserted.

     These reasons offered by critics (or "critical
reasons") are, of course, extremely varied. Here is
a small sampling:

     (On Haydn's Creation) "The work can be praised
for its boldness, originality, and unified conception.
But what remains so remarkable in this day and age is
its over-all spirit of joy, to which a serene religious faith, a love of this world and a sense of drama
contribute." (Raymond Ericson)

     (On the finale of Bruckner's Fifth Symphony)
"Perhaps this movement is the greatest of all sympho-
nic finales" because "It is a vision of apocalyptic
splendor such as no other composer, in my experience,

has ever painted." (Winthrop Sargeant)

(On a novel by Max Frisch) "Rarely has a pro-
vocative idea been spoiled more efficiently by excessive detail and over-decoration." (Richard Plant)

(On a motion picture of Pasolini's) "The sleeper
of the year is a bone bare, simple, and convincingly
honest treatment of the life of Jesus, The Gospel
According to St. Matthew." (Ernest Schier)

(On Edvard Munch's lithograph and oil painting,
"The Cry") "This cry of terror lives in most of
Munch's pictures. But I have seen faces like this in
life--in the concentration camp of Dachau...With "The
Cry," the Age of Anxiety found its first and perhaps
to this very day, its unmatched expression." (Alfred
Werner)

Probably the first question that will occur to
a philosopher who looks over such a list of reasons
is this: which of them are relevant? That is, which
of them really are grounds on which the judgment can
legitimately and defensibly be based? Just because
"The Cry" is an "unmatched expression" of the Age of
Anxiety, does that make it a good painting (or lithograph)? What reasons are there for supposing that
this reason counts in favor of the painting?

Many large and difficult issues in aesthetics will
loom ahead whenever this line of inquiry is pursued
very far--too many to cope with here. The task can
be somewhat simplified and clarified, however, if we
sort these issues into two main categories with the
help of an important distinction having to do with
reasons. There are reasons why something is a good
work of art (or a poor one), and reasons for supposing
that something is a good work of art (or a poor one);
in other words, there are reasons that serve to explain why the work of art is good or poor, and reasons that constitute logical support for a belief that
the work of art is good or poor. That these are not
the same can easily be shown. If Haydn's Creation
has a "unified conception," that would help to explain
why it is a good musical composition. On the other
hand, if we know that a large-scale musical work was
composed by Haydn in his mature years, this fact is
in itself a reason to believe that the work is proba-

bly very good, even though we have not yet heard
it; but this fact does not provide any explanation
of its goodness--being composed by Haydn is not one
of the things that is good about the work.

One way of setting aside some of the reasons offered by critics as irrelevant to the value-judgment
they accompany would then be to insist that relevant
critical reasons (or critical reaons in a strict
sense) be those that are reasons in both of the senses just distinguished. A relevant reason is one
that provides support to the value-judgment for which
it is a reason and also helps to explain why the
judgment is true. If the critic judges that a novel
is poor, or at least less good than some other novel
with which he compares it, and gives as one reason
that there is a great deal of "detail" and "decora-
tion," then this reason not only helps to lower our
estimate of the work's value but also points out part
of what is wrong with it.

If we insist that a relevant critical reason
must have both of these functions, it follows that
in order to be relevant, reasons must be statements
about the work itself, either descriptive statements
about its parts or internal relations (including
its form and regional qualities) or interpretive
statements about its "meaning" (taking this term
loosely enough to include such things as what it represents, symbolizes, signifies, expresses, says,
etc.). For statements about external matters, although
they may serve as indications of probable goodness
or poorness, do not explain that goodness or poorness
by telling us what in the work itself makes it good
or poor.

The class of relevant critical reasons in the
strict sense--those that are both explanations and
grounds--itself contains an enormous variety, the
range of which is only barely hinted at in the examples above, though it will be familiar to those who
have thought seriously about any of the arts. A miscellaneous collection like this is a challenge to the
philosophical aesthetician, who is bound to inquire
whether the items cannot be arranged in certain and
basic and illuminating categories, and whether there
is not a small set of principles at work here. Some
aestheticians are very dubious about this suggestion:

252

they say that by its very nature, art criticism is too complicated and too loose for any such attempt at classification to be feasible. But why not see how far we can go, if we are careful not to force reasons into categories where they don't fit? If it should in fact turn out to be the case (astonishingly, perhaps) that all relevant critical reasons in the strict sense fall into a few basic categories, that would not be without interest, and it might suggest further lines of inquiry of considerable philosophic importance.

One such classification I have proposed in Chapter 11 of my book Aesthetics: Problems in the Philosophy of Criticism. My procedure for constructing it is based on the observation that critical reasons are not all on the same level--that some are subordinate to others. We ask the critic, for example, "What makes the Max Frisch novel so poor?" He replies, "Among other things, excessive detail." We ask again, "What is so bad about the detail? Why is it excessive? How does it help to make the work poor?" If he is cooperative, the critic may reply once more: "The detail is excessive because it distracts the reader from those elements in the work (elements of plot, perhaps) that would otherwise give it a fairly high degree of unity," or perhaps, "The detail is excessive because it dissipates what would otherwise be strong dramatic and emotional qualities of the work." So it seems that the objectionableness of the detail is itself explained by an appeal to a more fundamental and general principle: that unity is desirable in the work, or that intensity of regional quality is desirable in the work.

If we press farther, however, and ask the critic why greater unity would help to make the work a better one, this question, too, deserves an answer, but it would have to be of a quite different sort. In explaining why excessive detail and over-decoration are objectionable, the critic appeals to other features of the work itself, which these features either increase or diminish. But what makes unity desirable is not what it does to other features of the work; thus, as far as the work itself is concerned, unity is a basic criterion. The fine arts critic could reasonably say that a particular group of shapes and colors in a painting is good because it creates a very subtle balance, and he could also say that balance is good because it is one way of unifying the painting; but he could not say that unity in a painting is a good thing because it makes the painting contain these particular shapes and colors.

In my view, there are exactly three basic criteria that are appealed to in relevant critical reasons, and all of the other features of works of art that are appealed to in such reasons are subordinate to these, or can be subsumed under them. There is unity, which is specifically mentioned in connection with Haydn's Creation and presupposed in the criticism of the Max Frisch novel. There is complexity, which I think is part of what Winthrop Sargeant admires in Bruckner's Fifth. (Insofar as the simplicity of Pasolini's film is regarded as a positive merit, I take it not as a low degree of complexity but as absence of "excessive detail and overdecoration.") And there is intensity of regional quality: the "over-all spirit of joy" in Haydn, the "cry of terror" in Edvard Munch.

Any such simplifying scheme as this ought to arouse immediate skepticism and protest. It is obviously too neat to be correct. It is tempting, no doubt, because it really does embrace and tidy up a very large number of critical reasons, and it enables us to distinguish the relevant ones from the irrelevant ones on a fairly clear principle. But certainly it needs to be examined and tested severely before it can be accepted.

Some searching questions can be asked about the three proposed criteria of judgment. First, are they sufficiently clear? Some aestheticians who have considered unity, for example, have expressed doubt (1) that it has a sufficiently well-defined meaning to be used in this highly general way, and (2) that it has the same meaning across the arts (the same, that is, for painting as for poetry or music). I do not know how to prove that I am right in rejecting both of these doubts. We can surely find examples of pairs of paintings or prints where it is perfectly evident that one is more unified than the other. And even though what tends to unify a painting is, of course, not identical to what tends to unify a poem or a musical composition, as far as I can tell I mean the same thing when I say that one poem is more unified than another or when I say that one painting is more unified than another.

I do not mean to imply, of course, that we can estimate infallibly the degree to which a basic aesthetic property (such as unity) is present in a particular painting. When we look at a painting and it fails to hang together, that may be because we are tired, or our perceptions are dulled by an adverse mood, or we are not attending closely enough, or we have had too little acquaintance with works of that sort. A negative conclusion must usually be somewhat tentative and rebuttable; for it may well be that if later we come to the painting again, in a more serene mood, with sharper faculties, and with greater willingness to give in to whatever the painting wishes to do to us, we may find that in fact it has a tight though subtle unity that is perfectly apparent to the prepared eye. But if we return again and again, under what we take to be the most favorable conditions, and it still looks incoherent, we have reasonable grounds for concluding that probably the painting cannot be seen as unified.

Even a positive conclusion may not be final. The painting may on one occasion fleetingly appear to us as unified. But suppose that unity turns out not to be a stable property--that it is hard to capture and to hold. Then we may decide that we were the victim of an illusion. The judgment of unity ultimately has to be based on a gestalt perception--on taking in the regional qualities and dominant patterns of the whole. But such perceptions can always be checked by analysis--by which I mean simply the minute examination of the parts of the work and their relationships with one another. A prima facie description of the work as having unity or disunity to some degree does have this kind of check: that it should hold up under analysis. For the perception that occurs after analysis may correct the earlier one: it may turn out that we have overlooked some parts or some internal relationships that, when taken into account in perception, make the work more unified--or less unified--than it at first appeared.

Second, are the three basic criteria really basic? One of the marks of being basic (as I have said)

255

is that the question "Why is X good (or poor) in the work?" seems to come to a turning-point in them, for at this point it takes one outside the work itself. Another mark is that the subordinate reasons are contextually limited. That is, the features they allude to may be desirable in some works but not necessarily in all. A particular cluster of shapes and colors may work well in one setting but badly in another; balance is not necessarily always a good thing; and details that would be excessive in one novel might not be excessive in another. But the basic criteria, I would claim, are all one-way. Unity, complexity, and intensity of regional quality never count against a work of art (we cannot say the painting is good because its regional quality is so insipid, or because it is so elementary a design, or because it falls apart into messiness), but always count in favor of it, to the extent to which they are present. The example of simplicity, which I mentioned earlier, might seem to refute at least part of this claim; but it seems to me that whenever simplicity is held up as a desirable feature, either it is not strictly simplicity (the opposite of complexity) that is referred to, but some sort of unity, or it is not the simplicity that is admired, but the intensity of some regional quality that happens to be obtainable in this case only by accepting simplicity.

Third, are the three proposed criteria really adequate to cover the entire range of relevant critical reasons? Consider "boldness" or "originality," for example, which are cited in the praise of Haydn's Creation. "Boldness" could no doubt benefit from further clarification: it could refer to a regional quality of the work, or it could refer in a somewhat roundabout way to originality (perhaps Haydn was bold to try out certain hitherto unheard of, or at least unfamiliar, ideas in it). But originality does not seem to fit under the three basic criteria. Or consider the description of Pasolini's film as "convincingly honest." Honesty, again, might be a certain quality of the work--absence of sentimentality and melodrama, etc. But it might be a correspondence between the film itself and the actual feelings of the film maker (even though he is a communist, he could still have certain feelings about this story, which he sincerely puts into his work); and honesty in that sense, like sincerity, does not seem relevant to unity or complexity or intensity of regional quality.

Criteria like originality and sincerity I have
already ruled out of the class of relevant critical
reasons by making the rule that a relevant critical
reason must not only support the critical judgment
but also (at least partially) explain why the judgment
is true. But here, of course, is a serious aesthetic
issue, since many critics regard originality and sincerity as highly relevant reasons. They would consider me wholly arbitrary in ruling them out.

This challenge leads into the fourth question
I intend to raise here: What good (philosophical)
reason is there for holding that any particular (critical) reason is relevant or irrelevant to the judgment of a particular work? If someone says that the
Bruckner Fifth is great because it presents a "vision
of apocalyptic splendor," there are always two questions we can ask: First, is it true that the work
presents such a vision? (Granted that the music is
splendid, and therefore splendor can be heard in it,
how do we know that it is apocalyptic?") Second,
if the statement is true, why is it a ground for
saying that the work is great? (How does apocalypti-
city make the music good?) To ask a question of the
second sort is to plunge us into some of the hardest
questions about the arts and art criticism. Without
pretending to dispose of them, I want at least to
face up to them.

Anything so complex as a work of art can usually
be regarded from more than one point of view: It is
(let us say) a visual design, an example of skilled
workmanship, a source of income for the painter and
(even more) for the art dealer, a political document,
an excellent example of a certain historical style,
and so forth. And one very broad way of sorting out
all the various remarks that people might want to
make about the painting is to say that they are made
from different points of view: economic, or art-historical, or political, or other. Then how are we
to distinguish between one point of view and another?
According to some philosophers, one point of view can
be distinguished from another only in terms of the
sort of reason given: thus if one says that the painting is costly, we can classify his point of view as
economic; and if another says that the painting is a

257

good example of Mannerism, we can classify his point of view as that of the art historian. But in that case, we could not use points of view to help us sort out the reasons, or we would be going in a circle. I would prefer to distinguish between one point of view and another in terms of a kind of value that one might take an interest in: market value or art-historical value (that is, usefulness in illuminating some phase of art history).

Speaking very broadly (and for some purposes too sweepingly), the various kinds of value that may be found in works of art can be classified under three headings. There is cognitive value (of which art-historical value would be a species). We often speak well of works of art if they contribute, in some way, to our knowledge. Perhaps Winthrop Sargeant is suggesting that Bruckner gives us a kind of insight into the nature of apocalypses, and perhaps Alfred Werner is suggesting that Munch gives us a better understanding of our Age of Anxiety. In any case, claims like these are frequently made, and if they are valid claims, then they certainly do show that the work is worth creating and preserving. But I do not think they are relevant reasons for saying that the work is good music or good painting--only that it is good as religious intuition or a social document.

Next there is what might be called moral and social value. Someone might follow Winthrop Sargeant's suggestion (and his remarks elsewhere) by saying that Bruckner's music is religiously significant, and under suitable circumstances can strengthen religious faith (assuming that this is desirable). Someone else might praise Pasolini's film because it can produce moral uplift or strengthen character. And, quite apart from whether or not "The Cry" is a good painting, it may be of great social worth as an "unmatched expression," a minatory reminder, of the ills of our age. But again, even if all these claims are admitted, they would not properly lead us to say that these are good works of art.

Finally, there is aesthetic value. This is the kind of value that we look for most especially and suitably in works of art, and the kind of value whose presence and degree we report when we say that the work is good or poor. If we set aside all those rea-

sons that clearly depend upon a cognitive or a moral/
social point of view, we may consider those that remain to be peculiarly aesthetic. They are, however,
not all equally relevant. Relevance depends on our
theory of aesthetic value. If we hold, as I do, that
the aesthetic value of an object is that value which
it possesses in virtue of its capacity to provide
aesthetic experience, then certain consequences follow. For the only way to support such a judgment
relevantly and cogently would be to point out features
of the work that enable it to provide an experience
having an aesthetic character. And thus the relevant
reasons, as I assumed above, will be those that both
support and explain.

There is one more set of distinctions that I
have found useful in dealing with critical reasons.
Any statement that a critic may make about a work of
art must be one of three kinds: (1) It may be a
statement about the relation of the work to its antecedent conditions—about the intentions of the artist,
or his sincerity, or his originality, or the social
conditions of the work, and so forth. If such a
statement is given as a reason for critical judgment,
it is a genetic reason. It may help explain why the
work has a particular feature that in turn helps explain why the work is good (as one might say that
something in Munch's childhood experience explains
the "cry of terror" in so much of his work, while the
presence of that "cry of terror," as an intense regional quality, helps explain why the works are good).
But the genetic reason itself does not explain directly why the work is good, and it is therefore not a
relevant reason: we cannot say that a work is good
because it is sincere, or original, or fulfills the
intention of the artist. (2) The critic's statement
may be a statement about the effects of the work on
individuals or groups: that it is morally uplifting,
or shocking, or popular at the box office. If such
a statement is given as a reason, it is an affective
reason. And since it does not say what in the work
makes it good, but itself has to be explained by what
is in the work (which is shocking because of the nu-
dity or the sadism or whatever), it is not a relevant
critical reason. (3) When the genetic and affective
reasons are set aside, what remain are descriptions
and interpretations of the work itself, as has already
been said. When given as reasons, such statements

may be called objective reasons, since they draw our attention to the object itself and its own merits and defects. These are the reasons, I would argue, that are properly the province of the critic.

---

from <u>Art Education</u> 20 (1967), 55-63.